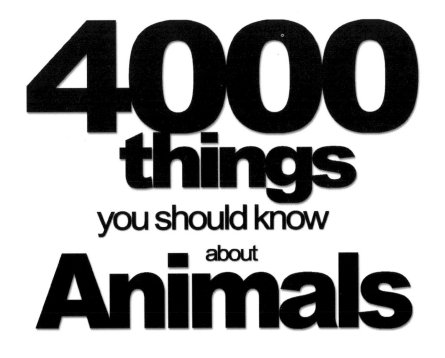

4000
things
you should know
about
Animals

First published by
Miles Kelly Publishing Ltd
Bardfield Centre, Great Bardfield, Essex, CM7 4SL

Copyright © Miles Kelly Publishing 2002

2 4 6 8 10 9 7 5 3 1

Project Manager: Ruth Boardman
Consultants: Dr Jim Flegg, Steve Parker
Picture Research: Liberty Newton
Assistant: Lisa Clayden
Production: Estela Godoy
Colour Reproduction: profile imaging – London

British Library Cataloguing-in-Publication Data
A catalogue record for this book is available from the British Library

ISBN 1-84236-150-3

Printed in Hong Kong

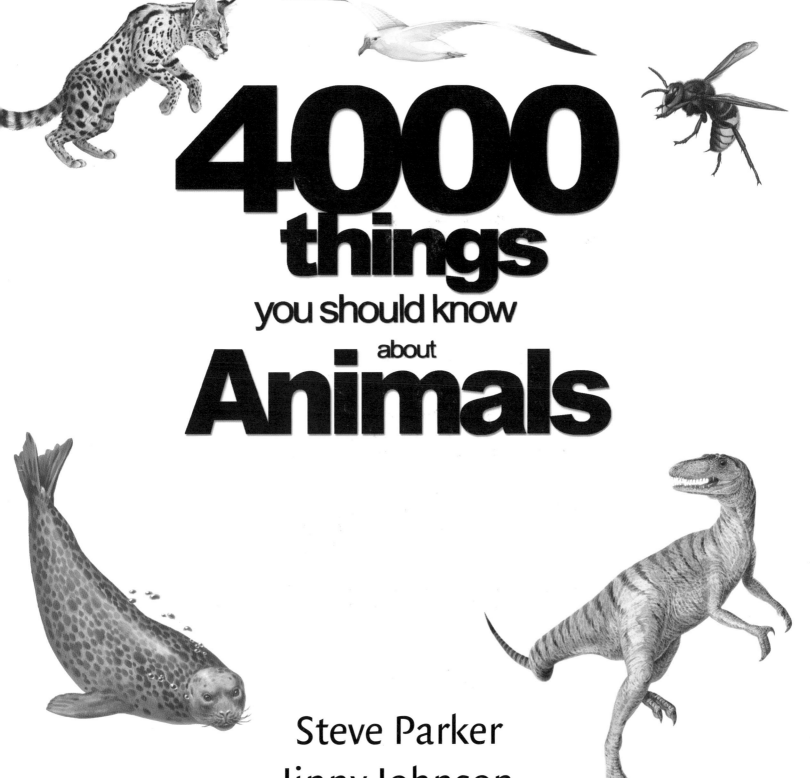

4000 things
you should know
about
Animals

Steve Parker

Jinny Johnson

John Farndon

Duncan Brewer

MILES KELLY

PUBLISHING

Contents

Dinosaurs 12–69

Contents

Birds 70–127

Contents

Wild Animals 128–185

Contents

Mammals 186–243

INDEX 244–255

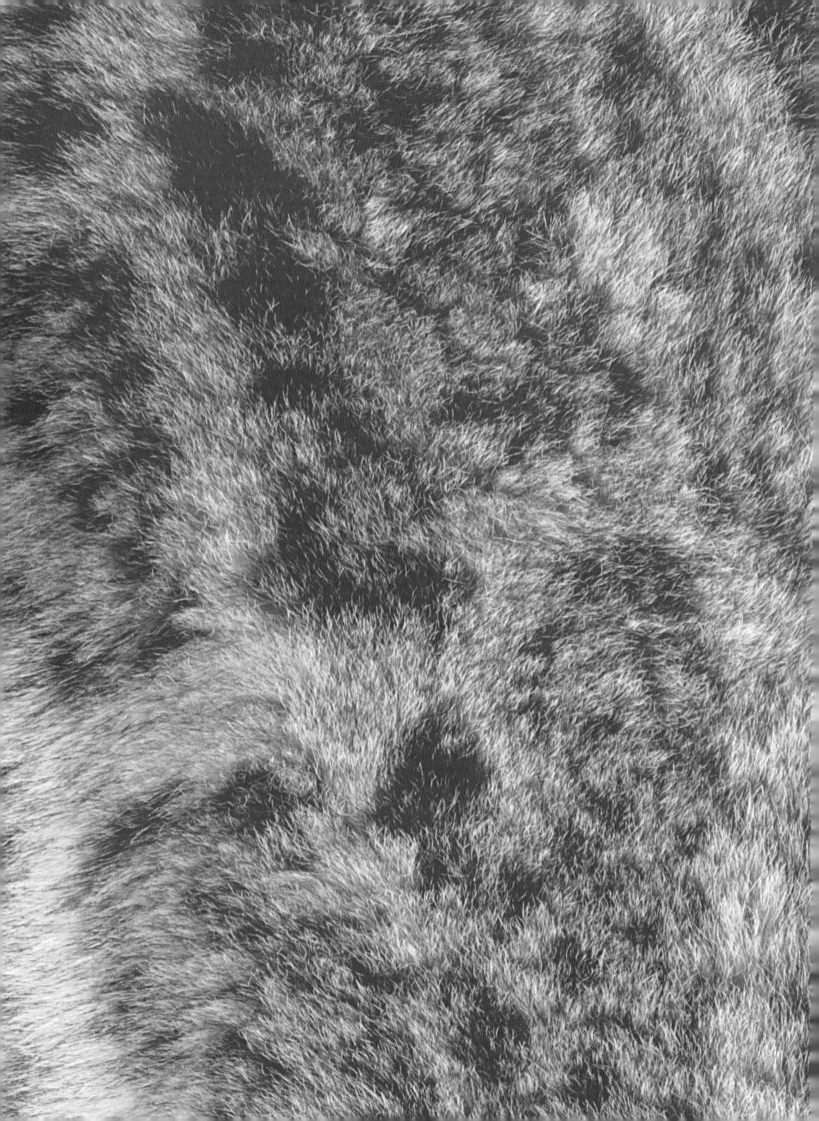

INTRODUCTION

4000 Things You Should Know About Animals provides a fantastic insight into the amazing world of the animal kingdom. Its 400 subject panels contain facts that will inform, astound and entertain. Dip into this amazing resource and you will find out about the dinosaurs who roamed the planet over 60 million years ago and the theories on their extinction.

You will be introduced to the fantastic variety of the world's animals – from the colourful and fascinating behaviour of birds, to the drama of mammals, the complex world of insects and spiders and the secretive life of reptiles and amphibians.

Animals have adapted to every imaginable environment on Earth, from the driest, sweltering deserts to the depths of the oceans.

The thousands of facts provided here will reveal the secrets of their survival.

Using this book

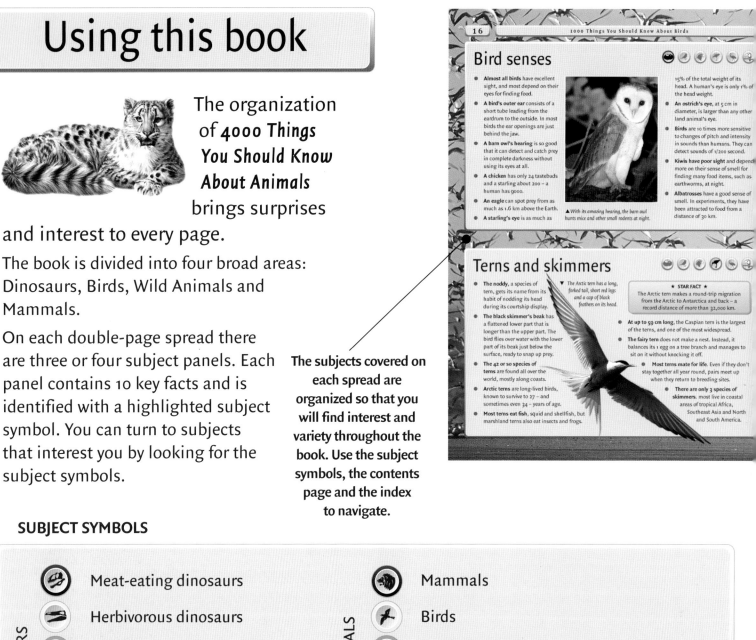

The organization of **4000 Things You Should Know About Animals** brings surprises and interest to every page.

The book is divided into four broad areas: Dinosaurs, Birds, Wild Animals and Mammals.

On each double-page spread there are three or four subject panels. Each panel contains 10 key facts and is identified with a highlighted subject symbol. You can turn to subjects that interest you by looking for the subject symbols.

The subjects covered on each spread are organized so that you will find interest and variety throughout the book. Use the subject symbols, the contents page and the index to navigate.

SUBJECT SYMBOLS

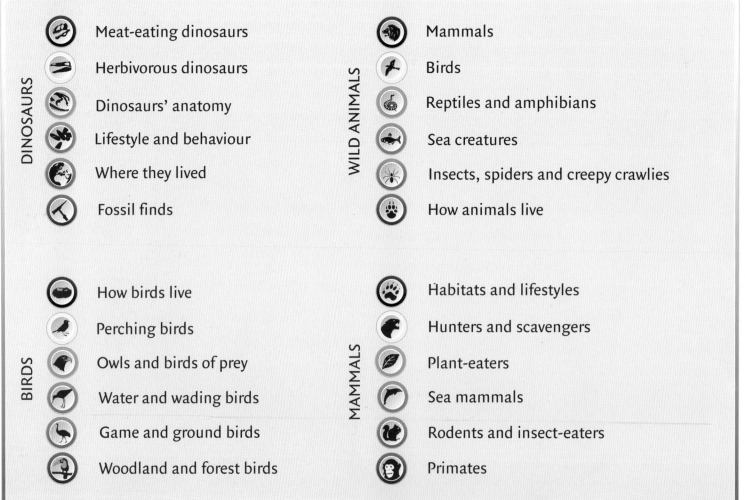

DINOSAURS
- Meat-eating dinosaurs
- Herbivorous dinosaurs
- Dinosaurs' anatomy
- Lifestyle and behaviour
- Where they lived
- Fossil finds

BIRDS
- How birds live
- Perching birds
- Owls and birds of prey
- Water and wading birds
- Game and ground birds
- Woodland and forest birds

WILD ANIMALS
- Mammals
- Birds
- Reptiles and amphibians
- Sea creatures
- Insects, spiders and creepy crawlies
- How animals live

MAMMALS
- Habitats and lifestyles
- Hunters and scavengers
- Plant-eaters
- Sea mammals
- Rodents and insect-eaters
- Primates

Weavers and relatives

- The **sociable weaver** nests in groups of up to 300 birds. The huge nest is made of sticks and grass, and may measure 4 m deep and weigh up to 1000 kg. Each pair of birds has its own hole in the nest.
- **Desert-living sociable weavers** use their nest all year round for shelter from sun, wind and cold. At night, when temperatures drop, the nest holes stay 20°C warmer than the outside air.
- **Whydah birds** do not make their own nests, but lay their eggs in the nests of other birds, usually waxbills.

▶ When the male cape weaver has finished making a nest, it calls to the female.

- **Young whydahs** make the same sounds and have the same mouth markings as their foster parents' own young, and because of this they get fed.
- The **baya weaver** makes a beautiful nest of woven grass and leaves that it hangs from a tree or roof.
- **In the breeding season**, the male paradise whydah grows 28 cm long tail feathers – almost twice the length of its body – for display in flight.
- **Most weavers** have short, strong beaks that they use for feeding on seeds and insects.
- The **red bishop** mates with three or four females, who all nest in his territory.
- The **red-vented malimbe** (a weaver) feeds mainly on the husks of oil palm nuts.

★ STAR FACT ★
As many as 500 pairs of red-billed queleas may nest together in one acacia tree.

Plovers and lapwings

- The **wrybill**, a New Zealand plover, has a unique beak that curves to the right. The bird sweeps its beak over sand to pick up insects.
- **If a predator** comes near a killdeer's nest, the bird moves away, trailing a wing to look as though it is injured. The predator, seeing what it thinks is an easy victim, follows the killdeer which, once far enough away, flies off.
- **Kentish plover chicks** have markings like the stones and pebbles of their nest site. If danger threatens, the chicks flatten themselves on the ground and are almost impossible to see.

▶ The wrybill breeds on New Zealand's South Island, but overwinters on North Island.

- There are 60 or so species of plovers and lapwings around the world.
- **Female dotterels** lay clutches of eggs for several males, which incubate the eggs.
- **To attract females**, the male lapwing performs a spectacular rolling, tumbling display flight in the air.
- **Spur-winged plovers** are often seen close to crocodiles in Africa and Asia – they may feed on small creatures that the crocodiles disturb.
- The **lapwing** is also known as the peewit.
- **Golden plovers** have been recorded flying at more than 113 km/h.

★ STAR FACT ★
Many plovers pat the ground with their feet to imitate the sound of rain. This attracts worms to the surface, where they are snapped up.

Subject symbols appear on every panel. Look for the ones that are highlighted.

Star facts are strange-but-true.

Over 300 photographs help illustrate the amazing facts.

Ten key facts are provided in each subject panel. There are 400 panels making 4000 facts in all.

Headings at the top of each double-page spread tell you which of the four areas of the book you are in – Dinosaurs, Birds, Wild Animals or Mammals.

Anchisaurus

- **Anchisaurus** was a prosauropod, a plant-eater with a small head, long neck and long tail.
- **Although officially named as a dinosaur** in 1912, Anchisaurus had in fact been discovered almost 100 years earlier.
- **Anchisaurus** was very small and slim compared to other prosauropods, with a body about the size of a large dog.
- **Fossils** of Anchisaurus date from the Early Jurassic times.
- **The remains** of Anchisaurus were found in Connecticut and Massachusetts, eastern USA, and in southern Africa.
- **With its small, serrated teeth**, Anchisaurus probably bit off the soft leaves of low-growing plants.
- **To reach leaves** on higher branches, Anchisaurus may

★ STAR FACT ★
Remains of Anchisaurus were the first fossils of a dinosaur to be discovered in North America in 1818.

have been able to rear up on its back legs.

- **Anchisaurus** had a large, curved claw on each thumb.
- **The thumb claws** of Anchisaurus may have been used as hooks to pull leafy branches towards the mouth, and/or as weapons for lashing out at enemies and inflicting wounds.

◀ The main body of Anchisaurus was about the size of a pet dog such as a labrador.

Cousins: Sea

- **Placodont reptiles** lived mainly during the Triassic Period. They were shaped like large salamanders or turtles, and probably ate shellfish.
- **The placodont** Placodus was about 2 m long and looked like a large, scaly newt.
- **The nothosaurs** were fish-eating reptiles of the Triassic Period. They had small heads, long necks and tails, and 4 flipper-shaped limbs.
- **Fossils** of the 3-m long nothosaur Nothosaurus have been found across Europe, Asia and Africa.

▼ Plesiosaurus was 2.5 m long, and was one of many plesiosaurs to thrive in Jurassic seas.

- **The dolphin-like ichthyosaur reptiles** had back fins, two-lobed tails and flipper-shaped limbs.
- **Many kinds of ichthyosaurs** thrived in the seas during the Triassic and Jurassic Periods, although they had faded away by the middle of the Cretaceous Period.
- **One of the biggest ichthyosaurs** was Shonisaurus, which measured up to 15 m long.
- **The plesiosaurs** were fish-eating reptiles of the Mesozoic Era, with small heads, tubby bodies, 4 flipper-shaped limbs and short, tapering tails.
- **The plesiosaur** Elasmosaurus was up to 14 m long, with more than half of this length being its extraordinarily long, snakelike neck.

★ STAR FACT ★
One of the biggest meat-eaters ever was the short-necked plesiosaur Liopleurodon, at possibly 20 m long and weighing 50 tonnes.

Dino-birds: 1

- **The earliest known bird** for which there is good fossil evidence, and which lived during the Age of Dinosaurs, is Archaeopteryx.
- **Archaeopteryx** lived in Europe during the Late Jurassic Period, about 155–150 million years ago.
- **At about 60 cm long** from nose to tail-tip, Archaeopteryx was about the size of a large crow.
- **Archaeopteryx** resembled a small, meat-eating dinosaur in many of its features, such as the teeth in its long, beaklike mouth, and its long, bony tail.

★ STAR FACT ★
Archaeopteryx was covered with feathers that had the same detailed designs found in feathers covering flying birds today.

- **In 1951**, a fossilized part-skeleton was identified as belonging to a small dinosaur similar to Compsognathus, but in the 1970s it was re-studied and named Archaeopteryx – showing how similar the two creatures were.
- **Three clawed fingers** grew halfway along the front of each of Archaeopteryx's wing-shaped front limbs.
- **The flying muscles** of Archaeopteryx were anchored to its large breastbone.
- **Archaeopteryx** probably flew, but not as fast or as skilfully as today's birds.
- **Archaeopteryx** probably fed by swooping on prey, running to catch small creatures such as insects and worms, or perhaps even by scavenging carrion.

Three clawed 'fingers' midway along front of wing

Long tail with tail backbones

Teeth in long, light jaws (all birds lack teeth today)

Flight feathers suited to agile manoeuvres in the air

▲ Archaeopteryx could probably glide well, swoop and turn as it pursued flying prey such as dragonflies. However, its long, strong legs suggest that it was also an able walker and runner. So it may have chased victims such as baby lizards and cockroaches on the ground.

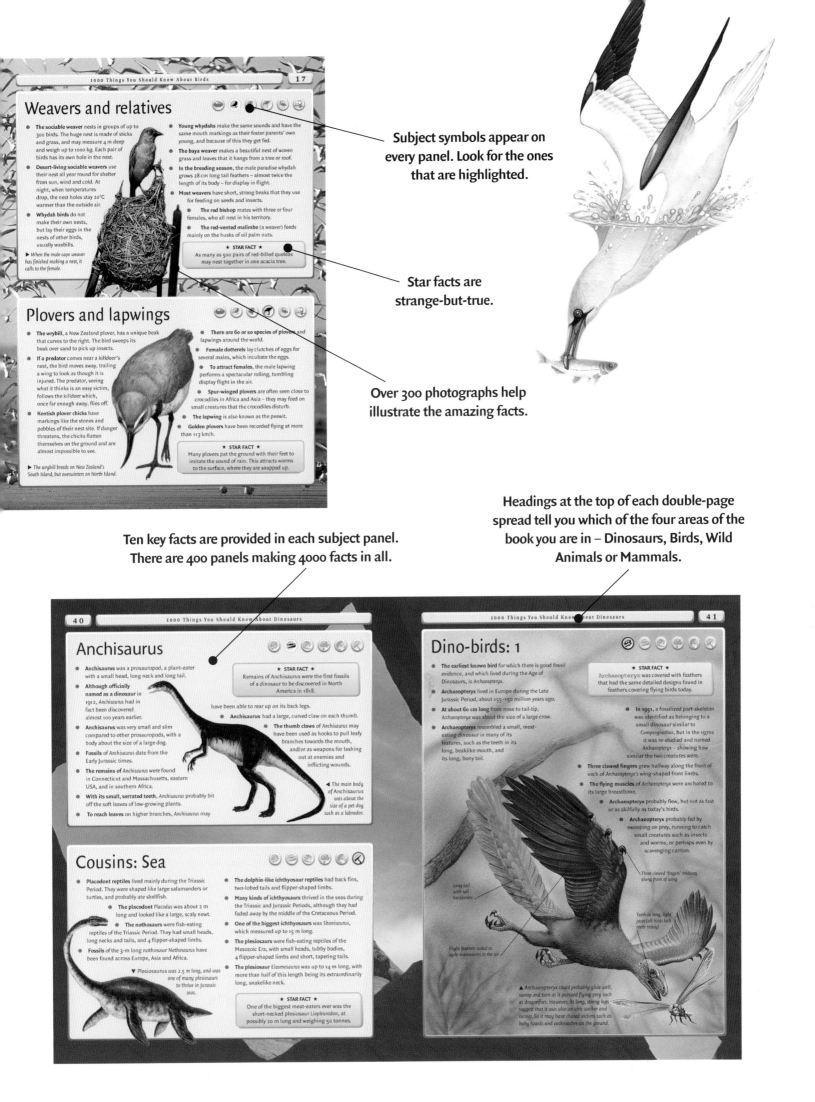

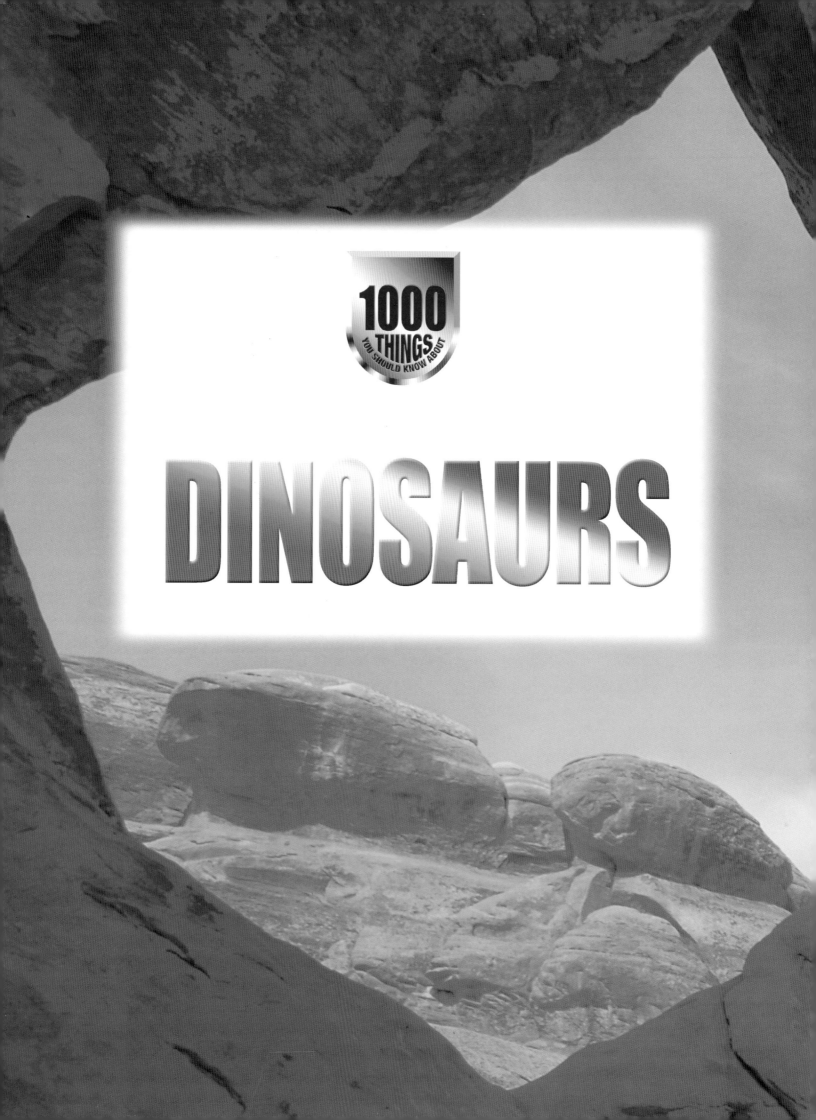

KEY

Meat-eating dinosaurs

Herbivorous dinosaurs

Dinosaurs' anatomy

Lifestyle and behaviour

Where they lived

Fossil finds

Age of Dinosaurs

- **The Age of Dinosaurs** corresponds to the time period that geologists call the Mesozoic Era, from about 248–65 million years ago.

- **The Mesozoic Era** is divided into three shorter time spans – the Triassic, Jurassic and Cretaceous Periods.

- **In the Triassic Period**, 248–208 million years ago, the dinosaurs began to evolve.

- **During the Jurassic Period** – about 208–144 million years ago – the dinosaurs reached their greatest size.

- **The Cretaceous Period** is when dinosaurs were at their most varied – about 144–065 million years ago.

- **In the Triassic Period**, all the continents were joined in one supercontinent – Pangaea.

- **In the Jurassic Period**, the supercontinent of Pangaea separated into two huge land-masses – Laurasia in the north and Gondwana in the south.

- **In the Cretaceous Period**, Laurasia and Gondwana split, and the continents as we know them began to form.

- **In the Mesozoic Era**, the major land-masses gradually moved across the globe in a process known as 'continental drift'.

MYA	ERA	PERIOD	
80			
100		CRETACEOUS	
120			
140	MESOZOIC	136 MYA	AGE OF REPTILES
160		JURASSIC	
180			
200		193 MYA	
220		TRIASSIC 225 MYA	

▲ Dinosaurs ruled the land for 160 million years – longer than any other animal group.

- **The joining and separating** of the continents affected which kinds of dinosaurs lived where.

Legs and posture

- **All dinosaurs had 4 limbs.** Unlike certain other reptiles, such as snakes and slow-worms, they did not lose their limbs through evolution.

- **Some dinosaurs**, such as massive, plant-eating sauropods like Janenschia, stood and walked on all four legs nearly all the time.

- **The all-fours method** of standing and walking is called 'quadrupedal'.

- **Some dinosaurs**, such as nimble, meat-eating dromaeosaurs like Deinonychus, stood and walked on their back limbs only. The front two limbs were used as arms.

- **The back-limbs-only method** of standing and walking is called 'bipedal'.

- **Some dinosaurs**, such as hadrosaurs like Edmontosaurus, could move on all four limbs or just on their back legs if they chose to.

- **The two-or-four-legs method** of standing and walking is called 'bipedal/quadrupedal'.

- **Reptiles** such as lizards and crocodiles have a sprawling posture, in which the upper legs join the body at the sides.

- **Dinosaurs** had an upright posture, with the legs directly below the body.

- **The more efficient upright posture** and gait may be one major reason why dinosaurs were so successful compared to other animals of the time.

▲ The small plant-eater Hypsilophodon was a bipedal dinosaur, walking and running on its two larger back legs.

Fabrosaurs

- **Fabrosaurs** were small dinosaurs that lived towards the beginning of the Jurassic Period, about 208–200 million years ago.

- **The group was named** from *Fabrosaurus*, a dinosaur that was itself named in 1964, from just the fossil of a piece of lower jaw bone, found in southern Africa.

- *Lesothosaurus* was a fabrosaur, the fossils of which were found in the Lesotho region of Africa, near the *Fabrosaurus* fossil. It was named in 1978.

- **The lightly built** *Lesothosaurus* was only 1 m long from nose to tail-tip, and would have stood knee-high to an adult human.

- *Lesothosaurus* had long, slim back legs and long toes, indicating that it was a fast runner.

- **The teeth and other fossils** of *Lesothosaurus* show that it probably ate low-growing plants such as ferns.

- *Lesothosaurus's* **teeth** were set inwards slightly from the sides of its skull, suggesting it had fleshy cheek pouches for storing or chewing food.

- *Lesothosaurus* may have crouched down to rest on its smaller front arms when feeding on the ground.

- *Lesothosaurus* probably lived in herds, grazing and browsing, and then racing away at speed from danger.

- **Some experts believe** that *Lesothosaurus* and *Fabrosaurus* were the same, and that the two sets of fossils were given different names.

◀ *Lesothosaurus's head and neck were small in relation to its body.*

Ancestors

- **Experts have many opinions** as to which group (or groups) of reptiles were the ancestors of the dinosaurs.

- **The earliest dinosaurs** appeared in the Middle Triassic Period, about 230–225 million years ago, so their ancestors must have been around before this.

- **Very early dinosaurs** walked and ran on their strong back limbs, so their ancestors were probably similar.

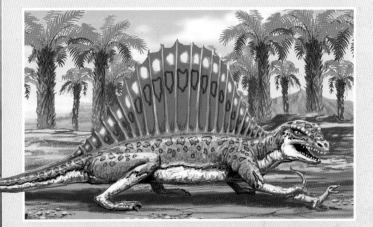

★ STAR FACT ★
Creatures similar to *Euparkeria* or *Lagosuchus* may have given rise to the first dinosaurs.

- **The thecodonts** or 'socket-toothed' group of reptiles may have been the ancestors of the dinosaurs.

- **A thecodont's teeth** grew from roots fixed into pit-like sockets in the jaw bone, as in dinosaurs.

- **Some thecodonts** resembled sturdy lizards. Others evolved into true crocodiles (still around today).

- **The ornithosuchian thecodonts** became small, upright creatures with long back legs and long tails.

- **The smaller thecodonts** included *Euparkeria*, at about 60 cm long, and *Lagosuchus*, at about 30 cm long.

- ***Euparkeria* and *Lagosuchus*** were fast-moving creatures that used their sharp claws and teeth to catch insects.

◀ *The early reptile Dimetrodon was a pelycosaur, not a dinosaur.*

Prosauropods

- **The prosauropods** were the first really big dinosaurs to appear on Earth. They were plant-eaters that thrived about 230–180 million years ago.

- **Prosauropods** had small heads, long necks and tails, wide bodies and four sturdy limbs.

- **One of the first prosauropods** was *Plateosaurus*, which lived about 220 million years ago in present-day France, Germany, Switzerland and other parts of Europe.

▶ Riojasaurus
*was South America's
first big dinosaur.*

- *Plateosaurus* usually walked on all fours, but it may have reared up on its back legs to reach high leaves.

- *Plateosaurus* was up to 8 m in total length, and weighed about 1 tonne.

- **Another prosauropod** was *Riojasaurus*. Its fossils are 218 million years old, and come from Argentina.

- *Riojasaurus* was 10 m long and weighed about 2 tonnes.

- *Anchisaurus* was one of the smallest prosauropods, at only 2.5 m long and about 30 kg. It lived in eastern North America about 190 million years ago.

- **Fossil evidence** suggests that 5-m long *Massospondylus* lived in southern Africa and perhaps North America.

- **The sauropods** followed the prosauropods and were even bigger, but had the same basic body shape, with long necks and tails.

Horns

- **A dinosaur's horns** got bigger as the animal grew – they were not shed and replaced each year like the antlers of today's deer.

- **Each horn** had a bony core and an outer covering of horny substance formed mainly from keratin.

- **Horns** were most common among the plant-eating dinosaurs. They were probably used for self-defence and to defend offspring against predators.

- **The biggest horns** belonged to the ceratopsians or 'horn-faces', such as *Triceratops*.

★ STAR FACT ★
Dinosaurs may have used their horns to push over plants or dig up roots for food.

- **In some ceratopsians**, just the bony core of the horn was about 1 m long, not including the outer sheath.

- **The ceratopsian** *Styracosaurus* or 'spiked reptile' had a series of long horns around the top of its neck frill, and a very long horn on its nose.

- **Horns may have been used** in head-swinging displays to intimidate rivals and make physical fighting less likely.

- **In battle**, male dinosaurs may have locked horns in a trial of strength, as antelopes do today.

- **Armoured dinosaurs** such as the nodosaur *Panoplosaurus* had horn-like spikes along the sides of its body.

◀ Styracosaurus's frill horns had bony centres.

Tyrannosaurus

- **Tyrannosaurus** is not only one of the most famous of the dinosaurs, but also one about which a great deal is known. Several discoveries have revealed fossilized bones, teeth, whole skeletons and other remains.

- **Tyrannosaurus** lived at the very end of the Age of Dinosaurs, about 68–65 million years ago.

- **The full name** of *Tyrannosaurus* is *Tyrannosaurus rex*, which means 'king of the tyrant reptiles'.

- **The head** of *Tyrannosaurus* was 1.2 m long and had more than 50 dagger-like teeth, some longer than 15 cm.

- **Tyrannosaurus** fossils have been found at many sites in North America, including Alberta and Saskatchewan in Canada, and Colorado, Wyoming, Montana and New Mexico in the USA.

> ★ STAR FACT ★
> *Tyrannosaurus*, when fully grown, was about 12–13 m long and stood taller than a two-decker bus. It weighed 6–7 tonnes.

- **The arms and hands** of *Tyrannosaurus* were so small that they could not pass food to its mouth, and may have had no use at all.

- **Recent fossil finds** of a group of *Tyrannosaurus*, includes youngsters, suggesting that they may have lived as families in small herds.

- **Tyrannosaurus** may have been an active hunter, pounding along at speed after its fleeing prey, or it may have been a skulking scavenger that ambushed old and sickly victims.

- **Until the 1990s**, *Tyrannosaurus* was known as the biggest meat-eating dinosaur, and the biggest meat-eating animal ever to walk the Earth, but its size record has been broken by *Giganotosaurus*.

▲ The huge skull of Tyrannosaurus *was deep from top to bottom, but relatively narrow from side to side. The jaw hinged at the rear of the head, giving a vast gape when the mouth was open.*

Curved neck allowed head to face forwards

Two-fingered 'hand'

Thick, heavy, muscular base to tail

Deep chest probably gave great stamina

Three-toed foot

▶ Tyrannosaurus's massive, *powerful rear legs contrasted greatly with its puny front limbs or 'arms'. As it pounded along, its thick-based tail balanced its horizontal body and the head, which was held low. The rear feet were enormous, each set of three toes supporting some 3–4 tonnes.*

Raptors

- **'Raptors'** is a nickname for the dromaeosaur group.

- **'Raptor'** is variously said to mean 'plunderer', 'thief' or 'hunter' (birds of prey are also called raptors).

- **Dromaeosaurs** were medium-sized, powerful, agile, meat-eating dinosaurs that lived mainly about 110–65 million years ago.

- **Most dromaeosaurs** were 1.5–3 m from nose to tail, weighed 20–60 kg, and stood 1–2 m tall.

- **Velociraptor** lived 75–70 million years ago, in what is now the barren scrub and desert of Mongolia in Central Asia.

- **Like other raptors**, *Velociraptor* probably ran fast and could leap great distances on its powerful back legs.

- **The dromaeosaurs** are named after the 1.8-m long *Dromaeosaurus* from North America – one of the least known of the group, from very few fossil finds.

- **The best-known raptor** is probably *Deinonychus*.

- **The large mouths of dromaeosaurs** opened wide and were equipped with many small, sharp, curved teeth.

> ★ **STAR FACT** ★
> On each foot, a dromaeosaur had a large, curved claw that it could swing in an arc to slash through its victim's flesh.

◄ *Velociraptor, the 'speedy thief', was a typical dromaeosaur. Fossils of it were found in Central Asia.*

Tails

- **All dinosaurs** evolved with tails – though some individuals may have lost theirs in attacks or accidents!

- **The length of the tail** relative to the body, and its shape, thickness and special features, give many clues as to how the dinosaur used it.

- **The longest tails**, at more than 17 m, belonged to the giant plant-eating sauropods such as *Diplodocus*.

- **Some sauropods** had a linked chain of more than

▶ *Compsognathus may have used its tapering, whiplike tail to slap its enemies.*

80 separate bones inside the tail – more than twice the usual number.

- **A sauropod** may have used its tail as a whip to flick at enemies.

- **Many meat-eating dinosaurs** that stood and ran on their back legs had thick-based tails to counterbalance the weight of their bodies and heads.

- **Small, fast, agile meat-eaters**, such as *Compsognathus*, used their tails for balance when leaping and darting about.

- **The meat-eater** *Ornitholestes* had a tail that was more than half of its 2-m length, and was used as a counterbalance-rudder to help it turn corners at speed.

- **The armoured dinosaurs** known as ankylosaurs had two huge lumps of bone at the ends of their tails, which they swung at their enemies like a club.

- **The tails of the duck-billed dinosaurs** (hadrosaurs) may have been swished from side to side in the water as an aid to swimming.

Gobi Desert

- **The Gobi** covers much of southern Mongolia and parts of northern China. During the Age of Dinosaurs, it was a land of scrub and scattered trees.

▲ The Gobi's fossil sites are far from any towns.

- **The first fossil-hunting expeditions** to the Gobi Desert took place in 1922–25, organized by the American Museum of Natural History.

- **The 1922–25 Gobi expeditions** set out to look for fossils of very early humans, but instead found some amazing dinosaur remains.

- **The first fossil dinosaur eggs** were found by the 1922–25 expeditions.

- *Velociraptor, Avimimus* and *Pinacosaurus* were discovered in the Gobi.

- **Russian fossil-hunting trips** into the Gobi Desert in 1946 and 1948–49 discovered new types of armoured dinosaurs, duck-billed dinosaurs, and the huge meat-eater *Tarbosaurus*.

- **More expeditions** to the Gobi in the 1960s–70s, especially to the fossil-rich area of the Nemegt Basin, found the giant sauropod *Opisthocoelicaudia* and the helmet headed *Prenocephale*.

- **Other dinosaurs** found in the Gobi include the ostrich-dinosaur *Gallimimus* and the strong-beaked 'egg thief' *Oviraptor*.

- **The inhospitable Gobi** can be -40°C in winter and 40°C in summer.

- **Despite the harsh conditions**, the Gobi Desert is one of the most exciting areas in the world for finding dinosaur fossils.

Brachiosaurus

- **Relatively complete** fossil remains exist of *Brachiosaurus*.

- *Brachiosaurus* was a sauropod – a huge plant-eater.

- **At 25-m long** from nose to tail, *Brachiosaurus* was one of the biggest of all dinosaurs.

- **Fossils** of *Brachiosaurus* have been found in North America, east and north Africa, and also possibly southern Europe.

- **Estimates of the weight** of *Brachiosaurus* range from about 30 to 75 tonnes.

- *Brachiosaurus* lived about 150 million years ago, and may have survived until 115 million years ago.

- **The name** *Brachiosaurus* means 'arm reptile' – it was so-named because of its massive front legs.

- **With its huge front legs and long neck**, *Brachiosaurus* could reach food more than 13 m from the ground.

- **The teeth** of *Brachiosaurus* were small and chisel-shaped for snipping leaves from trees.

- *Brachiosaurus's* nostrils were high on its head.

◄ *Brachiosaurus had similar body proportions to a giraffe, but was more than twice as tall and 50 times heavier.*

Europe

- **The first dinosaur fossils** ever discovered and given official names were found in England.

- **One of the first almost complete dinosaur skeletons** found was that

▲ *The dots indicate dinosaur fossils found in Europe.*

of the big plant-eater *Iguanodon*, in 1871, in southern England.

- **Some of the most numerous early fossils found** were those of *Iguanodon*, discovered in a coal mine in the Belgian village of Bernissart in 1878.

- **About 155–150 million years ago**, Solnhofen in southern Germany was a mosaic of lush islands and shallow lagoons – ideal for many kinds of life.

- **In sandstone** in the Solnhofen region of Germany, fossils of amazing detail preserved the tiny *Compsognathus* and the first known bird, *Archaeopteryx*.

- **Fossils** of tiny *Compsognathus* were found near Nice in southern France.

- **Many fossils** of the plant-eating prosauropod *Plateosaurus* were recovered from Trossingen, Germany, in 1911–12, 1921–23 and 1932.

- **Some of the largest fossil dinosaur eggs**, measuring 30 cm long (5 times longer than a hen's egg), were thought to have been laid by the sauropod *Hypselosaurus* near Aix-en-Provence in southern France.

- **The Isle of Wight** off southern England has provided so many dinosaur fossils that it is sometimes known as 'Dinosaur Island'.

- **Fossils** of *Hypsilophodon* have been found in eastern Spain, and those of *Camptosaurus* on the coast of Portugal.

Names: 1

- **Every dinosaur has a scientific name**, usually made up from Latin or Greek, and written in *italics*.

- **Many dinosaur names** end in *-saurus*, which some say means 'reptile' and others say means 'lizard' – even though dinosaurs were not lizards.

- **Dinosaur names** often refer to a feature that no other dinosaur had. *Baryonyx*, for example, means 'heavy claw', from the massive claw on its thumb.

- **The medium-sized meat-eater** *Herrerasaurus* from Argentina was named after Victorino Herrera, the farmer who first noticed its fossils.

- **Many dinosaur names are real**

▲ *Herrerasaurus was named after the Andean farmer who found it.*

tongue-twisters, such as *Opisthocoelicaudia*, pronounced 'owe-pis-thowe-see-lee-cord-ee-ah'.

- **Opisthocoelicaudia** means 'posterior tail cavity', and refers to the joints between the backbones in the tail.

- **Some dinosaurs** were named after the place where their fossils were found. *Minmi* was located near Minmi Crossing in Queensland, Australia.

- **Some dinosaur groups** are named after the first-discovered or major one of its kind, such as the tyrannosaurs or stegosaurs.

- **The fast-running ostrich-dinosaurs'** name, ornithomimosaurs, means 'bird-mimic reptiles'.

★ **STAR FACT** ★
Triceratops, or 'three-horned face', is one of the best known dinosaur scientific names.

Monsters

- **Dinosaurs** can be measured by length and height, but 'biggest' usually means heaviest or bulkiest.

- **Dinosaurs were not the biggest-ever living things** on Earth – some trees are more than 100 times their size.

- **The sauropod dinosaurs** of the Late Jurassic were the biggest animals to walk on Earth, as far as we know.

- **Sauropod dinosaurs** may not have been the biggest animals ever. Today's great whales, and perhaps the massive, flippered sea reptiles called pliosaurs of the Dinosaur Age, rival them in size.

- **For any dinosaur,** enough fossils must be found for a panel of scientists to be sure it is a distinct

▲ Seismosaurus is known from few fossils.

type, so they can give it a scientific name. They must also be able to estimate its size. With some giant dinosaurs, not enough fossils have been found.

- **Supersaurus** remains found in Colorado, USA, suggest a dinosaur similar to *Diplodocus*, but perhaps even longer, at 35 m.

- **Seismosaurus** fossils found in 1991 in the USA may belong to a 40-m long sauropod.

Long neck for reaching high leaves

- **Ultrasaurus** fossils found in South Korea suggest a dinosaur similar to *Brachiosaurus*, but smaller.

- **Ultrasaurus** fossils from the USA suggest a dinosaur similar to *Brachiosaurus*, but possibly even bigger.

- **Argentinosaurus** from South America may have weighed 100 tonnes or more.

Hips

- **All dinosaurs are classified** in one of two large groups, according to the design and shape of their hip bones.

- **One of the two large groups of dinosaurs** is the Saurischia, meaning 'reptile-hipped'.

- **In a saurischian dinosaur,** the lower front pair of rod-shaped bones in the pelvis project down and forwards.

- **All meat-eating dinosaurs** belonged to the Saurischia.

- **The biggest dinosaurs,** the plant-eating sauropods, belonged to the Saurischia.

- **The second of the two groups of dinosaurs** is the Ornithischia, meaning 'bird-hipped'.

◀ Saurischian ('reptile-hipped') bones.

▶ Ornithischian ('bird-hipped') bones.

> ★ STAR FACT ★
> One way experts assign a dinosaur to a main group is by the structure of its hip bones.

- **In an ornithischian dinosaur,** the lower front pair of rod-shaped bones in the pelvis, called the pubis bones, project down and backwards, lying parallel with another pair, the ischium bones.

- **All dinosaurs** in the group Ornithischia, from small *Heterodontosaurus* to huge *Triceratops*, were plant-eaters.

- **In addition to hips,** there are other differences between the Saurischia and Ornithischia, such as an 'extra' bone called the predentary at the front tip of the lower jaw in ornithischians.

Ostrich-dinosaurs

- **'Ostrich-dinosaurs'** is the common name of the ornithomimosaurs, because of their resemblance to today's largest bird – the flightless ostrich.

- **Ostrich-dinosaurs** were tall and slim, with two long, powerful back legs for very fast running.

- **The front limbs** of ostrich-dinosaurs were like strong arms, with grasping fingers tipped by sharp claws.

- **The eyes of ostrich-dinosaurs** were large and set high on the head.

- **The toothless mouth** of an ostrich-dinosaur was similar to the long, slim beak of a bird.

- **Ostrich-dinosaurs** lived towards the end of the Cretaceous Period, about 100–65

million years ago, in North America and Asia.

- **Fossils** of the ostrich-dinosaur *Struthiomimus* from Alberta, Canada, suggest it was almost 4 m in total length and stood about 2 m tall – the same height as a modern ostrich.

- **The ostrich-dinosaur** *Gallimimus* was almost 6 m long and stood nearly 3 m high.

- **Ostrich-dinosaurs probably ate** seeds, fruits and other plant material, as well as small animals such as worms and lizards, which they may have grasped with their powerful clawed hands.

- **Other ostrich-dinosaurs** included *Dromiceiomimus*, at 3–4 m long, and the slightly bigger *Ornithomimus*.

◀ Ostrich-dinosaurs such as Dromiceiomimus *were probably the fastest runners of their time, speeding along at 60–70 km/h.*

Sauropelta

- *Sauropelta* was a nodosaur – a type of armoured dinosaur.

- **The name** *Sauropelta* means 'shielded reptile', from the many large, conelike lumps of bone – some almost as big as dinner plates – on its head, neck, back and tail.

- **The larger lumps of bone** on *Sauropelta* were interspersed with smaller, fist-sized bony studs.

- *Sauropelta* had a row of sharp spikes along each side of its body, from just behind the eyes to the tail. The spikes decreased in size towards the tail.

- *Sauropelta* was about 7.5 m long, including the tail, and its

★ STAR FACT ★
Sauropelta lived 110–100 million years ago, in present-day Montana and Wyoming, USA.

bulky body and heavy, bony armour meant it probably weighed almost 3 tonnes.

- **The armour** of *Sauropelta* was flexible, almost like lumps of metal set into thick leather, so the dinosaur could twist and turn, but was unable to run fast.

- **Strong, sturdy, pillarlike legs** supported *Sauropelta's* great weight.

- *Sauropelta* probably defended itself by crouching down to protect its softer belly, or swinging its head to jab at an enemy with its long neck spines.

- **Using its beaklike mouth,** *Sauropelta* probably plucked its low-growing plant food.

▲ Sauropelta *was heavily armoured and protected on its upper side, but not on its belly.*

Fossil formation

- **Most of the information** we know, or guess, about dinosaurs comes from fossils.

- **Fossils are the remains of once-living things** that have been preserved in rocks and turned to stone, usually over millions of years.

- **Not just dinosaurs**, but many kinds of living things from prehistoric times have left fossils, including mammals, birds, lizards, fish, insects and plants such as ferns and trees.

- **The flesh, guts and other soft parts** of a dead dinosaur's body were probably eaten by scavengers, or rotted away, and so rarely formed fossils.

- **Fossils usually formed** when a dinosaur's remains were quickly covered by sediments such as sand, silt or mud, especially along the banks of a river or lake, or on the seashore.

- **The sand or other sediment** around a creature

▶ Fossil formation is a very long process, and extremely prone to chance and luck. Only a tiny fraction of animals that ever lived have left remains preserved by this process. Because of the way fossils are formed, animals that died in water or along banks and shores were most likely to become fossilized. It is very rare to find all the parts of an animal arranged as they were in life. Much more often, parts have been separated, jumbled, broken, crushed and distorted.

or plant's remains was gradually buried deeper by more sediment, squeezed under pressure, and cemented together into a solid mass of rock.

- **As the sediment turned to rock**, so did the plant or animal remains encased within it.

- **Information about dinosaurs** comes not only from fossils, but also from 'trace' fossils. These were not actual parts of their bodies, but other items or signs of their presence.

- **Trace fossils** include egg shells, footprints, marks made by claws and teeth, and coprolites – fossilized dinosaur droppings.

1) Animal dies and is covered by water

2) Animal's soft parts are scavenged or rot away

3) Sand, mud or other sediments cover the hard parts, such as the shell teeth, or bones

4) More layers build up as the minerals in the shell and other hard parts turn to rock

5) Erosion (wearing away) of upper rock layers exposes the fossil, which is now solid stone

Stegosaurus

- *Stegosaurus* was the largest of the stegosaurs group.

- **Fossils** of *Stegosaurus* were found mainly in present-day Colorado, Utah and Wyoming, USA.

- *Stegosaurus*, like most of its group, lived towards the end of the Jurassic Period, about 150 million years ago.

- **The mighty** *Stegosaurus* was about 8–9 m long from nose to tail-tip and probably weighed more than 2 tonnes.

- **The most striking feature** of *Stegosaurus* were the large roughly triangular bony plates along its back.

- **The name** *Stegosaurus* means 'roof reptile'. It was given this name because it was first thought that its 80-cm long bony plates lay flat on its back, overlapping slightly like the tiles on a roof.

- **It is now thought** that the back

▶ Stegosaurus's *shorter front limbs meant that it ate low-growing plants.*

plates of *Stegosaurus* stood upright in two long rows.

- **The back plates** of *Stegosaurus* may have been for body temperature control, allowing the dinosaur to warm up quickly if it stood side-on to the sun's rays.

- *Stegosaurus's* back plates may have been covered with brightly coloured skin, possibly to intimidate enemies – they were too flimsy for protection.

- *Stegosaurus's* tail was armed with 4 large spikes, probably for swinging at enemies in self defence.

Great meat-eaters

- **The large meat-eating dinosaurs** belonged to a general group known as the 'carnosaurs'.

- **All carnosaurs** were similar in body shape, and resembled the fearsome *Tyrannosaurus*.

- **Tarbosaurus** was very similar to *Tyrannosaurus*. It lived at the same time, 70–65 million years ago, but in Asia rather than North America.

- **Some experts believe** that *Tarbosaurus* was an Asian version of the North American *Tyrannosaurus*, and both should have been called *Tyrannosaurus*.

- **The carnosaur** *Albertosaurus* was about 8–9 m long and lived 75–70 million years

◀ Albertosaurus *had bony ridges on its eyebrows.*

★ **STAR FACT** ★

Giganotosaurus lived about 100 million years ago in today's Argentina, South America.

ago, in present-day Alberta, Canada.

- **Spinosaurus** was a huge carnosaur from North Africa, measuring 12 m long and weighing 4–5 tonnes. It had tall, rodlike bones on its back, which may have been covered with skin, like a 'sail'.

- **Daspletosaurus** was a 9-m long carnosaur that lived at the end of the Age of Dinosaurs in Alberta, Canada.

- **Biggest of all the carnosaurs** was *Giganotosaurus*, the largest meat-eater ever to walk the Earth.

- **Giganotosaurus** was up to 16 m long and weighed at least 8 tonnes.

◀ The Asian Tarbosaurus *was almost identical to Tyrannosaurus.*

Claws

- **Like reptiles today**, dinosaurs had claws or similar hard structures at the ends of their digits (fingers and toes).

- **Dinosaur claws** were probably made from keratin – the same hard substance that formed their horns, and from which our own fingernails and toenails are made.

- **Claw shapes and sizes** relative to body size varied greatly between dinosaurs.

- **In many meat-eating dinosaurs** that ran on two back legs, the claws on the fingers were long and sharp, similar to a cat's claws.

- **A small, meat-eating dinosaur** such as *Troodon* probably used its finger claws for grabbing small mammals and lizards, and for scrabbling in the soil for insects and worms.

- **Larger meat-eating dinosaurs** such as *Allosaurus* may have used their hand claws to hold and slash their prey.

- **Huge plant-eating sauropods** such as *Diplodocus* had claws on its elephant like feet that resembled nails or hooves.

- **Many dinosaurs** had 5 clawed digits on their feet, but some, such as *Tyrannosaurus*, had only 3 clawed toes on each foot to support their weight.

- **Some of the largest dinosaur claws** belonged to *Deinocheirus* – its massive finger claws were more than 35 cm long.

- ***Deinocheirus*** was probably a gigantic ostrich-dinosaur that lived in the Late Cretaceous Period in Mongolia. Only parts of its fossil hands and arms have been found, so the rest of it remains a mystery.

◀ *The long, relatively sharp finger claws of Troodon were used for extracting small prey and for self defence.*

Asia

- **Hundreds of kinds of dinosaurs** have been discovered on the continent of Asia.

- **In Asia**, most of the dinosaur fossils that have been found so far were located in the Gobi Desert, in Central Asia, and in present-day China. Some were also found in present-day India.

- **Remains of the huge plant-eating sauropod** *Titanosaurus* were uncovered near Umrer, in central India.

- ***Titanosaurus*** was about 12 m long and weighed 5–10 tonnes.

- ***Titanosaurus*** lived about 70 million years ago, and was very similar in shape to its close cousin of the same time, *Saltasaurus*, from South America.

- **Fossils** of the sauropod *Barapasaurus* were found in India. They date from the Early Jurassic Period, about 180 million years ago.

- ***Barapasaurus*** was 18 m long and probably weighed more than 20 tonnes.

- **Fossils** of the dinosaur *Dravidosaurus*, from the stegosaur group, were found near Tiruchirapalli in southern India.

- ***Dravidosaurus*** was about 3 m in total length. It lived much later than other stegosaurs, in the Late Cretaceous Period about 70 million years ago.

- ***Dravidosaurus*** had bony plates sticking up from its back, like *Stegosaurus*.

Gobi Desert Meileyingzi
Jingangkon
Taihezhen
Wujiabai
Umrer
Lufeng
Tiruchirapalli

▲ *Dinosaur fossil finds span this vast continent.*

Coelophysis

- **Coelophysis** was a small, agile dinosaur that lived early in the Age of Dinosaurs, about 220 million years ago.

- **A huge collection of fossils** of *Coelophysis* was found in the late 1940s, at a place now known as Ghost Ranch, New Mexico, USA.

- **Hundreds** of *Coelophysis* were preserved together at Ghost Ranch – possibly a herd that drowned as the result of a sudden flood.

- **Coelophysis** was almost 3 m in total length.

- **The very slim, lightweight build** of *Coelophysis* meant that it probably weighed only 25–28 kg.

- **Coelophysis** belonged to the group of dinosaurs known as coelurosaurs. It probably ate small animals such as insects, worms and lizards.

- **Long, powerful back legs** allowed *Coelophysis* to run fast.

- **The front limbs** of *Coelophysis* were like arms, each with a hand bearing three large, strong, sharp-clawed fingers for grabbing prey.

- **Coelophysis** means 'hollow form'. It was so-named because some of its bones were hollow, like the bones of birds, making it lighter.

- **Coelophysis** had many small, sharp teeth in its narrow, birdlike skull.

◄ *Coelophysis would have stood almost waist-high to a person as it darted about on its long back legs.*

Dinosaur fossil-hunters

- **Many dinosaurs** were found in the USA in the 1870s–90s by Othniel Charles Marsh and Edward Drinker Cope.

- **Marsh and Cope** were great rivals, each one trying to find bigger, better and more dinosaur fossils than the other.

- **The rivalry between Marsh and Cope** extended to bribing people to smash each other's fossils with hammers, planting fake fossils, and damaging food, water and other supplies at each other's camps in the Mid-West.

**Edward Drinker Cope
(1840-97)**   **Othniel Charles Marsh
(1831-99)**

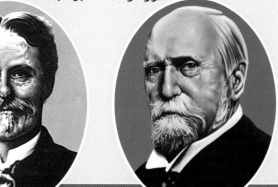

> ★ **STAR FACT** ★
> One of the first great fossil-hunters in the USA was Joseph Leidy, who found *Troodon* in 1856.

- **Cope and Marsh found and described** about 130 new kinds of dinosaurs between 1877 and 1897.

- **Joseph Tyrrell** discovered fossils of *Albertosaurus* in 1884, in what became a very famous dinosaur region, the Red Deer River area of Alberta, Canada.

- **Lawrence Lambe** found and described many North American dinosaur fossils, such as *Centrosaurus* in 1904.

- **German fossil experts** Werner Janensch and Edwin Hennig led expeditions to east Africa in 1908–12, and discovered *Brachiosaurus* and *Kentrosaurus*.

- **From 1933** Yang Zhong-jiang (also called CC Young) led many fossil-hunting trips in various parts of China.

- **José Bonaparte** from Argentina has found many fossils in that region, including *Carnotaurus* in 1985.

Size

- **The biggest dinosaurs** were the sauropods such as *Brachiosaurus* and *Argentinosaurus* – but working out how heavy they were when they were alive is very difficult.

- **Brachiosaurus** is known from many remains, including almost complete skeletons, so its length can be measured accurately.

- **A dinosaur's weight** is estimated from a scaled-down model of its skeleton 'fleshed out' with muscles, guts and skin on the bones, using similar reptiles such as crocodiles for comparison.

- **The size of a dinosaur** model is measured by immersing it in water to find its volume.

- **The volume of a model dinosaur** is scaled up to find the volume of the real dinosaur when it was alive.

▲ It is thought that despite its massive size, *Apatosaurus* would have been able to trot surprisingly quickly on its relatively long legs.

★ STAR FACT ★
The weights and volumes of reptiles alive today are used to calculate the probable weight of a dinosaur when it was alive.

- **The sauropod** *Apatosaurus* is now well known from about 12 skeletons, which between them have almost every bone in its body.

- **Different experts** have 'fleshed out' the skeleton of *Apatosaurus* by different amounts, so estimates of its weight vary from 20 tonnes to more than 50 tonnes.

- **The length of** *Apatosaurus* is known accurately to have been 21 m in total.

- **Fossils of a dinosaur called** *Brontosaurus* were found to be identical to those of *Apatosaurus*, and since the name *Apatosaurus* had been given first, this was the name that had to be kept – so, officially, there is no dinosaur called *Brontosaurus*.

Long neck allowed head to browse in treetops

Massive, heavy tail to swing at attackers

Human-sized meat-eaters present little threat

▶ Reconstruction of Argentinosaurus is based on relatively few of its own bones, combined with other bones from similar sauropod dinosaurs.

Heterodontosaurus

- **Heterodontosaurus** was a very small dinosaur at only 1.2 m in length (about as long as a large dog), and would have stood knee-high to a human.

- **Heterodontosaurus** lived about 205–195 million years ago, at the beginning of the Jurassic Period.

- **Probably standing partly upright** on its longer back legs, *Heterodontosaurus* would have been a fast runner.

- **Fossils** of *Heterodontosaurus* come from Lesotho in southern Africa and Cape Province in South Africa.

▶ *Tiny and slim, Heterodontosaurus looked outwardly similar to mini-meat-eaters such as Compsognathus.*

★ **STAR FACT** ★
The name *Heterodontosaurus* means 'different-toothed reptile'.

- **Most dinosaurs had teeth of only one shape** in their jaws, but *Heterodontosaurus* had three types of teeth.

- **The front teeth** of *Heterodontosaurus* were small, sharp and found only in the upper jaw. They bit against the horny, beak-like lower front of the mouth.

- **The four middle teeth** of *Heterodontosaurus* were long and curved, similar to the tusks of a wild boar, and were perhaps used for fighting rivals or in self-defence.

- **The back or cheek teeth** of *Heterodontosaurus* were long and had sharp tops for chewing.

- **Heterodontosaurus** probably ate low-growing plants such as ferns.

Speed

- **The fastest-running dinosaurs** had long, slim, muscular legs and small, lightweight bodies.

- **'Ostrich-dinosaurs'** were probably the speediest dinosaurs, perhaps attaining the same top speed as today's ostrich – 70 km/h.

- **The main leg muscles** of the ostrich-dinosaur *Struthiomimus* were in its hips and thighs.

- **The hip and leg design** of ostrich-dinosaurs meant that they could swing their limbs to and fro quickly, like those of a modern racehorse.

- **Large, powerful, plant-eating dinosaurs** such as the 'duck-bill' *Edmontosaurus* may have pounded along on their huge back legs at 40 km/h.

- **Plant-eaters** such as *Iguanodon* and *Muttaburrasaurus* may have trotted along at 10–12 km/h for many hours.

- **Some experts think** that the great meat-eater *Tyrannosaurus* may have been able to run at 50 km/h.

- **Other experts think** *Tyrannosaurus* was a relatively slow runner at 30 km/h (almost as fast as a human sprinter).

- **The slowest dinosaurs** were giant sauropods such as *Brachiosaurus*, which probably plodded at 4–6 km/h (about human walking speed).

- **Today's fastest runner**, the cheetah, would beat any dinosaur with its maximum burst of speed of more than 100 km/h.

◀ *In Struthiomimus's legs, the bulk of the muscle was in the hips and upper thighs, as in an ostrich or horse – both rapid runners.*

Allosaurus

- **Allosaurus** was a huge meat-eating dinosaur, almost as big as *Tyrannosaurus*.

- **Allosaurus** was about 11–12 m in total length.

- **The weight** of *Allosaurus* is variously estimated at 1.5–4 tonnes.

- **The head** of *Allosaurus* was almost 1 m long, but its skull was light, with large gaps or 'windows' that would have been covered by muscle and skin.

- **Allosaurus** could not only open its jaws in a huge gape, but it could also flex them so that the whole mouth became wider, for an even bigger bite.

- **Allosaurus** lived about 155–135 million years ago, during the Late Jurassic and Early Cretaceous Periods.

> ★ **STAR FACT** ★
> The remains of 60 *Allosaurus* were found in the Cleveland-Lloyd Dinosaur Quarry, Utah, USA.

- ◀ **Allosaurus** almost rivalled *Tyrannosaurus* in size, but lived 70 million years earlier.

- **Most** *Allosaurus* fossils come from the states in the American Midwest.

- **Allosaurus** may have hunted the giant sauropod dinosaurs such as *Diplodocus*, *Camarasaurus* and *Brachiosaurus*.

- **Fossils** of *Allosaurus* were identified in Africa, and a smaller or 'dwarf' version was found in Australia.

Armour

- **Many kinds of dinosaurs** had protective 'armour'.

- **Some armour** took the form of bony plates, or osteoderms, embedded in the skin.

- **A dinosaur with armour** might weigh twice as much as a same-sized dinosaur without armour.

- **Armoured dinosaurs** are divided into two main groups – the ankylosaurs and the nodosaurs.

- **The large sauropod** *Saltasaurus* had a kind of armour.

- ▶ **Ankylosaurus's** tail club was nearly 1 m across.

- **Saltasaurus** had hundreds of small, bony lumps, each as big as a pea, packed together in the skin of its back.

- **On its back**, *Saltasaurus* also had about 50 larger pieces of bone the size of a human hand.

- **Saltasaurus** is named after the Salta region of Argentina, where its fossils were found.

- **Uruguay** provided another site for *Saltasaurus* fossils.

- **Saltasaurus** was 12 m long and weighed about 3–4 tonnes.

Carnotaurus

- **The big, powerful, meat-eating** Carnotaurus is in the carnosaur group of dinosaurs.

- **Carnotaurus fossils come** mainly from the Chubut region of Argentina, South America.

- **Carnotaurus lived about** 100 million years ago.

- **A medium-sized dinosaur**, Carnotaurus was about 7.5 m in total length and weighed up to 1 tonne.

- **The skull of** Carnotaurus was relatively tall from top to bottom and short from front to back, compared to other carnosaurs like Allosaurus and Tyrannosaurus, giving it a snub-snouted appearance.

- **The name** Carnotaurus means 'meat-eating bull', referring partly to its bull-like face.

- **Carnotaurus had two curious, cone-shaped** bony crests or 'horns', one above each eye, where the horns of a modern bull would be.

- **Rows of extra-large scales**, like small lumps, ran along Carnotaurus from its head to its tail.

- **Like** Tyrannosaurus, Carnotaurus had very small front limbs that could not reach its mouth, and may have had no use.

◄ The fossils of Carnotaurus were first discovered in 1985.

- **Carnotaurus** probably ate plant-eating dinosaurs such as Chubutisaurus, although its teeth and jaws were not especially big or strong.

Ankylosaurs

- **Ankylosaurs** had a protective armour of bony plates.

- **Unlike the armoured nodosaurs**, ankylosaurs had a large lump of bone at the ends of their tails, which they used as a hammer or club.

- **One of the best-known ankylosaurs**, from the preserved remains of about 40 individuals, is Euoplocephalus.

► Euoplocephalus probably cropped low plants with its beaklike mouth.

- **Euoplocephalus**, or 'well-armoured head', had bony shields on its head and body, and even had bony eyelids. Blunt spikes ran along its back.

- **The hefty** Euoplocephalus was about 7 m long and weighed 2 tonnes or more.

- **Euoplocephalus** lived about 75–70 million years ago in Alberta, Canada and Montana, USA.

- **Specimens of** Euoplocephalus are usually found singly, so it probably did not live in herds.

- **The ankylosaur** Pinacosaurus had bony nodules like chain-mail armour in its skin, and rows of blunt spikes from neck to tail.

- **Ankylosaurs** had small, weak teeth, and probably ate soft, low-growing ferns and horsetails.

★ STAR FACT ★
Pinacosaurus was about 6 m long and lived in Asia some 80–75 million years ago.

Herbivores

- **Hundreds of kinds of dinosaurs** were herbivores, or plant-eaters. As time passed, the plants available for them to eat changed or evolved.

- **Early in the Age of Dinosaurs**, during the Triassic Period, the main plants for dinosaurs to eat were conifer trees, gingkoes, cycads and the smaller seed-ferns, ferns, horsetails and club-mosses.

- **A few cycads** are still found today. They resemble palm trees, with umbrella-like crowns of long green fronds on top of tall, unbranched, trunklike stems.

- **In the Triassic Period**, only prosauropod dinosaurs were big enough or had necks long enough to reach tall cycad fronds or gingko leaves.

- **In the Jurassic Period**, tall conifers such as redwoods and 'monkey-puzzle' trees became common.

- **The huge, long-necked sauropods** of the Jurassic Period would have been able to reach high into tall conifer trees to rake off their needles.

- **In the Middle Cretaceous Period**, a new type of plant food appeared – the flowering plants.

★ STAR FACT ★
Gingkoes are still found today in the form of the maidenhair tree, with fan-shaped leaves.

- **By the end of the Cretaceous Period** there were many flowering trees and shrubs, such as magnolias, maples and walnuts.

- **No dinosaurs ate grass**, because grasses did not appear on Earth until 30–20 million years ago, long after the dinosaurs had died out.

▼ During the warm, damp Jurassic Period, plants thrived in most areas, covering land that previously had been barren. Massive plant-eaters such as Barosaurus thrived on the high-level fronds, needles and leaves of towering tree-ferns, gingkoes and conifers.

Barosaurus, 26 m long and 25–30 tonnes

Triceratops

- **Many fossil remains** of *Triceratops* have been found. It is one of the most studied and best known dinosaurs.

- *Triceratops* was the largest of the plant-eating ceratopsians, or 'horn-faced' dinosaurs.

- *Triceratops* lived at the very end of the Age of Dinosaurs, 67–65 million years ago.

- **Fossils of 50 or so** *Triceratops* have been found in North America, though no complete skeleton has been found.

- *Triceratops* was about 9 m long and weighed 5–6 tonnes – as big as the largest elephants of today.

- **As well as a short nose horn** and two long eyebrow horns, *Triceratops* also had a wide, sweeping frill that covered its neck like a curved plate.

- **The neck frill** of *Triceratops* may have been an anchor for the dinosaur's powerful chewing muscles.

- **Acting as a shield**, the bony neck frill of *Triceratops* may have protected it as it faced predators head-on.

- *Triceratops*' neck frill may have been brightly coloured, to impress rivals or enemies.

- **The beak-like front** of *Triceratops*' mouth was toothless, but it had sharp teeth for chewing in its cheeks.

◀ The beak, head and neck frill of *Triceratops* made up almost a quarter of its length.

Earliest dinosaurs

- **The first known dinosaurs** appeared about 230–225 million years ago, in the Middle Triassic Period.

- **The earliest dinosaurs** were small-to-medium meat-eaters with sharp teeth and claws. They ran quickly on their two longer back legs.

- **Fossils** of *Herrerasaurus* date from 228 million years ago and were found near San Juan in Argentina, South America.

- *Herrerasaurus* was about 3 m in total length, and probably weighed some 90 kg.

▲ *Staurikosaurus was about 2 m in total length.*

- **At about the same time and in the same place** as *Herrerasaurus*, there lived a similar-shaped dinosaur named *Eoraptor*, at only 1.5 m long.

- **The name** *Eoraptor* means 'dawn plunderer' or 'early thief'.

- *Staurikosaurus* was a meat-eater similar to *Herrerasaurus*. It is known to have lived about the same time, in present-day Brazil, South America.

- *Procompsognathus* was another early meat-eater. It lived in the Late Triassic Period in Germany.

- *Pisanosaurus* lived in Argentina in the Late Triassic Period, and was only 1 m long. It may have been a plant-eater similar to *Lesothosaurus*.

★ STAR FACT ★
Eoraptor and *Herrerasaurus* hunted small animals such as lizards, insects and mammal-like reptiles.

Smallest dinosaurs

- **One of the smallest dinosaurs** was *Compsognathus*, which lived during the Late Jurassic Period, 155–150 million years ago.

- **Fossils** of *Compsognathus* come from Europe, especially southern Germany and southeastern France.

- *Compsognathus* was slim, with a long, narrow tail.It probably weighed less than 3 kg.

- **Each hand** of *Compsognathus* had two clawed fingers, and each foot had three long, clawed running toes, with another toe (the first or big toe) placed higher up in the 'ankle' region.

- *Compsognathus* had small teeth that were sharp and curved. It probably darted through the undergrowth

▼ *Very few fossils of* Compsognathus *have been found. They mainly belong to two individuals, one from Var, France, and the other from Bavaria, Germany. The larger specimen was about 1.2 m long, and was presumably an adult.*

★ STAR FACT ★
The little *Compsognathus* was only about 1 m long, and some specimens were even smaller, at 70 cm long.

after insects, spiders, worms and similar small prey.

- **Two other very small dinosaurs** were *Heterodontosaurus* and the 1-m long fabrosaur *Lesothosaurus*.

- **The smallest fossil dinosaur specimens** found to date are of *Mussaurus*, which means 'mouse reptile'.

- *Mussaurus* was a plant-eating prosauropod similar to *Plateosaurus*, which lived in the Late Triassic Period in South America.

- **The fossils of** *Mussaurus* measure just 20 cm long – but these are the fossils of babies, just hatched from their eggs. The babies would have grown into adults measuring 3 m long.

Africa

- **The first major discoveries** of dinosaur fossils in Africa were made from 1907, at Tendaguru in present-day Tanzania, east Africa.

- **Discoveries at Tendaguru** in east Africa included the giant sauropod *Brachiosaurus*, the smaller *Dicraeosaurus*, and the stegosaur-like *Kentrosaurus*.

- **Remains** of the massive sauropod *Cetiosaurus* were uncovered in Morocco, north Africa.

- **Camarasaurus**, a 20-tonne plant-eater, is known from fossils found in Niger, as well as from European and North American fossils.

- **Fossils** of the huge, sail-backed meat-eater *Spinosaurus* come from Morocco and Egypt.

- **The sail-backed plant-eater**

- **Ouranosaurus** is known from remains found in Niger.

- **Many sauropod fossils** were uncovered at sites in Zimbabwe, including *Barosaurus* and *Vulcanodon*.

- **Remains** of the medium-sized plant-eating prosauropod *Massospondylus* were extracted from several sites in southern Africa.

- **Fossils** thought to belong to the small prosauropod *Anchisaurus* were found in southern Africa, the only site for this dinosaur outside North America.

- **During the 1908–12 fossil-hunting expedition** to Tendaguru, more than 250 tonnes of fossil bones and rocks were carried by people for 65 km to the nearest port, for transport to Germany.

Wawmda
Bahariya
Gadoufaoua
Tendaguru
Lake Kariba
Kadzi
Ladybrand
Harrismith
Mafetang
Herschel

▲ In Africa, as elsewhere, fossils are easier to find in places with bare, rocky soils.

Mamenchisaurus

- *Mamenchisaurus* was a massive plant-eating dinosaur, a sauropod similar in appearance to *Diplodocus*.

- **The huge** *Mamenchisaurus* measured about 25 m from nose to tail tip.

- **The weight of** *Mamenchisaurus* has been estimated at 20–35 tonnes.

- **Mamenchisaurus** lived during the late Jurassic Period, from 160 to perhaps 140 million years ago.

- **The hugely long neck** of *Mamenchisaurus* had up to 19 vertebrae, or neckbones – more than almost any other dinosaur.

- **Mamenchisaurus** fossils were found in China.

- **The name** *Mamenchisaurus* is taken from the place

where its fossils were discovered – Mamen Stream.

- **Mamenchisaurus** may be a close cousin of other sauropod dinosaurs found in the region, including *Euhelopus* and *Omeisaurus*.

- **Mamenchisaurus** may have stretched its vast neck high into trees to crop leaves, or – less likely – it may have lived in swamps and eaten soft water plants.

- **Mamenchisaurus** had the longest neck, at up to 15 m, of any dinosaur yet discovered.

▲ The joints between the fossil bones of Mamenchisaurus's 15-m long neck show that the neck was not very flexible.

Deinonychus

- **Deinonychus** is one of the best-known members from the group of meat-eaters known as raptors.

- **The Middle Cretaceous Period**, about 115–100 million years ago, is when *Deinonychus* thrived.

- **Fossils** of *Deinonychus* come from the American

Midwest, mainly from Montana and Wyoming.

- **Deinonychus** was about 3 m long from nose to tail and weighed 60–70 kg, about the same as an adult human.

- **When remains of Deinonychus were dug up** and studied in the 1960s, they exploded the myth that dinosaurs were slow, small-brained and stupid.

- **Powerful, speedy and agile,** *Deinonychus* may have hunted in packs, like today's lions and wolves.

- **Deinonychus** had large hands with three powerful fingers, each tipped with a dangerous sharp claw.

- **On each foot**, *Deinonychus* had a massive, scythelike claw that it could flick in an arc to slice open prey.

- **The tail** of *Deinonychus* was stiff and could not be swished.

- **Deinonychus** and other similar dromaeosaurs, such as *Velociraptor*, were the basis for the cunning and terrifying raptors of the *Jurassic Park* films.

◀ Deinonychus *would often attack prey much larger than itself.*

Myths

- **Dinosaurs were the only animals alive** during the Age of Dinosaurs – false, there were many kinds of creatures, from worms, insects and fish to other kinds of reptiles.

- **Dinosaurs flew in the air** – false, although other reptiles called pterosaurs did fly.

- **Dinosaurs lived in the sea** – false, although other reptiles such as ichthyosaurs and plesiosaurs did.

- **Mammals appeared** on Earth after the dinosaurs died out – false. Small mammals lived all through the Age of Dinosaurs.

- **A single kind of dinosaur** survived all through the Age of Dinosaurs – false. A few

▶ Aquatic reptiles such as plesiosaurs and pliosaurs are sometimes mistakenly called 'dinosaurs'.

> ★ STAR FACT ★
> Dinosaurs and humans fought each other – false. The last dinosaurs died out more than 60 million years before humans appeared.

kinds may have lived for 10, 20 or even 30 million years, but none came close to 160 million years.

- **Dinosaurs were huge lizards** – false. Dinosaurs were reptiles, but not members of the lizard group.

- **Dinosaurs gave birth to babies** – false. As far as we know, dinosaurs laid eggs.

- **All dinosaurs were green** – false, probably.

- **Dinosaurs live on today** – false …

… unless you've found one!

Reconstructions

- **No complete fossilized dinosaur**, with all its skin, muscles, guts and other soft parts, has yet been found.

- **Most dinosaurs are reconstructed** from the fossils of their hard parts – chiefly teeth, bones, horns and claws.

- **The vast majority of dinosaurs** are known from only a few fossil parts, such as several fragments of bones.

- **Fossil parts** of other, similar dinosaurs are often used in reconstructions to 'fill in' missing bones, teeth, and even missing heads, limbs or tails.

- **Soft body parts** from modern reptiles such as lizards are used as a guide for the reconstruction of a dinosaur's muscles and guts, which are added to the fossils.

- **On rare occasions**, remains are found of a dinosaur

> ★ **STAR FACT** ★
> 'Sue', the part-mummified *Tyrannosaurus*, was sold in 1997 for more than $8.3 million to the Field Museum, Chicago, USA.

body that dried out rapidly so that quite a few parts were preserved as mummified fossils.

- **One of the best-known**, part-mummified dinosaur fossils is 'Sue', a specimen of *Tyrannosaurus* found in 1990 in South Dakota, USA.

- **'Sue' is the biggest** and most complete preserved *Tyrannosaurus* ever found.

- **'Sue'** was a female *Tyrannosaurus*. It was named after its discoverer, fossil-hunter Susan Hendrickson of the Black Hills Institute of Geological Research.

▼ At a fossil site or 'dig', scientists record every stage of excavation with measurements, maps, photographs and sketches.

Frame supports upper body

Fossil 'bones' on display are usually lightweight copies in GRP (glass-reinforced plastic)

▶ Some fragile fossils are wrapped in plaster bandages. These harden to support and protect the remains so that they can be moved.

▶ This early reconstruction shows an ornithopod dinosaur similar to Iguanodon in a fairly upright, kangaroo-like pose. As their knowledge increases, dinosaur experts change their views about how dinosaurs stood, walked and ran. Modern reconstructions tend to show Iguanodon on the move with its body almost horizontal.

Mini model shows fleshed-out appearance in life at much smaller scale

Male and female

- **In many living reptiles**, females are larger than males.

- **In dinosaur fossils**, the shapes of the hip bones and head crests can indicate if the creatures were male or female.

- **Head crest fossils** of different sizes and proportions belonging to the hadrosaur (duck-billed dinosaur) *Lambeosaurus* have been found.

- **Some** *Lambeosaurus* had short, rounded main crests with small, spikelike spurs pointing up and back.

- **Other** *Lambeosaurus* had a large, angular main crest with a large spur pointing up and back.

★ **STAR FACT** ★
In *Parasaurolophus* specimens, some head crests were twice as long as others – probably a male-female difference.

- **The head crest differences** in *Lambeosaurus* fossils may indicate that males and females looked different.

- **Remains of the hadrosaur** *Corythosaurus* show two main sizes of head crest, perhaps one belonging to females and the other to males.

- **New studies** in the variations of head crests led to more than 8 different species of dinosaurs being reclassified as one species of *Corythosaurus*.

- **In dinosaurs and other animals**, differences between the sexes – either in size or specific features – is known as sexual dimorphism.

◀ *The large, angular head crest shows this is a male Corythosaurus.*

Herds

- **When the fossils of many individuals** of the same type are found together, there are various possible causes.

- **One reason why** individuals of the same dinosaur type are found preserved together is because their bodies were swept to the same place by a flood.

- **A group of individuals** of the same type may have died in the same place if they had lived there as a group.

- **There is much evidence** that various dinosaur types lived in groups or herds, examples being *Diplodocus*, *Triceratops* and *Iguanodon*.

- **Some fossil groups** include dinosaurs of different ages, from newly hatched babies to youngsters and adults.

- **Fossil footprints** suggest some dinosaurs lived in herds.

- **Footprints** of a plant-eating dinosaur were found with the prints of a meat-eater to one side of them – perhaps evidence of a hunter pursuing its victim.

▶ *A mixed-age herd would have left similar footprints of different sizes.*

★ **STAR FACT** ★
At Peace River Canyon, British Columbia, Canada, some 1700 footprints were found.

- **Sometimes** the footprints of many dinosaurs of the same type are found together, suggesting a herd.

- **Sometimes larger footprints** are found to the sides of smaller ones, possibly indicating that adults guarded their young between them.

Stegosaurs

- **Stegosaurs** were a group of plant-eating dinosaurs that lived mainly during the Late Jurassic Period, 160–140 million years ago.

- **Stegosaurs are named after** the best-known of their group, *Stegosaurus*.

- **Stegosaurs are often called** 'plated dinosaurs', from the large, flat plates or slabs of bone on their backs.

- **Stegosaurs** probably first

◀ The back plates of Kentrosaurus were taller and narrower than those of Stegosaurus.

> ★ STAR FACT ★
> The back plates of *Kentrosaurus* were leaf- or diamond-shaped to about halfway along its back, and spike-shaped on its hips and tail.

appeared in eastern Asia, then spread to other continents, especially North America and Africa.

- **The stegosaur** *Kentrosaurus* was about 5 m long and weighed an estimated 1 tonne.

- **The name** *Kentrosaurus* means 'spiky reptile'.

- **Kentrosaurus** lived about 155–150 million years ago in east Africa.

- **Most stegosaurs had no teeth** at the fronts of their mouths, but had horny beaks, like those of birds, for snipping off leaves.

- **Most stegosaurs chewed** their food with small, ridged cheek teeth.

Cousins: Air

- **Many flying creatures** lived during the Age of Dinosaurs, especially insects such as flies and dragonflies, and also birds.

- **The main flying reptiles** during the Age of Dinosaurs were the pterosaurs, or 'winged reptiles'.

- **Hundreds of different kinds** of pterosaurs came and went through almost the entire Age of Dinosaurs, about 220–65 million years ago.

- **The arms of a pterosaur** resembled wings – a light, thin, stretchy wing membrane was held out mainly by the finger bones, especially the fourth finger.

- **Pterosaurs** are sometimes called pterodactyls,

▶ The wings of Quetzalcoatlus were as long as those of a four-seater airplane.

but *Pterodactylus* was just one kind of pterosaur.

- **Pterodactylus** had a wing span of 1–2 m. It lived 150–140 million years ago in southern Germany.

- **Some pterosaurs**, such as *Pterodactylus*, had very short tails, or no tail at all.

▲ Pteranodon had a long projection on the back of its head.

- **The pterosaur** *Rhamphorhynchus* had a long, trailing tail with a widened, paddle-shaped end.

- **Fossils** suggest that some pterosaurs, such as *Sordes*, had fur, and may have been warm-blooded, agile fliers rather than slow, clumsy gliders.

- **The biggest pterosaur**, and the largest flying animal ever, was *Quetzalcoatlus*. Its 'beak' was longer than an adult human, and its wings were almost 12 m across.

Noses

- **Dinosaurs breathed** through their mouths and/or noses, like many other creatures today.

- **Fossil dinosaur skulls** show that there were two nose openings, called nares, in the bone.

- **A dinosaur's two nasal openings**, or nares, led to nasal chambers inside the skull, where the smell organs were located.

- **Some meat-eaters**, especially carnosaurs such as *Allosaurus* and *Tyrannosaurus*, had very large nasal chambers

▲ The nasal openings of Baryonyx were towards the front of its snout, rather than at the tip.

and probably had an excellent sense of smell.

- **In most dinosaurs** the nasal openings were at the front of the snout, just above the upper jaw.

- **In some dinosaurs**, especially sauropods such as *Mamenchisaurus* and *Brachiosaurus*, the nasal openings were higher on the skull, between the eyes.

- **Fossils** show that air passages led from the nasal chambers rearwards into the head for breathing.

- **The nasal openings** in a dinosaur's skull bone led to external openings, or nostrils, in the skin.

- **New evidence** from animals alive today suggests that a dinosaur's nostrils would have been lower down than the nares (the openings in the skull bone), towards the front of the snout.

Nests and eggs

▶ Most dinosaur eggs were elongated and had tough, flexible shells, like stiff leather.

- **There are hundreds of discoveries** of fossil dinosaur eggs and nests, found with the parent dinosaurs.

- **Eggs and nests** are known of the pig-sized plant-eater *Protoceratops*, an early kind of horned dinosaur.

- **Many** *Protoceratops*' nests were found in a small area, showing that these dinosaurs bred in colonies.

- ***Protoceratops*' nests** were shallow, bowl-shaped pits about 1 m across, scraped in the dry, sandy earth and surrounded by low walls.

- **At the Protoceratops site**, it was discovered that new nests had been made on top of old ones, showing that the colony was used again year after year.

- **The female** *Protoceratops* laid a clutch of 20 or so tough-

shelled, sausage-shaped eggs.

- ***Protoceratops*' eggs** were probably covered with earth and incubated by the heat of the sun.

- **Nests and eggs** of the small plant-eater *Orodromeus* have been found in Montana, USA.

- **In each nest** about 20 *Orodromeus* eggs were arranged neatly in a spiral, starting with one in the centre and working outwards.

- ***Protoceratops*** arranged its eggs neatly in its nest, in a circle or spiral shape resembling the spokes of a wheel.

▶ Protoceratops was about 1.8 m long.

Names: 2

- **More than 100 kinds of dinosaurs** have been named after the people who first discovered their fossils, dug them up, or reconstructed the dinosaur.

- **The very large duck-bill (hadrosaur)** *Lambeosaurus* was named after Canadian fossil expert Lawrence Lambe.

- **Lawrence Lambe** worked mainly during the early 1900s, and named one of his finds *Stephanosaurus*.

- **In the 1920s**, *Stephanosaurus* was re-studied and renamed, along with *Didanodon*, as *Lambeosaurus*, in honour of Lambe's great work.

- **The full name** of the 'heavy-claw' meat-

▲ *The first fossil find of Baryonyx was its huge thumb claw.*

★ **STAR FACT** ★
Australian *Leaellynasaura* was named after Lea Ellyn, the daughter of its discoverers.

eater *Baryonyx* is *Baryonyx walkeri*, after Bill Walker, the discoverer of its massive claw.

- **Part-time fossil-hunter** Bill Walker found the claw of *Baryonyx* in a clay pit quarry in Surrey, England.

- **Some dinosaur names** are quite technical, such as *Diplodocus*, which means 'double beam' – it was named for its tail bones, which have two long projections like a pair of skis.

- **The 4-m long plant-eater** *Othnielia*, related to *Hypsilophodon*, was named after the late 19th-century American fossil-hunter Othniel Charles Marsh.

- **Parksosaurus**, a 2.5-m long plant-eater related to *Hypsilophodon*, was named in honour of Canadian dinosaur expert William Parks.

Diplodocus

- **Diplodocus** was a huge plant-eating dinosaur belonging to the group known as the sauropods.

- **Diplodocus** lived during the Late Jurassic Period, about 155–145 million years ago.

- **The first discovery** of *Diplodocus* fossils was in 1877, near Canyon City, Colorado, USA.

- **The main fossils** of *Diplodocus* were found in the Midwest of the USA, in Colorado, Utah and Wyoming.

- **At an incredible 27 m** or more in length, *Diplodocus* is one of the longest dinosaurs known.

- **Although so long**, *Diplodocus* was quite lightly built – it probably weighed 'only' 10–12 tonnes!

- **Diplodocus** probably swung its tiny head on its enormous neck to reach fronds and foliage in the trees.

- **The teeth** of *Diplodocus* were slim rods that formed a comblike fringe only around the front of its mouth.

- **Diplodocus** may have used its comblike teeth to strip leaves from twigs and swallow them without chewing.

- **Diplodocus's** nostrils were so high on its skull (almost above its eyes) that experts once thought it had a trunk like an elephant's.

▶ Diplodocus *was long but light for a sauropod, weighing 'only' about 10 tonnes.*

Colours

- **No one knows** for certain what colours dinosaurs were.

- **There are several good fossil specimens** of dinosaur skin, but all of them are stone coloured, because fossils are living things that have turned to stone.

- **Some experts believe** that dinosaurs were similar in colour to crocodiles – dull greens and browns.

- **Dinosaurs** that were dull greens and browns would have been well camouflaged among trees, rocks and earth.

- **According to some experts**, certain dinosaurs may have been bright yellow, red or blue, and possibly striped or patched, like some of today's lizards and snakes.

- **Some dinosaurs** may have been brightly coloured to frighten off predators or to intimidate rivals at breeding time.

- **The tall 'sails'** of skin on the backs of the plant-eater *Ouranosaurus* and the meat-eater *Spinosaurus* may have been for visual display, as well as for (or instead of) temperature control.

- **The large, bony back plates** on stegosaurs may have been used for colourful displays to rivals.

- **The large neck frills** of horned dinosaurs such as *Triceratops* were possibly very colourful and used for display.

- **Recent finds** of dinosaur skin and scales with microscopic ridges and patterns on their surface may show how the scales reflected light, and so what colour they would have appeared.

◄ *Like all reconstructions from fossils, the colours of feathered dinosaur Caudipteryx are intelligent guesswork.*

Ornitholestes

- **Ornitholestes** was a smallish meat-eating dinosaur in the group known as coelurosaurs.

- **The name** *Ornitholestes* means 'bird robber' – experts who studied its fossils in the early 1900s imagined it chasing and killing the earliest birds.

- **Ornitholestes** lived about 150 million years ago, at the same time as the first birds.

- **Present-day Wyoming, USA,** was the home of *Ornitholestes*, a continent away from the earliest birds in Europe.

- **Only one specimen** of *Ornitholestes* has been found, along with parts of a hand at another site.

- **Ornitholestes** was about 2 m long from nose to tail-tip.

> ★ STAR FACT ★
> According to some experts, *Ornitholestes* may have had a slight ridge or crest on its nose. Other experts disagree.

- **Slim and lightweight,** *Ornitholestes* probably weighed only about 12–15 kg.

- **The teeth** of *Ornitholestes* were small and well-spaced, but also slim and sharp, well suited to grabbing small animals for food.

- **Ornitholestes** had very strong arms and hands, and powerful fingers with long claws, ideal for grabbing baby dinosaurs newly hatched from their eggs.

◄ *Ornitholestes relied for survival on speed and its good senses of sight and smell.*

Duck-bills

- **'Duck-bills'** is the common name for the group of dinosaurs called hadrosaurs.

- **Hadrosaurs were big plant-eaters** that walked mainly on their two large, powerful rear legs.

- **Hadrosaurs** were one of the last main dinosaur groups to appear on Earth, less than 100 million years ago.

- **Hadrosaurs were named after** *Hadrosaurus*, the first dinosaur of the group to be discovered as fossils, found in 1858 in New Jersey, USA.

- **Most hadrosaurs had wide mouths** that were flattened and toothless at the front, like a duck's beak.

- **Huge numbers of cheek teeth** filled the back of the hadrosaur's mouth, arranged in rows called batteries. They were ideal for chewing tough plant food.

- **Some hadrosaurs** had tall, elaborate crests or projections of bone on their heads, notably *Corythosaurus*, *Tsintaosaurus*, *Saurolophus* and *Parasaurolophus*.

- **Hadrosaurs that lacked bony crests** and had low, smooth heads included *Anatosaurus*, *Bactrosaurus*, *Kritosaurus* and *Edmontosaurus*.

- **The name** *Hadrosaurus* means 'big reptile'.

▶ Parasaurolophus may have had a 'web' of brightly coloured skin extending from its bony head crest to the back of its neck – perhaps part of a visual display for mating, herd dominance or gaining territory. Alternatively, the bony crest may have lacked skin and simply projected upwards and backwards like a pole.

Possible inflatable bag of skin on snout and forehead

Tall, relatively narrow tail with muscular tail base to swish tail from side to side

▲ Asian Saurolophus was about 12 m long – larger than its North American counterparts. It also had a relatively larger, horn-like head crest, which may have supported a balloon-like pouch of skin that the dinosaur could inflate to make a trumpeting call.

Powerful rear legs for rapid walking and trotting

★ STAR FACT ★

Edmontosaurus may have had a loose bag of skin on its nose that it blew up like a balloon to make a honking or trumpeting noise – perhaps a breeding call.

Warm or cold blood?

- **If dinosaurs were cold-blooded** and obtained heat only from their surroundings, like reptiles today, they would have been slow or inactive in cold conditions.

- **If dinosaurs were warm-blooded**, like birds and mammals today, they would have been able to stay warm and active in cold conditions.

- **Some time ago** experts believed that all dinosaurs were cold-blooded, but today there is much disagreement.

- **One type of evidence** for warm-bloodedness comes from the detailed structure of the insides of very well-preserved fossil bones.

- **The inside structure** of some fossil dinosaur bones is more like that of warm-blooded creatures than reptiles.

▲ The detailed microscopic structure inside bones can give clues as to warm- or cold-bloodedness.

- **Certain small, meat-eating dinosaurs** may have evolved into birds, and since birds are warm-blooded, these dinosaurs may have been, too.

- **In a 'snapshot' count** of dinosaur fossils, the number of predators compared to prey is more like that in mammals than in reptiles.

- **Some dinosaurs** were thought to live in herds and raise families, as many birds and mammals do today. In reptiles, such behaviour is rare.

- **Most dinosaurs stood upright** on straight legs, a posture common to warm-blooded creatures, but not to other, cold-blooded reptiles.

- **If dinosaurs had been warm-blooded**, they would probably have needed to eat at least 10 times more food than if they were cold-blooded, to 'burn' food energy and make heat.

Eustreptospondylus

- **Eustreptospondylus** was a large meat-eater that lived in present-day Oxfordshire and Buckinghamshire, in central southern England.

- **Eustreptospondylus** lived about 165 million years ago.

- **In the 1850s**, a fairly complete skeleton of a young Eustreptospondylus was found near Wolvercote, Oxford, but was named as Megalosaurus, the only other big meat-eater known from the region.

- **In 1964**, British fossil expert Alick Walker showed that the Wolvercote dinosaur was not Megalosaurus, and gave it a new name, Eustreptospondylus.

- **Eustreptospondylus** means 'well curved, or true reversed, backbone'.

- **A full-grown** Eustreptospondylus measured about 7 m in total length.

- **Eustreptospondylus** is estimated to have weighed a massive 200–250 kg.

- **In its enormous mouth**, Eustreptospondylus had a great number of small, sharp teeth.

- **Eustreptospondylus** may have hunted sauropods such as Cetiosaurus and stegosaurs, two groups that roamed the region at the time.

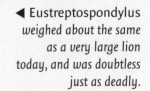

◄ Eustreptospondylus weighed about the same as a very large lion today, and was doubtless just as deadly.

★ STAR FACT ★

For more than 100 years, the fossil Eustreptospondylus from near Oxford was known by the name Megalosaurus.

Pachycephalosaurs

- **The pachycephalosaurs** are named after one of the best-known members of the group, *Pachycephalosaurus*.

- *Pachycephalosaurus* means 'thick-headed reptile', due to the domed and hugely thickened bone on the top of its skull – like a cyclist's crash helmet.

- **Pachycephalosaurs** were one of the last dinosaur groups to thrive. They lived 75–65 million years ago.

Extra thick skull bone

◀ Typical of its group, Pachycephalosaurus had a thickened layer of bone on the top of its head.

★ STAR FACT ★
Pachycephalosaurs are often known as the 'bone-heads' or 'helmet-heads'.

- **Pachycephalosaurs were plant-eaters** that stood up and ran on their longer back legs.

- *Pachycephalosaurus* was about 4.5 m long from nose to tail, and lived in the American Midwest.

- *Stegoceras*, also from the American Midwest, was about 2.5 m long with a body the size of a goat.

- *Homalocephale*, another pachycephalosaur, was about 3 m long and had a flatter skull. It lived in east Asia.

- **Pachycephalosaurs** may have defended themselves by lowering their heads and charging at their enemies.

- **At breeding time**, the males may have engaged in head-butting contests, as some sheep and goats do today.

Baryonyx

- *Baryonyx* was a large meat-eating dinosaur that lived about 120 million years ago.

- **The first fossil find** of *Baryonyx* was its huge thumb claw, discovered in Surrey, England, in 1983.

- **The total length** of *Baryonyx* was 10–11 m.

- *Baryonyx* had a slim shape and long, narrow tail, and probably weighed less than 2 tonnes.

- **The head** of *Baryonyx* was unusual for a meat-eating dinosaur in having a very long, narrow snout, similar to today's slim-snouted crocodiles.

- **The teeth** of *Baryonyx* were long and slim, especially at the front of its mouth.

- **The general similarities** between *Baryonyx* and a crocodile suggest that *Baryonyx* may have been a fish-eater.

- *Baryonyx* may have lurked in swamps or close to rivers, darting its head forwards on its long, flexible neck to snatch fish.

- **The massive thumb claw** of *Baryonyx* may have been used to hook fish or amphibians from the water.

- **The long thumb claw** of *Baryonyx* measured about 35 cm in length.

▶ Fossils of Baryonyx were found associated with remains of fish scales, suggesting this dinosaur was a semi-aquatic fish-catcher.

Footprints

- **Thousands of fossilized dinosaur footprints** have been found all over the world.

- **Some dinosaurs left footprints** when they walked on the soft mud or sand of riverbanks. Then the mud baked hard in the sun, and was covered by more sand or mud, which helped preserve the footprints as fossils.

- **Some fossil footprints** were made when dinosaur feet left impressions in soft mud or sand that was then

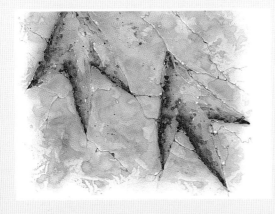

◀ The relative positions of footprints indicate how a dinosaur stood or moved.

> ★ STAR FACT ★
> Hadrosaur footprints 135 cm long and 80 cm wide were found near Salt Lake City, Utah, USA.

covered by volcanic ash, which set hard.

- **Many footprints** have been found together in lines, called 'trackways'. These suggest that some dinosaurs lived in groups, or used the same routes regularly.

- **The distance between same-sized footprints** indicates whether a dinosaur was walking, trotting or running.

- **Footprints of big meat-eaters** such as *Tyrannosaurus* show 3 toes with claws, on a forward-facing foot.

- **In big plant-eaters** such as *Iguanodon*, each footprint shows 3 separate toes, but less or no claw impressions, and the feet point slightly inwards.

- **In giant plant-eating sauropods**, each footprint is rounded and has indentations of nail-like 'hooves'.

- **Some sauropod footprints** are more than 1 m across.

Archosaurs

- **Archosaurs** were a very large group of reptiles that included the dinosaurs as one of their subgroups.

- **Other archosaur subgroups** included thecodonts, flying reptiles called pterosaurs, and crocodiles.

- **The thecodonts** included a smaller reptile group, the ornithosuchians – possibly the dinosaurs' ancestors.

- **One of the most dinosaur-like of the archosaurs** was the thecodont *Ornithosuchus*.

- **The 4-m long** *Ornithosuchus* stood almost upright.

- ***Ornithosuchus*** fossils were found in Scotland.

- **Sharp-toothed** *Ornithosuchus* was probably a powerful predator.

▶ Ornithosuchus *had a mix of features, both non-dinosaur (hips, back plates) and dinosaur (legs, skull).*

- **Features** in *Ornithosuchus*'s backbone, hips and feet indicate that it was almost certainly not a dinosaur.

- **The archosaur** *Longisquama* was a lizard-like reptile only 15 cm long, with tall scales forming a V-shaped row along its back.

- **Archosaur means 'ruling reptile'**, and archosaurs did indeed rule the land, swamps and skies for over 170 million years.

Teeth

- **Some of most common fossil remains** of dinosaurs are their teeth – the hardest parts of their bodies.

- **Dinosaur teeth** come in a huge range of sizes and shapes – daggers, knives, shears, pegs, combs, rakes, filelike rasps, crushing batteries and vices.

- **In some dinosaurs**, up to three-quarters of a tooth was fixed into the jaw bone, so only one-quarter showed.

- **The teeth of plant-eaters** such as *Iguanodon* had angled tops that rubbed past each other in a grinding motion.

- **Some duck-bill dinosaurs** (hadrosaurs) had

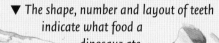

★ STAR FACT ★
Troodon, or 'wounding tooth', was named on the evidence of just 1 or 2 teeth.

more than 1000 teeth, all at the back of the mouth.

- **Like modern reptiles**, dinosaurs probably grew new teeth to replace old, worn or broken ones.

- **Individual teeth** were replaced at different times.

- **Some of the largest teeth** of any dinosaur belonged to 9-m long *Daspletosaurus*, a tyrannosaur-like meat-eater.

- **Some of** *Daspletosaurus*'s teeth were 18 cm long.

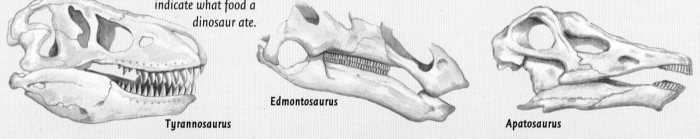

▼ *The shape, number and layout of teeth indicate what food a dinosaur ate.*

Tyrannosaurus

Edmontosaurus

Apatosaurus

Plateosaurus

- **Plateosaurus**, a prosauropod, was one of the first really big dinosaurs to appear, some 220 million years ago.

- **The name** *Plateosaurus* means 'flat reptile'.

- **Groups of** *Plateosaurus* have been found at various sites, including one in Germany and one in France.

- **Plateosaurus** used its many small, serrated teeth to crop and chew plant food.

- **Plateosaurus** had very flexible, clawed fingers, which it perhaps used to pull branches of food to its mouth.

- **Plateosaurus** could bend its fingers 'backwards', allowing it to walk on its hands and fingers, in the same posture as its feet and toes.

- **Plateosaurus's thumbs** had especially large, sharp claws, perhaps used as weapons to jab and stab enemies.

- **Fossil experts** once thought that *Plateosaurus* dragged its tail as it walked.

- **Experts today** suggest that *Plateosaurus* carried its tail off the ground, to act as a balance to its head, long neck and the front part of its body.

- **Plateosaurus** was one of the earliest dinosaurs to be officially named, in 1837, even before the term 'dinosaur' had been invented.

▲ *Plateosaurus may have reared up to chomp on leaves 2–3 m above the ground.*

Growth and age

- **No one knows for sure** how fast dinosaurs grew, how long they took to reach full size, or how long they lived.

- **Most estimates** of dinosaur growth rates and ages come from comparisons with today's reptiles.

- **Some reptiles today** continue to grow throughout their lives, although their growth rate slows with age.

- **Dinosaurs** may have grown fast as youngsters and slower as adults, never quite stopping until they died.

- **Estimates for the age of a full-grown meat-eater** such as *Tyrannosaurus* range from 20 to more than 50 years.

- **Full-grown, small meat-eaters** such as *Compsognathus* may have lived to be only 3–10 years old.

- **A giant sauropod** probably lived to be 50 years old, or even over 100 years old.

- **Like many reptiles today**, a dinosaur's growth rate probably depended largely on its food supply.

- **Dinosaurs** probably ate a lot and grew fast when food was plentiful, and slowed down when food was scarce.

- **During its lifetime**, a big sauropod such as *Brachiosaurus* would have increased its weight 2000 times (compared to 20 times in a human).

▶ Tyrannosaurus *may have taken 20–50 years to reach adult size.*

Cousins: Land

◀ Protosuchus, *a North American crocodile, lived 200 million years ago.*

- **Land animals** during the Age of Dinosaurs included insects, spiders, other reptiles, birds and mammals.

- **Dinosaurs** had many large, fierce, reptile enemies.

- **One of the biggest** non-dinosaur land reptiles was *Deinosuchus* (or *Phobosuchus*), a type of crocodile.

- **Deinosuchus** lived in the Late Cretaceous Period, in present-day Texas, USA.

- **The fossil skull** of *Deinosuchus* measures about 2 m long, much bigger than any crocodile of today.

- **The first mammals** appeared on Earth at about the same time as the early dinosaurs.

- **Various kinds of mammals** survived all through the Age of Dinosaurs, although none grew larger than a pet cat.

- **One of the first mammals** known from fossils is *Megazostrodon*, which resembled a shrew of today.

- **Megazostrodon** was just 12 cm long and its fossils, from 220–210 million years ago, come from southern Africa.

- **If Deinosuchus's body** was in proportion to its skull, it would have been 15 m long!

▶ Megazostrodon *probably fed like the shrews of today.*

Anchisaurus

- **Anchisaurus** was a prosauropod, a plant-eater with a small head, long neck and long tail.

- **Although officially named as a dinosaur** in 1912, *Anchisaurus* had in fact been discovered almost 100 years earlier.

- **Anchisaurus** was very small and slim compared to other prosauropods, with a body about the size of a large dog.

- **Fossils** of *Anchisaurus* date from the Early Jurassic times.

- **The remains of** *Anchisaurus* were found in Connecticut and Massachusetts, eastern USA, and in southern Africa.

- **With its small, serrated teeth**, *Anchisaurus* probably bit off the soft leaves of low-growing plants.

- **To reach leaves** on higher branches, *Anchisaurus* may have been able to rear up on its back legs.

★ STAR FACT ★
Remains of *Anchisaurus* were the first fossils of a dinosaur to be discovered in North America in 1818.

- **Anchisaurus** had a large, curved claw on each thumb.

- **The thumb claws** of *Anchisaurus* may have been used as hooks to pull leafy branches towards the mouth, and/or as weapons for lashing out at enemies and inflicting wounds.

◀ The main body of Anchisaurus was about the size of a pet dog such as a labrador.

Cousins: Sea

- **Placodont reptiles** lived mainly during the Triassic Period. They were shaped like large salamanders or turtles, and probably ate shellfish.

- **The placodont** *Placodus* was about 2 m long and looked like a large, scaly newt.

- **The nothosaurs** were fish-eating reptiles of the Triassic Period. They had small heads, long necks and tails, and 4 flipper-shaped limbs.

- **Fossils** of the 3-m long nothosaur *Nothosaurus* have been found across Europe, Asia and Africa.

▼ Plesiosaurus *was 2.5 m long, and was one of many plesiosaurs to thrive in Jurassic seas.*

- **The dolphin-like ichthyosaur reptiles** had back fins, two-lobed tails and flipper-shaped limbs.

- **Many kinds of ichthyosaurs** thrived in the seas during the Triassic and Jurassic Periods, although they had faded away by the middle of the Cretaceous Period.

- **One of the biggest ichthyosaurs** was *Shonisaurus*, which measured up to 15 m long.

- **The plesiosaurs** were fish-eating reptiles of the Mesozoic Era, with small heads, tubby bodies, 4 flipper-shaped limbs and short, tapering tails.

- **The plesiosaur** *Elasmosaurus* was up to 14 m long, with more than half of this length being its extraordinarily long, snakelike neck.

★ STAR FACT ★
One of the biggest meat-eaters ever was the short-necked plesiosaur *Liopleurodon*, at possibly 20 m long and weighing 50 tonnes.

Dino-birds: 1

- **The earliest known bird** for which there is good fossil evidence, and which lived during the Age of Dinosaurs, is *Archaeopteryx*.

- *Archaeopteryx* lived in Europe during the Late Jurassic Period, about 155–150 million years ago.

- **At about 60 cm long** from nose to tail-tip, *Archaeopteryx* was about the size of a large crow.

- *Archaeopteryx* resembled a small, meat-eating dinosaur in many of its features, such as the teeth in its long, beaklike mouth, and its long, bony tail.

★ STAR FACT ★
Archaeopteryx was covered with feathers that had the same detailed designs found in feathers covering flying birds today.

- **In 1951**, a fossilized part-skeleton was identified as belonging to a small dinosaur similar to *Compsognathus*, but in the 1970s it was re-studied and named *Archaeopteryx* – showing how similar the two creatures were.

- **Three clawed fingers** grew halfway along the front of each of *Archaeopteryx*'s wing-shaped front limbs.

- **The flying muscles** of *Archaeopteryx* were anchored to its large breastbone.

- *Archaeopteryx* probably flew, but not as fast or as skilfully as today's birds.

- *Archaeopteryx* probably fed by swooping on prey, running to catch small creatures such as insects and worms, or perhaps even by scavenging carrion.

Long tail with tail backbones

Flight feathers suited to agile manoeuvres in the air

Three clawed 'fingers' midway along front of wing

Teeth in long, light jaws (all birds lack teeth today)

▲ *Archaeopteryx* could probably glide well, swoop and turn as it pursued flying prey such as dragonflies. However, its long, strong legs suggest that it was also an able walker and runner. So it may have chased victims such as baby lizards and cockroaches on the ground.

Skin

- **Several fossils of dinosaur skin** have been found, revealing that dinosaurs had scales, like today's reptiles.

- **As in crocodiles**, the scales of a dinosaur were embedded in its thick, tough, leathery hide, rather than lying on top of its skin and overlapping, as in snakes.

- **When the first fossils** of dinosaur skin were found in the mid 1800s, scientists thought they were from giant prehistoric crocodiles.

- **Fossil skin** of the horned dinosaur *Chasmosaurus* has been found.

- ***Chasmosaurus*** had larger bumps or lumps, called tubercles, scattered among its normal-sized scales.

- **Samples of fossil skin** belonging to the

▶ Fossil skin, such as this piece from Edmontosaurus, is a relatively rare find.

> ★ STAR FACT ★
> Many dinosaur scales were roughly six-sided, like the cells in a bee's honeycomb.

duck-bill hadrosaur *Edmontosaurus* have been found.

- ***Edmontosaurus*** was covered in thousands of small scales, like little pebbles, with larger lumps or tubercles spaced among them.

- **Various specimens** of fossil skin show that the scales of *Iguanodon*-type dinosaurs were larger than those of same-sized, similar duck-bill dinosaurs.

- **Scaly skin** protected a dinosaur against the teeth and claws of enemies, accidental scrapes, and the bites of small pests such as mosquitoes and fleas.

Camarasaurus

- ***Camarasaurus*** is one of the best known of all big dinosaurs, because so many almost-complete fossil skeletons have been found.

- ***Camarasaurus*** was a giant plant-eating sauropod.

- ***Camarasaurus*** lived during the Late Jurassic Period, about 155–150 million years ago.

- **The famous American fossil-hunter** Edward

Drinker Cope gave *Camarasaurus* its name in 1877.

- **The name** *Camarasaurus* means 'chambered reptile', because its backbones, or vertebrae, had large, scoop-shaped spaces in them, making them lighter.

- **The huge** *Camarasaurus* was about 18 m long.

- **Compared to other sauropods**, such as *Diplodocus*, *Camarasaurus* had a relatively short neck and tail, but a very bulky, powerful body and legs.

- **North America, Europe and Africa** were home to *Camarasaurus*.

- **A large, short-snouted, tall head**, like that of *Brachiosaurus*, characterized *Camarasaurus*.

- **A fossil skeleton** of a young *Camarasaurus* was uncovered in the 1920s, and had nearly every bone in its body lying in the correct position, as they were in life – an amazingly rare find.

◀ Compared to other sauropods, Camarasaurus had a short neck and tail.

Could dinosaurs live again?

- **The Jurassic Park movies** showed dinosaurs being recreated as living creatures in the modern world.

- **The instructions**, or genes, of all animals, including dinosaurs, are in the form of the genetic substance known as DNA (de-oxyribonucleic acid).

- **In Jurassic Park**, dinosaur DNA came not from dinosaur fossils, but from mosquitoes that had sucked the blood of living dinosaurs, and then been preserved.

- **Scientists** in Jurassic Park combined the DNA of dinosaurs with DNA from living amphibians such as frogs.

- **Tiny bits of DNA** have been recovered from fossils formed in the Age of Dinosaurs.

- **The bits of dinosaur DNA found so far** represent a tiny amount of the DNA needed to recreate a living thing.

- **Most scientists** doubt that living dinosaurs could really be made from bits of fossilized DNA.

- **Plants today** might not be suited to 'modern' dinosaurs.

- **'Modern' dinosaurs** might die from today's diseases.

- **The task of recreating** a living dinosaur from tiny fragments of DNA has been compared to writing all the plays of Shakespeare starting with couple of words.

◀ The heroes of Jurassic Park find a sick Triceratops.

Oviraptor

- **Oviraptor** was an unusual meat-eater from the dinosaur group known as theropods.

- **Fossils of** Oviraptor were found in the Omnogov region of the Gobi Desert in Central Asia.

- **From beak to tail-tip**, Oviraptor was about 2 m long.

- **Oviraptor** lived during the Late Cretaceous Period about 85–75 million years ago.

- **Oviraptor** was named 'egg thief' because the first of its fossils was found lying among the broken eggs possibly of another dinosaur Protoceratops.

- **The mouth of** Oviraptor had no teeth. Instead, it had a strong, curved beak, like that of a parrot or eagle.

- **On its forehead**, Oviraptor had a tall, rounded piece of bone, like a crest or helmet, sticking up in front of its eyes.

- **Oviraptor's** bony head crest resembled that of today's flightless bird, the cassowary.

- **Oviraptor** may have eaten eggs, or cracked open shellfish with its powerful beak.

◀ Oviraptor's unusual features included its parrot-like beak.

> ★ STAR FACT ★
> Oviraptor had two bony spikes inside its mouth that it may have used to crack eggs when it closed its jaws.

Pack-hunters

- **Dinosaurs were reptiles**, but no reptiles today hunt in packs in which members cooperate with each other.

- **Certain types of crocodiles and alligators** come together to feed where prey is abundant, but they do not coordinate their attacks.

- **Fossil evidence** suggests that several kinds of meat-eating dinosaurs hunted in groups or packs.

- **Sometimes** the fossils of several individuals of the same type of dinosaur have been found in one place, suggesting the dinosaurs were pack animals.

- **The fossil bones** of some plant-eating dinosaurs

- have been found with many tooth marks on them, apparently made by different-sized predators, which may have hunted in packs.

- ***Tyrannosaurus*** may have been a pack-hunter.

- **In southwest Montana, USA**, the remains of three or four *Deinonychus* were found near the fossils of a much larger plant-eater named *Tenontosaurus*.

- **One** *Deinonychus* probably would not have attacked a full-grown *Tenontosaurus*, but a group of three or four might have.

◀ The raptors could probably hunt alone, but also bring down larger prey in packs, as hyaenas or lions do today.

> **★ STAR FACT ★**
> Some meat-eaters may have had fairly large brains, enabling them to hunt as a group.

Ceratopsians

- **Ceratopsians** were large plant-eaters that appeared less than 90 million years ago.

- **Most ceratopsian fossils** come from North America.

- **'Ceratopsian' means 'horn-face'**, after the long horns on their snouts, eyebrows or foreheads.

- **Most ceratopsians** had a neck shield or frill that swept sideways and up from the back of the

- head to cover the upper neck and shoulders.

- **Well-known ceratopsians** included *Triceratops, Styracosaurus, Centrosaurus, Pentaceratops, Anchiceratops, Chasmosaurus* and *Torosaurus*.

- **The neck frills of some ceratopsians**, such as that of *Chasmosaurus*, had large gaps or 'windows' in the bone.

- **In life**, the windows in the neck frill of a ceratopsian were covered with thick, scaly skin.

- **Ceratopsians** had no teeth in the fronts of their hooked, beaklike mouths.

- **Using rows of powerful cheek teeth**, ceratopsians sheared their plant food.

▶ Centrosaurus was a Late Cretaceous 'horn-face', about 6 m long.

> **★ STAR FACT ★**
> *Torosaurus* had the longest skull of any land animal ever, at about 2.5 m from the front of the snout to the rear of the neck frill.

Babies

- **As far as we know**, female dinosaurs laid eggs, from which their babies hatched.

- **The time between** eggs being laid and babies hatching out is called the incubation period.

- **Incubation periods** for dinosaur eggs probably varied by weeks or months depending on the temperature, as in today's reptiles.

- **Many fossils** of adult *Maiasaura* (a duck-bill dinosaur, or hadrosaur) have been found, together with its nests, eggs and hatchlings (just-hatched babies).

- **Fossils of** *Maiasaura* come mainly from Montana, USA.

> ★ **STAR FACT** ★
> Some preserved nests of *Maiasaura* babies contain traces of fossil buds and leaves – perhaps food brought to them by a parent?

- **The name** *Maiasaura* means 'good mother reptile'.

- **The teeth of** *Maiasaura* babies found in the nest are slightly worn, showing that they had eaten food.

- **The leg bones and joints** of the *Maiasaura* babies were not quite fully formed, showing that they were not yet able to move about to gather their own food.

- **Evidence** from *Maiasaura* and other nesting sites shows that dinosaurs may have been caring parents, protecting and feeding their young.

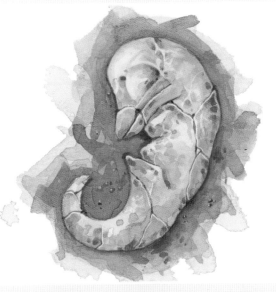

▶ Various clues from fossil evidence show that the hadrosaur Maiasaura may have brought food back to its newly hatched young in the nest. Whether one parent or both did this is not known.

▲ Some fossil dinosaur eggs contain preserved embryos, still in the process of development. They use nutrients stored as egg yolk. Dinosaurs did not suckle their babies on milk, as mammals do.

Some eggs were still not hatched

Preserved eggshells showed signs of trampling by young in the nest

Dinosaur eyes

- **No fossils have been found of dinosaur eyes**, because eyes are soft and squishy, and soon rot away after death, or are eaten by scavengers.

- **The main clues** to dinosaur eyes come from the hollows, or orbits, in the skull where the eyes were located.

- **The orbits** in fossil dinosaur skulls show that dinosaur eyes were similar to those of reptiles today.

- **The 6-m long sauropod** Vulcanodon had tiny eyes relative to the size of its head.

- **Small-eyed dinosaurs** probably only had good vision in the daytime.

- **The eyes** of many plant-eating dinosaurs, such as Vulcanodon, were on the sides of their heads, giving them all-round vision.

- **The small meat-eater** Troodon had relatively large eyes, and it could probably see well even in dim light.

- **Troodon's** eyes were on the front of its face and pointed forwards, allowing it to see detail and judge distance.

- **Dinosaurs that had large bulges**, called optic lobes, in their brains – detectable by the shapes of their skulls – could probably see very well, perhaps even at night.

> ★ STAR FACT ★
> The plant-eater Leaellynasaura had large optic lobes, and probably had good eyesight.

◀ Leaellynasaura had very large eyes for the size of its skull, suggesting it was active at dusk or at night.

Coprolites: Dino-dung

- **Coprolites** are the fossilized droppings, or dung, of animals from long ago, such as dinosaurs.

- **Dinosaur coprolites** are not soft and smelly – like other fossils, they have become solid rock.

- **Many thousands** of dinosaur coprolites have been found at fossil sites all over the world.

- **Cracking or cutting open** coprolites sometimes reveals what the dinosaur had recently eaten.

- **Coprolites** produced by large meat-eaters such as

◀ Fossilized droppings are no longer squishy or smelly.

> ★ STAR FACT ★
> One of the largest dinosaur coprolites found measures 44 cm long and was probably produced by Tyrannosaurus.

Tyrannosaurus contain bone from their prey.

- **The microscopic structure** of the bones found in coprolites shows the age of the prey when it was eaten. Most victims were very young or old, as these were the easiest creatures for a predator to kill.

- **Coprolites produced by small meat-eaters** such as Compsognathus may contain the hard bits of insects, such as the legs and wing-cases of beetles.

- **Huge piles of coprolites** found in Montana, USA, were probably produced by the large plant-eater Maiasaura.

- **Maiasaura** coprolites contain the remains of cones, buds and the needlelike leaves of conifer trees, showing that these dinosaurs had a tough diet.

Scelidosaurus

- **Scelidosaurus** was a medium-sized armoured dinosaur, perhaps an early member of the group called the ankylosaurs.

- **Fossils of** *Scelidosaurus* have been found in North America, Europe and possibly Asia.

- **Scelidosaurus** lived during the Early Jurassic Period, about 200 million years ago.

- **From nose to tail**, *Scelidosaurus* was about 4 m long.

▶ Scelidosaurus *was a widespread dinosaur, and a forerunner of bigger, more heavily armoured dinosaur types.*

- **Scelidosaurus** probably moved about on 4 legs, although it could perhaps rear up to gather food.

- **A plant-eater**, *Scelidosaurus* snipped off its food with the beaklike front of its mouth, and chewed it with its simple, leaf-shaped teeth.

- **Scelidosaurus** is one of the earliest dinosaurs known to have had a set of protective, bony armour plates.

- **A row of about 50 bony plates**, or scutes, stuck up from *Scelidosaurus*'s neck, back and tail.

- **Scelidosaurus** had rows of conical bony plates along its flanks, resembling limpets on a rock.

- **Scelidosaurus** was described in 1859, and named in 1863, by Richard Owen, who also invented the name 'dinosaur'.

Australia

- **In the past 40 years**, some of the most exciting discoveries of dinosaur fossils have come from Australia.

- **Remains of the large plant-eater** *Muttaburrasaurus* were found near Muttaburra, Queensland.

- **Muttaburrasaurus** was about 7 m long and similar in some ways to the well-known plant-eater *Iguanodon*.

- **Fossils of** *Rhoetosaurus*, a giant plant-eater, were found in 1924 in southern Queensland.

- **The sauropod** *Rhoetosaurus* was about 17 m long and lived 170 million years ago.

- **Near Winton, Queensland**, more than 3300 footprints

▶ Many exciting fossils have been found in Australia over the past 40 years - many found nowhere else.

★ STAR FACT ★
Dinosaur Cove is difficult to reach, and many of the fossils are in hard rocks in the middle of sheer cliffs with pounding waves far beneath.

show where about 130 dinosaurs once passed by.

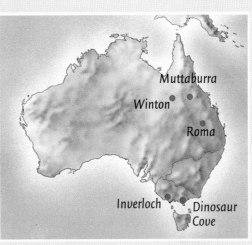

Muttaburra

Winton

Roma

Inverloch   Dinosaur Cove

- **One of the major new fossil sites** in Australia is 'Dinosaur Cove', on the coast near Melbourne, Victoria.

- **Fossil-rich rocks** at 'Dinosaur Cove' are part of the Otway-Strzelecki mountain ranges, and are 120–100 million years old.

- **Remains** found at 'Dinosaur Cove' include *Leaellynasaura* and a smaller version of the huge meat-eater *Allosaurus*.

Sauropods

- **The sauropods** were the biggest of all the dinosaurs.

- **The huge plant-eating sauropods** lived mainly during the Jurassic Period, 208–144 million years ago.

- **A typical sauropod** had a tiny head, a very long neck and tail, a huge, bulging body and 4 massive legs, similar to those of an elephant, but much bigger.

- **Sauropods** included the well-known *Mamenchisaurus*, *Cetiosaurus*, *Diplodocus*, *Brachiosaurus* and *Apatosaurus*.

- **Rebbachisaurus** fossils were found in Morocco, Tunisia and Algeria.

▶ *Sauropods could browse in tree-tops.*

- *Rebbachisaurus* lived 120 million years ago.

- *Cetiosaurus* was about 18 m long and weighed 30 tonnes.

- *Cetiosaurus*, or 'whale reptile', was so-named because French fossil expert Georges Cuvier thought that its giant backbones came from a prehistoric whale.

- *Cetiosaurus* was the first sauropod to be given an official name, in 1841 – the year before the term 'dinosaur' was invented,

- **The first fossils** of *Cetiosaurus* were found in Oxfordshire, England, in the 1830s.

Dinosaur feet

- **Dinosaur feet differed**, depending on the animal's body design, weight and lifestyle.

- **A typical dinosaur's front feet** had metacarpal bones in the lower wrist or upper hand, and 2 or 3 phalanges bones in each digit (finger or toe), tipped by claws.

- **The rear feet** of a typical dinosaur had metatarsal (instead of metacarpal) bones in the lower ankle.

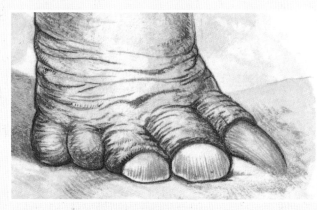

▲ *Each foot of Apatosaurus supported more than 5 tonnes.*

★ STAR FACT ★
The dinosaur group that includes all the meat-eaters, both large and small, is named the theropods, or 'beast feet'.

- **Some dinosaurs had 5 toes** per foot, like most other reptiles (and most birds and mammals).

- **Sauropods** probably had feet with rounded bases supported by a wedge of fibrous, cushion-like tissue.

- **Most sauropods** had claws on their first 3 toes, and smaller, blunter 'hooves' on the other 2 toes.

- **Ostrich-dinosaurs** such as *Gallimimus* had very long feet and long, slim toes for fast running.

- **Many fast-running dinosaurs** had fewer toes, to reduce weight – *Gallimimus* had 3 toes per back foot.

- **The dinosaur group** that includes *Iguanodon*, duck-billed dinosaurs, *Heterodontosaurus* and many other plant-eaters is named the ornithopods, or 'bird feet'.

Extinction

- **All dinosaurs on Earth** had died out, or become extinct, by 65 million years ago.

- **Many other reptiles**, such as pterosaurs and plesiosaurs, and many other animals and plants disappeared with the dinosaurs, in a 'mass extinction'.

- **A possible cause** of the mass extinction was a new kind of disease that swept across the land and seas.

- **The mass extinction** of the dinosaurs and other animals may have been due to a series of huge volcanic eruptions that filled the air with poisonous fumes.

- **Climate change** is another possible cause of the mass extinction – perhaps a period of global warming that lasted for a few hundred years, or even longer.

▼ We can only guess at the havoc caused when a massive meteorite hit Earth 65 million years ago. Whether this was the main cause of the mass extinction, or the 'last straw' following other problems, is not clear from evidence found so far.

> ★ STAR FACT ★
> Scientists found a huge crater – the Chixulub Crater – under sea-bed mud off the coast of Yucatan, Mexico. This could be where a giant meteorite hit Earth 65 million years ago.

- **One theory** for the mass extinction is that a giant lump of rock from space – a meteorite – hit Earth.

- **A giant meteorite** 10 km across smashing into Earth would have set off earthquakes and volcanoes, and thrown up vast amounts of dust to darken the skies.

- **Skies darkened by dust for 1 year or more** would mean the death of many plants, and so the death of plant-eating animals, and consequently the meat-eaters.

- **One great puzzle** about the disappearance of the dinosaurs is why similar reptiles, such as crocodiles, lizards and turtles, survived.

Dilophosaurus

- **Dilophosaurus** was a large meat-eating dinosaur in the group known as the ceratosaurs.

- **About 200 million years ago**, *Dilophosaurus* roamed the Earth in search of prey.

- **Fossils** of *Dilophosaurus* were found in Arizona, USA, and possibly Yunnan, China.

- **The remains** of *Dilophosaurus* in Arizona, USA, were discovered by Jesse Williams, a Navajo Native American, in 1942.

- **Studying the fossils** of *Dilophosaurus* proved very difficult, and the dinosaur was not given its official name until 1970.

- **Dilophosaurus** measured about 6 m from its nose to the end of its very long tail.

- **The name** *Dilophosaurus* means 'two ridged reptile', from the two thin, rounded, bony crests on its head, each shaped like half a dinner plate.

- **The crests** of *Dilophosaurus* were too thin and fragile to be used as weapons for head-butting.

- **Brightly coloured skin** may have covered *Dilophosaurus's* head crests, as a visual display to rivals or enemies.

> ★ **STAR FACT** ★
> *Dilophosaurus* probably weighed about 500 kg – as much as the biggest polar bears today.

◀ The fearsome *Dilophosaurus* was one of the first large meat-eating dinosaurs. It gained the nickname 'terror of the Early Jurassic'.

Mysteries

- **Some dinosaurs have been named** on very scant evidence, such as a single bit of fossil bone, or just one tooth or claw.

- **The small meat-eater** *Troodon* was named in 1856 on the evidence of a single tooth.

- **The first tooth** of *Troodon* was found in the Judith River region of Montana, USA.

- **At first**, the tooth of *Troodon* was thought to have come from a lizard such as a monitor lizard.

- **In the early 1900s**, more *Troodon*-like teeth were found in Alberta and Wyoming, and were believed to have come from a pachycephalosaur or 'bone-head' dinosaur.

- **In the 1980s**, a fuller picture of *Troodon* was built up by putting its teeth together with other fossils, including bones.

- **Only parts of the hands and arms** of *Deinocheirus* have been found. They were discovered in Mongolia, Central Asia, in the 1970s.

- **It is possible** that *Deinocheirus* was a gigantic ostrich-dinosaur, perhaps as tall as a giraffe, at 5–6 m.

- **Therizinosaurus**, or 'scythe reptile', was a huge dinosaur known only from a few parts of its limbs. It lived in the Late Cretaceous Period in Mongolia, Central Asia.

- **A mysterious fossil claw** was found, thought possibly to belong to *Therizinosaurus*, and measuring about 90 cm around its outer curve.

▶ Deinocheirus, *known only from a few fossil pieces of arm and hand, may have been an ostrich-dinosaur like this – but as tall as a giraffe.*

Psittacosaurus

- **Psittacosaurus** was a plant-eater in the group known as the ceratopsians, or horn-faced dinosaurs.

- **Living in the Middle Cretaceous Period**, *Psittacosaurus* walked the Earth about 115–110 million years ago.

- **Psittacosaurus** was named in 1923 from fossils found in Mongolia, Central Asia.

- **Fossils** of *Psittacosaurus* have been found at various sites across Asia, including ones in Russia, China and Thailand.

- **The rear legs** of *Psittacosaurus* were longer and stronger than its front legs, suggesting that this dinosaur may have reared up to run fast on its rear legs, rather than running on all 4 legs.

- **Psittacosaurus** measured about 2 m long.

- **On each foot** *Psittacosaurus* had 4 toes.

- **The name** *Psittacosaurus* means 'parrot reptile', after the dinosaur's beak-shaped mouth, like that of a parrot.

- **Inside its cheeks**, *Psittacosaurus* had many sharp teeth capable of cutting and slicing through tough plant material.

◄ *Psittacosaurus had two small ridges or horns, one on each cheek.*

> ★ STAR FACT ★
> Fossil evidence shows that when newly hatched from their eggs, baby *Psittacosaurus* were hardly longer than a human hand.

Beaks

- **Several kinds of dinosaurs** had a toothless, beak-shaped front to their mouths.

- **Beaked dinosaurs** included ceratopsians (horn-faces) such as *Triceratops*, ornithopods such as *Iguanodon* and the hadrosaurs (duck-bills), stegosaurs, segnosaurs, ankylosaurs (armoured dinosaurs) and fast-running ostrich-dinosaurs.

- **Most beaked dinosaurs** had chopping or chewing teeth near the backs of their mouths, in their cheeks, but ostrich-dinosaurs had no teeth.

- **A dinosaur's beak** was made up of the upper (maxilla) and the lower (mandible) jaw bones.

- **Ornithischian (bird-hipped) dinosaurs** had what is called a 'predentary' bone at the front tip of the lower jaw.

> ★ STAR FACT ★
> Some of the largest beaks in relation to body size belonged to *Oviraptor* and *Psittacosaurus*.

- **Ceratopsian (horn-faced) dinosaurs** had a 'rostral' bone at the front tip of the upper jaw.

- **In life**, the bones at the front of a dinosaur's jaw would have been covered with horn, which formed the outer shape of the beak.

- **Dinosaurs almost certainly** used their beaks for pecking, snipping, tearing and slicing their food.

- **Dinosaurs may have** used their beaks to peck fiercely at any attackers.

◄ *Ornithomimus's long, toothless jaws would have been covered by horny beak.*

Massospondylus

- **Massospondylus** was a medium-sized plant-eater belonging to the group known as the prosauropods.

- **Africa and perhaps North America** were home to Massospondylus, about 200 million years ago.

- **In total**, Massospondylus was about 5 m long, with almost half of this length being its tail.

- **The rear legs** of Massospondylus were bigger and stronger than its front legs, so it may have reared up to reach high-up food.

▶ All day, Massospondylus would have been kept busy eating to fuel its bulky body.

- **The name** Massospondylus means 'huge backbone'.

- **Fossils of more than 80** Massospondylus have been found, making it one of the best-studied dinosaurs.

- **Massospondylus** had a tiny head compared to its large body, and it must have spent many hours each day gathering enough food to survive.

- **The front teeth** of Massospondylus were surprisingly large and strong for a plant-eater, with ridged edges more like meat-eating teeth.

- **The cheek teeth** of Massospondylus were too small and weak for chewing large amounts of plant food, so perhaps the dinosaur's food was mashed mainly in its stomach.

- **In the 1980s**, some scientists suggested that Massospondylus may have been a meat-eater, partly because of the ridged edges on its front teeth.

Stomach stones

- **Some dinosaur fossils** are found with unusually smooth, rounded stones, like seashore pebbles, jumbled up among or near them.

- **Smoothed pebbles** occur with dinosaur fossils far more than would be expected by chance alone.

- **Smooth stones** are mainly found with or near the remains of large plant-eating dinosaurs, especially those of prosauropods such as Massospondylus, Plateosaurus and Riojasaurus, sauropods such as Brachiosaurus and Diplodocus, the parrot-beaked Psittacosaurus and the stegosaurs.

- **Some plant-eating dinosaurs** may have used smooth stones to help process their food.

▶ Gastroliths range from pea- to football-sized.

- **The smoothed pebbles** associated with dinosaur remains are known as gastroliths, gastric millstones or gizzard stones.

- **Gastroliths** were stones that a dinosaur found on the ground and deliberately swallowed into its stomach.

- **In the dinosaur's stomach**, gastroliths acted as 'millstones', crushing and churning plant food, and breaking it down into a soft pulp for better digestion.

- **As gastroliths churned and rubbed** inside a dinosaur's guts, they became very rounded, smoothed and polished.

- **Gastroliths as small as a pea** and as large as a football have been found.

- **Gastroliths may be the reason why** many big plant-eaters, especially sauropods, had no chewing teeth – the mashing was done inside the guts.

Migration

- **Almost no land reptiles today** go on regular, long-distance journeys, called migrations.

- **Over the past 30 years**, scientists have acquired evidence that some dinosaurs regularly migrated.

- **Evidence for migrating dinosaurs** comes from the positions of the continents at the time. In certain regions, cool winters would have prevented the growth of enough plants for dinosaurs to eat.

- **Fossil evidence suggests** that some plants stopped growing during very hot or dry times, so some dinosaurs would have had to migrate to find food.

- **The footprints or tracks** of many dinosaurs travelling in herds is possible evidence that some dinosaurs migrated.

- **Dinosaurs that may have migrated** include *Centrosaurus* and *Pachyrhinosaurus*, sauropods such as *Diplodocus*, and ornithopods such as *Iguanodon* and *Muttaburrasaurus*.

- **One huge fossil site** in Alberta, Canada, contains the fossils of about 1000 *Pachyrhinosaurus* – perhaps a migrating herd that got caught in a flood.

- **In North America**, huge herds of *Centrosaurus* migrated north for the brief sub-Arctic summer, when plants were abundant, providing plentiful food.

- **In autumn**, *Centrosaurus* herds travelled south again to overwinter in the forests.

◀ *Pachyrhinosaurus may have migrated.*

> ★ STAR FACT ★
> Migrating *Centrosaurus* may have walked 100 km a day.

China

- **For centuries**, dinosaur fossils in China were identified as belonging to folklore creatures such as dragons.

- **The first dinosaur fossils** studied scientifically in China were uncovered in the 1930s.

- **Because of China's political isolation in the past**, many dinosaur fossils found there remained unknown to scientists in other countries.

- **From the 1980s**, dinosaur discoveries in almost every province of China have amazed scientists around the globe.

- **A few exciting dinosaur finds** in China have been fakes, such as part of a bird skeleton that was joined to the part-skeleton of a dinosaur along a natural-looking crack in the rock.

- **Some better-known Chinese finds**

> ★ STAR FACT ★
> Of all the world's countries, probably only the USA has more fossil dinosaurs than China.

of dinosaurs include *Mamenchisaurus*, *Psittacosaurus*, *Tuojiangosaurus* and *Avimimus*.

Meileyingzi
Jingangkon
Wujiabai
Taihezhen
Lufeng

- **Remains** of the prosauropod *Lufengosaurus* were uncovered in China's southern province of Yunnan, in 1941.

- **China's** *Lufengosaurus* lived during the Early Jurassic Period, and measured about 6–7 m long.

- **Many recently found fossils** in China are of feathered dinosaurs.

◀ *Recent fossil finds in China are causing scientists to change many long-held ideas.*

South America

- **Many of the most important discoveries** of dinosaur fossils in the last 30 years were made in South America.

- **Dinosaur fossils have been found** from the north to the south of the continent, in the countries of Colombia, Peru, Chile, Brazil, Uruguay and Argentina.

- **Most dinosaur fossils in South America** have been found on the high grassland, scrub and semi-desert of southern Brazil and Argentina.

- **Some of the earliest known dinosaurs**, such as

Herrerasaurus and *Eoraptor*, lived more than 225 million years ago in Argentina.

- **Some of the last dinosaurs**, such as the sauropods *Saltasaurus* and *Titanosaurus*, lived in Argentina.

- **Fossils of the meat-eating predator** *Piatnitzkyosaurus* come from Cerro Condo in southern Argentina.

- ***Piatnitzkyosaurus*** was similar to the great predator *Allosaurus* of North America, but at 4–5 m long was less than half its size.

- **Like many dinosaurs in Argentina**, *Piatnitzkyosaurus* lived during the Middle Jurassic Period.

- **Remains of about 10 huge** *Patagosaurus* sauropods were found in the fossil-rich region of Chubut, Argentina, from 1977.

▼ The high, windswept, stony, grassy plains of southern Argentina are especially rich in Jurassic and Cretaceous fossils, including those of the vast plant-eating sauropods *Argentinosaurus*. The plains slope upwards to the west, finally reaching the foothills of the Andes, where sun, wind and rain constantly erode the rocks and reveal new remains.

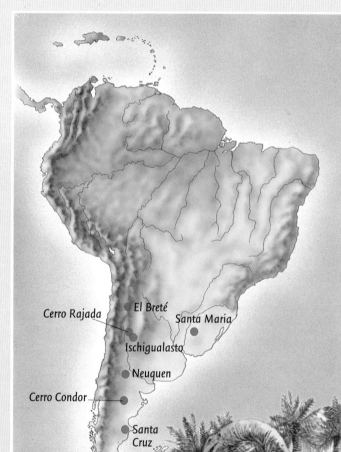

Cerro Rajada
El Breté
Santa Maria
Ischigualasto
Neuquen
Cerro Condor
Santa Cruz

▲ Dinosaur fossils found in South America since the 1970s reveal unique kinds of meat-eaters, the biggest predatory dinosaurs, some of the earliest members of the dinosaur group, and possibly the largest of all dinosaurs.

Tuojiangosaurus

- **Tuojiangosaurus** was a member of the group called plated dinosaurs, or stegosaurs.

- **The first nearly complete dinosaur skeleton** to be found in China was of a *Tuojiangosaurus*, and excellent fossil skeletons are on display in several Chinese museums.

- **The name** *Tuojiangosaurus* means 'Tuo River reptile'.

- **Tuojiangosaurus** lived during the Late Jurassic Period, about 155 million years ago.

- **Tuojiangosaurus** was 7 m long from nose to tail-tip.

- **The weight of** *Tuojiangosaurus* was probably about 1 tonne.

- **Like other stegosaurs,** *Tuojiangosaurus* had tall slabs or plates of bone on its back.

- **The back plates of** *Tuojiangosaurus* were roughly triangular and probably stood upright in 2 rows that ran from the neck to the middle of the tail.

- **Tuojiangosaurus** plucked low-growing plant food with the beak-shaped front of its mouth, and partly chewed the plant material with its leaf-shaped, ridge-edged cheek teeth.

- **On its tail,** *Tuojiangosaurus* had 4 long spikes arranged in two Vs, which it could swing at enemies to keep them at a distance or inflict wounds.

◀ *Tuojiangosaurus had about 15 pairs of tall plates along its neck, back and tail.*

Head crests

- **Many dinosaurs** had lumps, bumps, plates, bulges, ridges or other shapes of bone on their heads, called head crests.

- **Head crests** may have been covered with brightly coloured skin in life, for visual display.

- **Meat-eaters with head crests** included *Carnotaurus* and *Dilophosaurus*.

- **The dinosaurs with the largest** and most complicated head crests were the hadrosaurs.

- **The largest dinosaur head crest** was probably a long, hollow, tubular shape of bone belonging to the hadrosaur *Parasaurolophus*.

- **The head crests of hadrosaurs** may have been involved in making sounds.

- **Some years ago** the hadrosaur *Tsintaosaurus* was thought to have a very unusual head crest – a hollow tube sticking straight up between the eyes, like a unicorn's horn.

- **The so-called head crest** of *Tsintaosaurus* is now thought to be the fossil part of another animal, and not part of *Tsintaosaurus* at all.

- **Tsintaosaurus** is now usually known as *Tanius*, a hadrosaur with a small crest or no crest at all!

▲ *Dilophosaurus was one of the few meat-eaters with a large head crest.*

★ STAR FACT ★
The head crests of some large
Parasaurolophus, perhaps full-grown males,
reached an incredible 1.8 m in length.

Sails

- **Long, bony extensions**, like rods or spines, stuck up from the backs of some dinosaurs.

- **In life**, a dinosaur's bony extensions may have held up a large area of skin, commonly called a back sail.

- **Dinosaurs with back sails** included the huge meat-eater *Spinosaurus* and the large plant-eater *Ouranosaurus*.

- **Spinosaurus** and *Ouranosaurus* both lived over 100 million years ago.

- **Fossils of** *Spinosaurus* and *Ouranosaurus* were found in North Africa.

- **The skin** on a dinosaur's back sail may have been brightly coloured, or may even have changed colour, like the skin of a chameleon lizard today.

▲ Apart from its sail, *Ouranosaurus was similar to its close cousin, the plant-eater Iguanodon.*

- **A dinosaur's back sail** may have helped to control its body temperature.

- **Standing sideways** to the sun, a back sail would absorb the sun's heat and allow the dinosaur to warm up quickly, ready for action.

▲ Spinosaurus *was almost as large as* Tyrannosaurus.

- **Standing in the shade**, a back sail would lose warmth and help the dinosaur to avoid overheating.

- **The bony back rods** of *Spinosaurus* were up to 1.6 m tall.

North America

- **North America** is the continent where most dinosaur fossils have been found.

- **Most dinosaur fossils** in North America come from the dry, rocky 'badlands' of the Midwest region, which includes Alberta in Canada, and the US states of Montana, Wyoming, Utah, Colorado and Arizona.

- **Fossils of the most famous dinosaurs** come from North America, including *Allosaurus*, *Tyrannosaurus*, *Diplodocus*, *Triceratops* and *Stegosaurus*.

- **Several fossil-rich sites** in North America are now national parks.

- **The US Dinosaur National Monument**, on the border of Utah and Colorado, was established in 1915.

- **The Cleveland-Lloyd Dinosaur Quarry** in Utah contains fossils of stegosaurs, ankylosaurs, sauropods and meat-eaters such as *Allosaurus*.

- **Along the Red Deer River** in Alberta, a large area with thousands of dinosaur fossils has been designated the Dinosaur Provincial Park.

- **Fossils found in Alberta** include those of the meat-eater *Albertosaurus*, armoured *Euoplocephalus* and the duck-bill *Lambeosaurus*.

- **The Dinosaur Provincial Park** in Alberta is a United Nations World Heritage Site – the same status as the pyramids of ancient Egypt.

- **A huge, 20-m long plant-eater** was named *Alamosaurus* after the famous Battle of the Alamo in Texas in 1836.

▲ *Some of the most famous dinosaurs lived in the areas marked above.*

Iguanodon

- **Iguanodon** was a large plant-eater in the dinosaur group known as ornithopods.

- **Numerous fossils** of Iguanodon have been found in several countries in Europe, including England, Belgium, Germany and Spain.

- **Iguanodon** measured about 9 m from nose to tail.

- **It is estimated** that an Iguanodon weighed about the same as a large elephant - 4–5 tonnes.

- **Iguanodon** lived during the Early to Middle Cretaceous Period, 140–110 million years ago.

- **Iguanodon** probably walked and ran on its large, powerful back legs for much of the time, with its body held horizontal.

- **A cone-shaped spike** on Iguanodon's thumb may have been a weapon for jabbing at rivals or enemies.

> ★ STAR FACT ★
> Iguanodon was one of the very first dinosaurs to be given an official scientific name, in 1825.

- **The 3 central fingers** on Iguanodon's hands had hooflike claws for occasional four-legged walking.

- **The fifth or little finger** of Iguanodon was able to bend across the hand for grasping objects, and was perhaps used to pull plants towards the mouth.

▲ Iguanodon is very well known from many fossils.

Hibernation

- **Dinosaurs may have gone into an inactive state** called hibernation during long periods of cold conditions, as many reptiles do today.

- **Dinosaurs** such as the small plant-eater Leaellynasaura, found at 'Dinosaur Cove', Australia, may have had to hibernate due to the yearly cycle of seasons there.

- **Dinosaur Cove, Australia**, was nearer the South Pole when dinosaurs lived there, 120–100 million years ago.

▶ Leaellynasaura may have slept through the cold season, perhaps protected in a cave or burrow.

- **The climate** was relatively warm 120–100 million years ago, with no ice at the North or South Poles.

- **Dinosaurs at Dinosaur Cove, Australia**, would have had to cope with long hours of darkness during winter, when few plants grew.

- **Australia's Dinosaur Cove dinosaurs** may have hibernated for a few months each year to survive the cool, dark conditions.

- **The eyes and brain shape** of Leaellynasaura from Dinosaur Cove, Australia, suggest that this dinosaur had good eyesight.

- **Leaellynasaura** may have needed good eyesight to see in the winter darkness, or in the dim forests.

- **Dinosaur fossils** have been found in the Arctic region near the North Pole.

- **Arctic dinosaurs** either hibernated during winter, or migrated south to warmer regions.

Sounds

- **Few reptiles today make sounds**, except for simple hisses, grunts and coughs.

- **Fossils suggest that dinosaurs** made a variety of sounds in several different ways.

- **The bony, hollow head crests** of duck-bills (hadrosaurs) may have been used for making sounds.

- **The head crests of some hadrosaurs** contained tubes called respiratory airways, used for breathing.

- **Air** blown forcefully through a hadrosaur's head crest passages could have made the whole crest vibrate.

- **A hadrosaur's vibrating head crest** may have made a loud sound like a honk, roar or bellow – similar to an elephant trumpeting with its trunk.

- **Fossil skulls** of some hadrosaurs, such as *Edmontosaurus* and *Kritosaurus*, suggest

that there was a loose flap of skin, like a floppy bag, between the nostrils and the eyes.

- ***Kritosaurus*** may have inflated its loose nasal flap of skin like a balloon to make a honking or bellowing sound, as some seals do today.

- **Dinosaurs may have made sounds** to keep in touch with other members of their herd, to frighten away enemies, to intimidate rivals and to impress potential mates at breeding time.

◀ In a battle between predator and prey, Tyrannosaurus may have been startled or even warned off by the trumpeting of Parasaurolophus. The effect of the sudden noise on the predator may have given the plant-eating hadrosaur time to escape. Its noise may also have summoned members of its herd, for massed defence against the huge meat-eater.

Tyrannosaurus may have been startled by the noise of its prey

Long, hollow crest may have resonated to make a loud call

★ STAR FACT ★
By blowing through models of hadrosaur head crests, a wide range of sounds can be made – a bit like those of brass and wind instruments!

Powerful rear legs used for kicking in self defence

Tail used for lashing out

Nodosaurs

- **Nodosaurs** were a subgroup of armoured dinosaurs, in the main ankylosaur group.

- **The nodosaur subgroup** included *Edmontonia*, *Sauropelta*, *Polacanthus* and *Nodosaurus*.

- **Nodosaurs were slow-moving**, heavy-bodied plant-eaters with thick, heavy nodules, lumps and plates of bone in their skin for protection.

- **Most nodosaurs lived** during the Late Jurassic and the Cretaceous Periods, 150–65 million years ago.

- *Edmontonia* lived in North America during the Late Cretaceous Period, 75–70 million years ago.

- *Edmontonia* was about 7 m long, but its bony armour made it very heavy for its size, at 4–5 tonnes.

★ **STAR FACT** ★
Like many nodosaurs, *Edmontonia* and *Polacanthus* probably had long, fierce spikes on their shoulders, used to 'spear' enemies.

- **Along its neck, back and tail** *Edmontonia* had rows of flat and spiky plates.

- **The nodosaur** *Polacanthus* was about 4 m long and lived 120–110 million years ago.

- **Fossils** of *Polacanthus* come from the Isle of Wight, southern England, and perhaps from North America, in South Dakota, USA.

◄ *Edmontonia, one of the last dinosaurs, was covered in many sharp lumps of bone that gave it some protection from its enemies.*

Inventing the 'dinosaur'

- **When fossils of dinosaurs were first studied** by scientists in the 1820s, they were thought to be from huge lizards, rhinoceroses or even whales.

- **The first dinosaur** to be given an official name was *Megalosaurus*, by English clergyman William Buckland in 1824.

- **Fossils of dinosaurs** were found and studied in 1822 by Gideon Mantell, a country doctor in Sussex, southern England.

- **In 1825**, Englishman Gideon Mantell named his creature *Iguanodon*, because its fossil teeth were very similar in shape to, but larger than, the teeth of the iguana lizard.

- **In the late 1830s**, British scientist Richard Owen realized that some fossils did not belong to lizards, but to an as yet unnamed group of reptiles.

- **In 1841–42**, Richard Owen invented a new name for

the group of giant prehistoric reptiles – Dinosauria.

- **The name 'dinosaur'** means 'terrible reptile'.

- **Life-sized models** of several dinosaurs were made by sculptor Waterhouse Hawkins in 1852–54.

- **Hawkins' models** were displayed in the gardens of the Crystal Palace Exhibition in London, and caused a public sensation – the first wave of 'Dino-mania'.

- **The three main dinosaurs** of the Dinosauria in the 1840s were *Iguanodon*, the big meat-eater *Megalosaurus* and the nodosaur *Hyaelosaurus*.

◄ *Megalosaurus was the first dinosaur to be given an official scientific name, even though the term 'dinosaur' had not yet been invented.*

Brains

- **There is a broad link** between the size of an animal's brain compared to the size of its body, and the level of intelligence it shows.

- **Some fossil dinosaur skulls** have preserved the hollow where the brain once was, revealing the approximate size and shape of the brain.

- **In some cases** a lump of rock formed inside a fossil skull, taking on the size and shape of the brain.

- **The tiny brain** of *Stegosaurus* weighed about 70–80 g, while the whole dinosaur weighed up to 2 tonnes.

- **The brain** of *Stegosaurus* was only 1/25,000th of the weight of its whole body (in a human it is 1/50th).

- ***Brachiosaurus's*** brain was perhaps only 1/100,000th of the weight of its whole body.

- **The brain of the small meat-eater** *Troodon* was about 1/100th the weight of its whole body.

▶ Troodon *may have been fairly 'intelligent' for a dinosaur.*

- **The brain-body size comparison** for most dinosaurs is much the same as the brain-body size for living reptiles.

- **Small and medium sized meat-eaters** such as *Troodon* may have been as 'intelligent' as parrots or rats.

- **It was once thought** that *Stegosaurus* had a 'second brain' in the base of its tail! Now this lump is thought to have been a nerve junction.

Segnosaurs

- **Little is known** about the segnosaur group of dinosaurs – the subject of much disagreement among experts.

- **Segnosaurs** are named after almost the only known member of the group, *Segnosaurus*.

- **The name** *Segnosaurus* means 'slow reptile'.

- ***Segnosaurus*** lived during the Mid to Late Cretaceous Period, about 90 million years ago.

- **Fossils** of *Segnosaurus* were found mainly in the Gobi Desert in Central Asia in the 1970s. The dinosaur was named in 1979 by Mongolian scientist Altangerel Perle.

- ***Segnosaurus*** had a narrow head and probably a toothless, beaklike front to its mouth.

- **Experts have variously described** *Segnosaurus* as a predatory meat-eater, a swimming or wading fish-eater, a rearing-up leaf-eater, or even an ant-eater.

- **Different experts have said** *Segnosaurus* was a theropod, a prosauropod and an ornithopod.

- **Some scientists have suggested** that *Segnosaurus* was a huge dinosaur-version of today's anteater that ripped open the nests of termites and ants with its powerful claws.

▶ Segnosaurus *remains a mystery – even its diet is hotly debated by the experts.*

★ STAR FACT ★
Segnosaurus was a sizeable dinosaur, probably about 6 m long and standing 2 m tall.

Dino-birds: 2

- **Fossils found during the last 20 years** show that some dinosaurs may have been covered with feathers or fur.

- **Sinosauropteryx** was a small, 1-m long meat-eater that lived 135 million years ago in China.

- **Fossils** of Sinosauropteryx show that parts of its body were covered not with the usual reptile scales, but with feathers.

- **The overall shape** of Sinosauropteryx shows that, despite being feathered, it could not fly.

- **The feathers** of Sinosauropteryx may have been for camouflage, for visual display, or to keep it warm – suggesting it was warm-blooded.

- **Avimimus** was a small, light dinosaur. Its fossils come from China and Mongolia, and date from 85–82 million years ago.

▲ Avimimus may have evolved feathers for warmth or for camouflage.

- **The 1.5-m long** Avimimus had a mouth shaped like a bird's beak for pecking at food.

- **The fossil arm bones** of Avimimus have small ridges of the same size and shape as the ridges on birds' wing bones, where feathers attach.

- **In modern science**, any animal with feathers is a bird, so some experts say that feathered dinosaurs were not actually dinosaurs or even reptiles, but birds.

- **Some experts say** that birds are not really a separate group of animals, but a subgroup of dinosaurs that lives on today, and they should be regarded as feathered dinosaurs.

After dinosaurs

- **The Age of Dinosaurs** came to a fairly sudden end 65 million years ago. We know this from rocks and fossils, which changed dramatically at that time.

- **The Cretaceous Period** ended 65 million years ago.

- **There are no dinosaur fossils** since 65 million years ago.

- **Many animal groups**, including fish, crocodiles, turtles, lizards, birds and mammals, survived the extinction that took place 65 million years ago.

- **Birds and mammals** in particular underwent rapid changes after the dinosaurs disappeared.

- **Within 10 million years** of the dinosaurs' demise, bats, primates, armadillos, hoofed mammals and rodents such as rats had all appeared.

- **The land mammal** that came closest to rivalling the great size of the dinosaurs was Indricotherium, also known as Baluchitherium.

- **Indricotherium** was 8 m long, 5 m tall and weighed perhaps 25 tonnes.

- **Indricotherium** was less than half the size of the biggest dinosaurs.

▶ Indricotherium was 3 times bigger than elephants of today.

★ STAR FACT ★
Some people believe that dinosaurs may still be alive today, deep in tropical forests or in remote valleys – but no firm evidence exists.

1000
THINGS
YOU SHOULD KNOW ABOUT

BIRDS

KEY

 How birds live

Perching birds

Owls and birds of prey

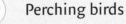 Water and wading birds

Game and ground birds

Woodland and forest birds

The world of birds

- **There are more than 9000 species** of birds.

- **One of the most widespread** of all birds is the osprey, which is found nearly all over the world.

- **More than a third of all known bird species** live and breed in South and Central America.

▲ *Ospreys make a large nest at the top of a tree or on a cliff. They feed mostly on fish, which they snatch up with their feet.*

- **A species** is a particular type of bird. Birds of the same species can mate and have young, and these can themselves have offspring.

- **The 9000 bird species** are organized into about 180 families. Species in a family share certain characteristics such as body shape.

- **Bird families** are organized into 28 or 29 larger groups called orders. Largest is the perching bird order, with more than 5000 bird species.

- **The wandering albatross** is one of the longest-lived birds. Individuals may live as long as 50 years.

- **The red-billed quelea** is probably the most common wild bird. There are thought to be at least 1.5 billion.

- **The largest bird**, the ostrich, weighs almost 80,000 times more than the smallest, the bee hummingbird.

- **All birds** lay hard-shelled eggs, in which their young develop. If a mother bird had young that developed inside her body instead, she would be too heavy to fly.

Cormorants and anhingas

- **The 4 species of anhinga** also called darters all live in freshwater in tropical parts of the world.

- **The flightless cormorant** lives on two of the Galapagos Islands. Its tiny wings are useless for flight, but it is an expert swimmer.

- **The feathers** of cormorants and darters lack waterproofing and quickly get soaked through. This makes the birds heavier in water and better able to dive for fish.

- **After diving for food**, cormorants stand on a rock with wings outstretched to dry.

▶ *The cormorant's long, hooked beak is an ideal shape for catching fish, its main food.*

- **In parts of Asia**, fishermen use cormorants to catch fish – the birds dive for the fish but do not swallow them.

- **Cormorant colonies** may number 100,000 birds or more. Their droppings, known as guano, are collected and used as fertilizer.

- **The biggest species** of cormorant, the great cormorant, is up to 1 m long.

- **A great cormorant eats** about 15% of its body weight in fish a day. That's like an adult human eating more than 80 hamburgers a day.

- **The American darter**, or snake bird, swims with its neck held in a snakelike curve above the water's surface.

> ★ STAR FACT ★
> Cormorants can dive to an incredible 50 m or more in their hunt for fish.

Ducks

- **The female eider duck** lines her nest with soft down feathers that she pulls from her breast. Humans use the feathers, too, to make quilts and sleeping bags.

- **Torrent ducks** live by fast-flowing streams in South America's Andes mountains. When new ducklings hatch, they leap straight into the swirling waters.

- **There are more than 100 duck species**, living all over the world, except Antarctica.

- **Steamer ducks** get their name from their habit of paddling over water with their wings as well as their feet, at speeds of up to 28 km/h.

- **Ducks have been domesticated** for more than 2000 years for their meat and eggs.

- **Ducks** feed on fish, shellfish, leaves and seeds.

- **Like cuckoos**, the black-headed duck lays its eggs in the nests of other birds, such as herons.

- **The merganser** has a serrated beak like the blade of a bread knife, to help it hold slippery fish.

- **The wood duck** was hunted nearly to extinction in the 19th century for the male's colourful feathers, which were used as fishing flies and hat decorations.

- **The red-breasted merganser** is one of the fastest-flying birds. It can reach speeds of more than 65 km/h – and possibly even 100 km/h.

▼ The beautiful wood duck breeds in North America.

Hoopoes and relatives

- **Rollers** have a spectacular courtship flight, rolling and somersaulting as they dive towards land.

- **The 8 noisy, insect-eating woodhoopoe species** live in forests in central and southern Africa.

- **A light, coin-shaped mark** on each wing of the broad-billed roller is the reason for its other common name – 'dollar bird'.

- **The cuckoo-roller** lives only in Madagascar and the Comoros Islands, where it catches chameleons and insects.

- **Groups of woodhoopoes** make loud calls and rocking movements, and pass bark to each other, in a display of territorial ownership.

- **The 16 or so species of roller** and ground roller live in southern Europe, Asia, Africa and Australia.

- **The broad-billed roller** catches winged termites in the air. A roller will eat as many as 800 termites an evening.

- **If threatened** by birds of prey, the hoopoe hides by flattening itself on the ground with its wings and tail spread out.

- **The hoopoe** was a symbol of gratitude in ancient Egyptian hieroglyphics. The Egyptians believed that the hoopoe comforted its parents in their old age.

- **The hoopoe lines its nest** with animal excrement, perhaps so that the smell will keep enemies away!

◀ With its decorative crest and striking plumage, the hoopoe is easy to recognize. It lives in Europe, Asia and Africa.

Starlings

- **The male wattled starling** loses his head feathers in the breeding season. Scientists investigating cures for human baldness are researching the bird's ability to regrow its head feathers each year.

- **When kept in captivity**, hill mynahs mimic human speech, but wild birds do not imitate the calls of other bird species, only the calls of other hill mynahs.

- **The largest starlings** are up to 43 cm long and weigh just over 100 g.

- **European starlings** feed their young on caterpillars, earthworms and beetle

▶ *The male starling has glossy, iridescent plumage. The female is much plainer, with brownish feathers.*

grubs, and may make 400 feeding trips a day.

- **Male starlings** bring fresh green leaves to the nest, which release a substance that deters parasites.

- **The Brahminy starling** has a brush-like tip on its tongue, used for collecting pollen and nectar.

- **There are about 113 species of starling** in Europe, Africa and Asia. Starlings have also been introduced into Australasia and North America.

- **Some 100 years ago**, 60 pairs of European starlings were released in New York. Fifty years later, starlings were one of the most common birds in the USA.

- **Locusts** are the favourite food of the rose-coloured starling. Large flocks fly to wherever they are plentiful.

> ★ STAR FACT ★
> In some cities, flocks of as many as 1 million starlings gather for the night.

The structure of birds

- **Birds are the only creatures** to have feathers. These keep them warm and protected from the weather and allow them to fly.

- **Like mammals, fish and reptiles**, a bird is a vertebrate animal – it has a backbone.

- **Birds** have a body temperature of 40°C to 44°C – higher than other warm-blooded animals.

- **A bird's bones** have a honeycomb structure. The bones are so light that they account for only about 5% of its total weight.

- **Birds** do not have teeth. Instead their food is ground down by a

▲ *Thrushes are adaptable birds, able to feed on fruit as well as insects. Many have beautiful songs.*

part of the digestive system called the gizzard. Some birds swallow small stones to help the action of the gizzard.

- **A bird's nostrils** are usually at the base of the beak, but in the kiwi, which has a better sense of smell than most birds, they are at the tip.

- **Birds' muscles** make up 30–60% of their total weight. The biggest are the flight and leg muscles.

- **Small birds** have about 15 neck vertebrae, while the mute swan has 23. (Mammals have only 7.)

- **The skeleton** of a bird's wings has bones similar to those in the hand and arm of mammals, but there are much reduced bones for only three fingers not five.

- **The heart rate** of a tiny hummingbird reaches an astonishing 615 beats a minute.

Swifts

- **Once a young swift** has left its nest, it may not come to land again until it is about 2 years old and ready to breed. In this time it may fly 500,000 km.

- **The edible-nest swiftlet** makes a nest of its own spit (saliva) and a few feathers on a cave wall. Birds nest soup made from this nest is considered a delicacy in China

- **Swifts** do almost everything in the air. They eat, drink, court and even mate on the wing.

- **There are about 74 species of swifts** found all over the world, except in the very far north and south.

- **The largest swift**, the white-naped swift, is about 25 cm long and weighs 175 g – about the weight of a lemon.

- **Trials with ringed birds** have shown that a young common swift that has only just left the nest can fly from London to Madrid in 3 days.

- **A swift's legs** and feet are so small and weak that it cannot move on the ground. It must land on a cliff ledge or building so it can launch itself into the air again.

- **The cave swiftlet** finds its way in totally dark caves by using a form of echolocation.

- **The African palm swift** glues its nest to the underneath of a palm leaf with its own spit, and glues its eggs to the nest. The parents cling on with their claws while incubating the clutch.

- **When a swift regurgitates** a mouthful of food for its young to eat, it may contain as many as 1000 tiny insects and spiders.

◄ *The Eurasian swift is seen in Europe in the summer, swooping overhead on sunny days. It flies to tropical Africa for the winter.*

Partridges and relatives

- **The Himalayan snowcock** (partridge family) lives on the lower slopes of the Himalayas, where its grey and white feathers hide it among rocks and snow.

- **Tiny quail chicks** are born with their eyes open and their bodies covered in warm, downy feathers. They are able to follow their mother within 1 hour of hatching.

- **A mother quail** helps her chicks to learn how to find food by pointing at food items with her beak.

- **At about 50 cm long**, the vulturine guineafowl is the largest of the 6 species of guineafowl. It lives in Africa and eats fallen fruit.

- **The female red-legged partridge** lays one clutch of eggs for her mate to incubate, and another to incubate herself.

- **The partridge family** includes more than 90 species of partridges and francolins. They feed mainly on seeds.

- **In parts of Europe and North America**, partridges are reared in captivity and then released and shot for sport.

- **The helmeted guineafowl**, originally from Africa, was domesticated in Europe more than 2500 years ago.

- **A group of partridges** is called a 'covey'. A covey usually contains a family of male, female and young, plus a few other birds.

- **The grey partridge** lays the largest clutch of any bird – on average about 19 or 20 eggs, but some birds lay as many as 25.

◄ *The crested wood partridge lives in woodland and forest in Southeast Asia. It feeds on insects, snails, fruit and seeds.*

Birds of paradise

- **Birds of paradise**, of which there are about 44 species, live only in New Guinea and northeastern Australia.

- **The king of Saxony** bird of paradise has two 50 cm head plumes decorated with small, sky-blue squares, so unusual-looking they were first thought to be fake.

- **The magnificent riflebird** gets its name from its loud whistling call, which sounds like a passing bullet.

- The **Female bird** makes a cup or dome-shaped nest and lays 1–2 eggs.

- **During courtship**, the blue bird of paradise hangs upside-down from a branch with his splendid blue feathers and tail plumes spread over his head.

- **Fruit and insects** are the main foods of

◄ *The blue bird of paradise is one of the rarer birds of the species.*

the birds of paradise. Some also eat leaves and buds.

- **New Guinea tribesmen** traditionally wear bird of paradise feathers in their head-dresses.

- **During the early 19th century**, 100,000 bird of paradise feathered skins were sold each year in Europe for hat and dress decorations.

- **The first bird of paradise skins** brought to Europe from New Guinea did not have feet, so some people thought the birds never landed.

► *The male king bird of paradise has long tail feathers for display.*

Geese and swans

- **Whooper, trumpeter and mute swans** are among the heaviest flying birds, weighing up to 16 kg.

- **Snow geese** breed in the Arctic tundra, but fly south to spend the winter months around the Gulf of Mexico – a journey of some 3500 km.

- **The black swan** makes a nest of sticks and other plant material in shallow water and lays up to 6 eggs. Both parents help to incubate the eggs.

- **Geese** feed mostly on leaves, and can eat as many as 100 blades of grass in 1 minute.

- **Tundra swans** mate for life, returning year after year to the same nesting site. They usually make their nest on marshland and lay 3–5 eggs.

- **Although quieter than other swans**, the mute swan is not really

mute, but makes many snorting and hissing calls.

- **The Hawaiian goose** is the world's rarest goose. Fifty years ago there were only about 30 left. Now it is protected and numbers are increasing.

- **Red-breasted geese** often make their nests near those of peregrines and buzzards. This gives them protection, and they don't seem to get attacked by the birds of prey.

- **Male swans** are known as 'cobs', females as 'pens' and baby swans are called 'cygnets'.

▼ *Swans generally stay faithful to one mate.*

Tyrant flycatchers

- **The tyrant flycatcher family** includes at least 390 species of birds. They range from northern Canada through the USA to the tip of South America.

- **Not all flycatchers** feed only on insects. The great kiskadee dives into water for fish and tadpoles, as well as catching flying insects in the air.

- **The vermilion flycatcher** is one of the few brightly coloured flycatchers. The male has bright red plumage, which it shows off in his courtship display.

- **In 1976**, ornithologists – bird-watchers – in Peru found a previously unknown flycatcher, which they named the cinnamon-breasted tody-tyrant. It lives only in cloud forests on a few mountain peaks in Peru.

- **The royal flycatcher** is a plain, brownish bird, but it has an amazing crest of feathers on its head that it sometimes unfurls and shows off. Males have red crests and females yellow or orange crests.

- **Smallest of all the tyrant flycatchers** is the short-tailed pygmy tyrant, at only 6.5 cm long. It lives in northern South America.

▶ The vermilion flycatcher brings a flash of colour to the desert and dry scrub of the southwestern USA, Central America and tropical South America.

- **The eastern phoebe** makes a nest of mud mixed with grass and plant stems. The female lays 3–7 eggs, and incubates them for 14–16 days. The young leave the nest when they are about 17 days old.

- **The boat-billed flycatcher** has a larger beak than other flycatchers, and eats frogs and other small animals, as well as insects.

- **Some flycatchers**, including the great crested flycatcher, line their nests with snakeskins that have been cast off.

1

2

3

▲ The tyrant flycatchers are the largest bird family in North and South America. Shown here are: (1) the buff-breasted flycatcher, (2) the lesser flycatcher and (3) the great-crested flycatcher.

★ STAR FACT ★
Well-known for its fierce behaviour, the eastern kingbird (a flycatcher) attacks larger birds that dare to approach its territory, sometimes even landing on their backs.

Nightjars and relatives

- **After hunting** for insects at night, the common potoo rests by day in a tree, where its position and coloration make it look like a broken branch.

- **The 12 species of frogmouth** live in the rainforests of Southeast Asia and Australia.

- **The common poorwill** (nightjar family) is one of the few birds known to hibernate. It sleeps in a rock crevice.

- **The bristle-fringed beak** of the nightjar opens very wide to help it snap up moths and beetles at night.

- **The oilbird** is the only bird to feed

◀ *The potoo lives in forests and woodlands in Mexico and Central and South America.*

★ STAR FACT ★
So as not to give themselves away by their droppings, potoos squirt out their faeces so that they land well away from their perches.

on fruit at night. Its excellent sense of smell helps it find the oily fruits of palms and laurels in the dark.

- **Oilbird chicks** put on so much weight from their rich diet that they may weigh much more than their parents when they are only a couple of months old.

- **There are about 70 species of nightjars**, found in most warmer parts of the world except New Zealand and southern South America.

- **The oilbird** nests in dark caves, and uses echolocation.

- **An old name** for nightjars is goatsuckers, because people mistakenly thought they saw the birds feeding on goats' milk, when in fact they were snapping up insects disturbed by the animals.

Oystercatchers and relatives

- **The oystercatcher** uses its strong, bladelike beak to prise mussels off rocks and open their shells.

- **Oystercatcher chicks** stay with their parents for up to 1 year while they learn how to find and open shellfish.

- **The Egyptian plover** (courser family) buries its eggs in sand and leaves them to be incubated by the warmth of the sun. The parents sit on the eggs at night and if the weather is cool.

- **The cream-coloured courser** has pale, sandy feathers that help to keep it hidden in its desert home.

- **The 17 species in the courser and pratincole family**

▶ *The common oystercatcher breeds in Europe and Asia, but spends the winter in South Africa and southern Asia.*

live in southern Europe, Asia, Africa and Australia.

- **The common pratincole** nests on sand or rocks, and lays 2–4 mottled, well-camouflaged eggs. The parents take turns to incubate the eggs for 17–18 days.

- **The 9 species in the thick-knee family** include the stone curlew and the dikkop. These long-legged birds usually feed at night on insects, worms and shellfish.

- **The thick-knees** get their common name from the knobbly joints on their legs – actually between the ankle and shin bones.

- **If the Egyptian plover's chicks** get too hot, the parent birds soak their own belly feathers with water and give their young a cooling shower.

- **The pygmy seed-snipe** of southern South America blends in with the plains landscape so well that it is almost invisible when it crouches on the ground.

Fairy-wrens and relatives

- **The 26 species of fairy-wrens** live in Australia and New Guinea, where they forage for insects on the ground.

- **Young fairy-wrens** often stay with their parents and help them raise the next brood of young. Pairs with helpers can raise more young than those without.

- **The rock warbler** makes its nest in a dark cave or mine-shaft, attaching the nest to the walls with spiderwebs.

- **During its courtship display**, the male superb fairy-wren may present his mate with a yellow flower petal.

- **If a predator** comes too close to a fairy-wren's nest, the parent birds make a special 'rodent run' away from the nest, squeaking and trailing their tails to confuse and distract the enemy.

- **The 50 or so species of thickhead** live in rainforests and scrub in Southeast Asia and Australasia.

- **The white-throated gerygone's nest** hangs from a eucalyptus branch and is made from bark strips and plant fibres woven together with spiderwebs.

- **The hooded pitohui** (thickhead family) is one of the very few poisonous birds known. Its feathers and skin contain a poison that protects it from predators.

- **The Australasian warbler** family includes 65 species of gerygone, thornbills and scrubwrens.

- **The golden whistler** is probably the most variable of birds – the 70 or more races all have slightly different feather patterns or beak shapes.

◄ *The male superb fairy-wren is easily recognized by the bright blue plumage around its head and neck.*

Beaks and feet

- **No bird** has more than four toes, but some have three and the ostrich has only two.

- **Four-toed birds** have different arrangements of toes: in swifts, all four point forwards; in most perching birds, three point forwards and one backwards; and in parrots, two point forwards and two backwards.

- **A beak** is made up of a bird's projecting jaw bones, covered in a hard horny material.

- **The hyacinth macaw** has one of the most powerful beaks of any bird, strong enough to crack brazil nuts.

- **Webbed feet** make all waterbirds efficient paddlers.

- **The Australian pelican** has the largest beak of any bird, at up to 50 cm long.

★ STAR FACT ★
A baby bird has a spike called an 'egg-tooth' on its beak for breaking its way out of its egg.

- **Nightjars** have the shortest beaks, at 8–10 mm long.

- **A bird stands** on the tips of its toes – the backward bending joint halfway down its leg is the ankle joint.

- **A bird's beak** is extremely sensitive to touch. Birds that probe in the ground for food have extra sensory organs at the beak tip.

▼ *When a chick is ready to hatch, it makes a tiny hole in the shell with its 'egg-tooth' – a process called 'pipping' – and then struggles its way out.*

First tiny hole

Egg cracks

Chick appears

Chick breaks free of egg

Divers and grebes

- **The great crested grebe** is best known for its amazing courtship dance, during which male and female perform a series of movements in water and exchange pieces of weed.

- **At 90 cm long**, the white-billed diver is the largest of the 4 species of diver.

- **The short-winged grebe** lives on lakes high in the mountains of Peru and Bolivia, and cannot fly. It basks in the sun to warm its body after the cold nights.

- **Divers feed only on fish**, which they catch underwater. The great northern diver can dive

◀ The great crested grebe lives in parts of Europe, Asia, Africa and Australasia.

★ STAR FACT ★
Grebes have up to 20,000 feathers to keep their bodies warm and dry as they dive for food.

as deep as 20 m or more below the water's surface.

- **In the 19th century**, the breast feathers of grebes were used to make muffs to keep ladies' hands warm.

- **There are about 20 species of grebes** (three flightless). They live near freshwater lakes and marshes.

- **Divers** are so specialized for diving and swimming that adult birds cannot walk upright on land.

- **Grebes** feed on fish, insects and shellfish. They also swallow moulted feathers, which may help them to regurgitate waste such as fish bones and keep their gut free of parasites.

- **The great crested grebe** makes a nest of water plants floating near the water's edge. It lays 3–6 eggs, which both male and female incubate.

Falcons

- **The peregrine** is the fastest bird, diving through the air at 180 km/h to catch prey.

- **The peregrine's hunting technique** is so exacting that only one in ten attacks is successful.

- **At up to 60 cm long**, the gyr falcon is the largest of the falcon family, and can catch ducks and hares.

- **The common kestrel** hovers above the ground on fast-beating wings while it searches for small mammals.

- **Falconets and pygmy falcons** are the smallest birds of prey. The Philippine falconet is only 15 cm long.

- **Falcons** have adapted well to city life – kestrels hover above rubbish bins to watch for mice, and peregrines dive down between New York skyscrapers.

- **Eleonora's falcon** is named after a 14th-century

★ STAR FACT ★
Kestrels can see ultra-violet light, which reflects off the urine a rodent uses to mark its tracks.

Sardinian princess, who brought in laws to protect it.

- **The earliest known records** of falconry come from 2nd-century BC China.

- **In winter**, both male and female kestrels spend about a quarter of their day hunting. But when the female is incubating eggs, the male hunts for longer.

▲ The peregrine kills with its talons and rips prey apart with its hooked beak.

Parrots

- **The only flightless parrot** is the New Zealand kakapo or owl parrot, which is now extremely rare.

- **The palm cockatoo** has an amazing courtship display. The male bird holds a stick in its foot and makes a loud drumming noise by beating the stick against the side of a tree.

- **At about 85 cm long**, the scarlet macaw of South and Central America is one of the largest of the parrot family.

- **Unlike most parrots**, the kea of New Zealand eats meat as well as fruit and insects. It feasts on carrion – animals that are already dead – and also hunts young shearwaters in their burrows.

- **Macaws nest in tree holes** high in rainforest trees. The female lays two eggs which her mate helps to incubate. The young macaws stay with their parents for up to 2 years.

- **The little blue-crowned hanging parrot** gets its name from its strange habit of hanging upside down from a branch when at rest.

- **Macaws** swallow beakfuls of clay from riverbanks. The clay may help to protect the birds from the effects of some plants and seeds that they eat, many of which are poisonous to other creatures.

- **There are about 350 species in the parrot order**, including birds such as macaws, budgerigars, lories and cockatoos. They live in Central and South America, Africa, southern Asia and Australasia

- **As early as 400 BC**, a Greek author wrote of owning a pet parrot – a bird that could speak words in both Indian and Greek!

▶ With its bright red feathers, the scarlet macaw is one of the most beautiful of all the parrots. It can fly at up to 56 km/h as it searches the rainforest for fruit, nuts and seeds to eat.

★ STAR FACT ★
The pattern of feathers on each side of the red-and-green macaw's face is unique – no two birds look identical.

Bird senses

- **Almost all birds** have excellent sight, and most depend on their eyes for finding food.

- **A bird's outer ear** consists of a short tube leading from the eardrum to the outside. In most birds the ear openings are just behind the jaw.

- **A barn owl's hearing** is so good that it can detect and catch prey in complete darkness without using its eyes at all.

- **A chicken** has only 24 tastebuds and a starling about 200 – a human has 9000.

- **An eagle** can spot prey from as much as 1.6 km above the Earth.

- **A starling's eye** is as much as

▲ With its amazing hearing, the barn owl hunts mice and other small rodents at night.

15% of the total weight of its head. A human's eye is only 1% of the head weight.

- **An ostrich's eye**, at 5 cm in diameter, is larger than any other land animal's eye.

- **Birds** are 10 times more sensitive to changes of pitch and intensity in sounds than humans. They can detect sounds of 1/200 second.

- **Kiwis have poor sight** and depend more on their sense of smell for finding many food items, such as earthworms, at night.

- **Albatrosses** have a good sense of smell. In experiments, they have been attracted to food from a distance of 30 km.

Terns and skimmers

- **The noddy**, a species of tern, gets its name from its habit of nodding its head during its courtship display.

- **The black skimmer's beak** has a flattened lower part that is longer than the upper part. The bird flies over water with the lower part of its beak just below the surface, ready to snap up prey.

- **The 42 or so species of terns** are found all over the world, mostly along coasts.

- **Arctic terns** are long-lived birds, known to survive to 27 – and sometimes even 34 – years of age.

- **Most terns eat fish**, squid and shellfish, but marshland terns also eat insects and frogs.

▼ The Arctic tern has a long, forked tail, short red legs and a cap of black feathers on its head.

★ **STAR FACT** ★
The Arctic tern makes a round-trip migration from the Arctic to Antarctica and back – a record distance of more than 32,000 km.

- **At up to 59 cm long**, the Caspian tern is the largest of the terns, and one of the most widespread.

- **The fairy tern** does not make a nest. Instead, it balances its 1 egg on a tree branch and manages to sit on it without knocking it off.

- **Most terns mate for life**. Even if they don't stay together all year round, pairs meet up when they return to breeding sites.

- **There are only 3 species of skimmers**. most live in coastal areas of tropical Africa, Southeast Asia and North and South America.

Weavers and relatives

- **The sociable weaver** nests in groups of up to 300 birds. The huge nest is made of sticks and grass, and may measure 4 m deep and weigh up to 1000 kg. Each pair of birds has its own hole in the nest.

- **Desert-living sociable weavers** use their nest all year round for shelter from sun, wind and cold. At night, when temperatures drop, the nest holes stay 20°C warmer than the outside air.

- **Whydah birds** do not make their own nests, but lay their eggs in the nests of other birds, usually waxbills.

▶ When the male cape weaver has finished making a nest, it calls to the female.

- **Young whydahs** make the same sounds and have the same mouth markings as their foster parents' own young, and because of this they get fed.

- **The baya weaver** makes a beautiful nest of woven grass and leaves that it hangs from a tree or roof.

- **In the breeding season**, the male paradise whydah grows 28 cm long tail feathers – almost twice the length of its body – for display in flight.

- **Most weavers** have short, strong beaks that they use for feeding on seeds and insects.

- **The red bishop** mates with three or four females, who all nest in his territory.

- **The red-vented malimbe** (a weaver) feeds mainly on the husks of oil palm nuts.

★ STAR FACT ★
As many as 500 pairs of red-billed queleas may nest together in one acacia tree.

Plovers and lapwings

- **The wrybill**, a New Zealand plover, has a unique beak that curves to the right. The bird sweeps its beak over sand to pick up insects.

- **If a predator** comes near a killdeer's nest, the bird moves away, trailing a wing to look as though it is injured. The predator, seeing what it thinks is an easy victim, follows the killdeer which, once far enough away, flies off.

- **Kentish plover chicks** have markings like the stones and pebbles of their nest site. If danger threatens, the chicks flatten themselves on the ground and are almost impossible to see.

▶ The wrybill breeds on New Zealand's South Island, but overwinters on North Island.

- **There are 60 or so species of plovers** and lapwings around the world.

- **Female dotterels** lay clutches of eggs for several males, which incubate the eggs.

- **To attract females**, the male lapwing performs a spectacular rolling, tumbling display flight in the air.

- **Spur-winged plovers** are often seen close to crocodiles in Africa and Asia – they may feed on small creatures that the crocodiles disturb.

- **The lapwing** is also known as the peewit.

- **Golden plovers** have been recorded flying at more than 113 km/h.

★ STAR FACT ★
Many plovers pat the ground with their feet to imitate the sound of rain. This attracts worms to the surface, where they are snapped up.

Penguins

- **Not all of the 18 species of penguin** live in Antarctica. A few species live around Australia and South Africa, and there is even one resident in the Galapagos Islands on the equator.

- **Penguins have wings**, but cannot fly. They spend as much as 85% of their time in water, where they use their wings like flippers to help push themselves through the water.

- **The king penguin** has been known to dive down to 250 m in search of prey.

- **An emperor penguin** may travel at least 900 km

An emperor penguin stands about 110 cm high

◄ *An emperor chick spends the first 2 months of its life on its parent's feet, protected from the cold by a pouch of skin. If it falls off, it freezes to death in seconds.*

★ **STAR FACT** ★
The male emperor penguin incubates his mate's eggs for 60 days, eating nothing and losing as much as 45% of his body weight.

on one feeding expedition.

- **Like many other penguins**, gentoos nest in a simple scrape on the ground, but they surround it with a ring of pebbles. A courting gentoo shows its mate an example of the sort of pebbles it will provide.

- **The emperor penguin** keeps its egg warm on its feet, where it is covered by a fold of skin. The temperature there stays at 36°C, despite the freezing surroundings.

- **Penguins** eat fish, squid and shellfish. They have spiny tongues to help them hold on to slippery prey.

- **A dense covering** of three layers of feathers keeps penguins warm. An emperor penguin has about 12 feathers per square cm of his body.

- **Penguins** usually swim at 5–10 km/h, but can reach speeds of up to 24 km/h.

Emperor penguin chick

▲ *Emperor penguins are highly streamlined, allowing them to dive to depths of 500 m when they hunt. They can stay underwater for more than fifteen minutes, using their strong flippers to propel them forward.*

Bird song and calls

- **Birds** make two sorts of sounds – simple calls, giving a warning or a threat, and the more complicated songs sung by some males at breeding time.

- **Birds' songs** have a definite dialect. The songs of a group of chaffinches in one area, will sound slightly different from those of a group somewhere else.

- **A songbird** reared in captivity away from its family produces a weak version of its parents' song, but cannot perform the whole repertoire.

- **Gulls and parrots** do not sing, but they do make various calls to attract mates or warn off enemies.

- **A bird sings** by vibrating the thin muscles in its syrinx – a special organ in its throat.

- **A sedge warbler** may use at least 50 different sounds in its songs.

- **Male and female boubou shrikes** sing a duet together, performing alternate parts of the song.

- **Songbirds** may make as many as 20 calls; gulls make only about 10.

- **Birds** make other sounds, too. During courtship flights, male woodpigeons make a loud clapping with their wings.

◀ The chaffinch is the commonest of Europe's finches.

> **★ STAR FACT ★**
> A baby songbird starts to learn to sing about 10 days after it hatches, and continues to learn for about 40 days.

Shrikes and vangas

- **If it has plenty of prey**, such as lizards, frogs or insects, the northern shrike will store items for later by impaling them on a thorn bush or barbed wire fence.

- **Shrikes** are also known as 'butcher birds', because of their habit of hanging prey in trees.

- **The 14 species of vanga** live only on Madagascar and the neighbouring Comoros Islands.

- **The fiscal shrike** is an aggressive bird that kills other birds which come near it.

- **During its courtship display**, the male puffback (a shrike) fluffs up the long feathers on its lower back like a powder puff.

▲ The beautiful crimson-breasted shrike often uses strips of acacia bark to build its nest.

- **There are about 65 species of shrikes** found in Africa, Europe, Asia and North America, as well as 72 species of cuckoo-shrikes and 9 species of helmet shrikes.

- **All shrikes** have powerful hooked beaks that they use for killing insects, lizards and frogs.

- **The call of the brubru shrike** sounds just like a phone ring.

- **The loggerhead shrike** makes a nest of twigs and grass in a thorny bush or tree, where the female incubates 5–7 eggs.

- **The sickle-billed vanga** uses its long, curved beak to probe bark for insects. It hangs upside down by its claws while it feeds.

Tits

- **The blue tit** is only 10–11 cm long, but lays as many as 15 eggs – more than any other bird that feeds its young.

- **The largest of the tits** is the Asian sultan tit, at about 22 cm long and 30 g in weight – twice the size of most tits.

- **The penduline tit** makes an amazing nest woven from plant fibres and suspended from the end of a twig. The walls of the nest may be 2.5 cm thick.

- **There are about 50 species of true tits** found in Europe, Africa, Asia and North America. There are also 7 species of long-tailed tits and 10 species of penduline tits.

◄ Agile little blue tits and their relatives can often be seen clinging to wire bird feeders in gardens during the winter.

★ STAR FACT ★
The willow tit may bury up to 1000 nuts and seeds a day, to eat later when food is scarce.

- **The black-capped chickadee** gets its name from its call, which sounds like a 'chick-a-dee-dee', and is one of the most complex of any bird songs.

- **The female great tit** lays 8–13 eggs, each of which is about 10% of her body weight.

- **Great tits** hatch blind and helpless, and are fed by their parents for about 3 weeks. The parents may make 1000 feeding trips a day to the young.

- **The long-tailed tit** makes its nest from feathers and moss that it collects – one nest may contain as many as 2000 feathers in all.

- **The long-tailed tit** is only about 14 cm long, and more than half of its length is its tail feathers.

Pigeons and sandgrouse

- **The passenger pigeon** was once one of the most common birds in North America – one flock was 480 km long and 1.6 km wide. But overhunting made the birds rare, and the last passenger pigeon died in captivity in 1914.

- **Both male and female pigeons** can make a milky substance in their crops that they feed to their young.

- **Wood pigeons** feed on leaves, seeds, nuts, berries and some insects, but those living near humans also eat bread and food scraps.

- **At about 74 cm long** (nearly as big as a turkey), the Victoria crowned pigeon of New Guinea is the largest member of its family.

- **Pigeon 'races'** are held

▲ Sandgrouse usually have grey or brownish feathers with mottled patterns that blend with their desert surroundings.

in which birds return to their homes from 1000 km away.

- **The 16 or so species of sandgrouse** live in southern Europe, Africa and parts of Asia.

- **One adult sandgrouse** was found to have 8000 seeds in its crop.

★ STAR FACT ★
A male sandgrouse soaks his belly feathers at a desert waterhole, then flies back to his nest so the chicks can drink from his plumage.

- **In Christianity**, a dove is often used to symbolize the Holy Spirit. Doves are often released as a gesture of peace and goodwill.

- **There are more than 300 species of pigeon**, and they occur all over the world, except in the far north and Antarctica.

Hawks and harriers

- **The female sparrowhawk** is almost twice the size of the male. At breeding time she defends the nest while the more agile male brings the family food.

- **The marsh harrier** flies close to the ground searching for mice, rats, frogs, rabbits and even fish. When it sights prey, it swoops down, seizes the victim in its sharp talons and tears it apart with its beak.

- **Tiny spines** on the underside of the black-collared hawk's toes help it catch and hold slippery fish prey.

- **The African harrier hawk** likes to feed on baby birds. It has long, double-jointed legs that allow it to reach into other birds' nests and grab the chicks.

- **There are about 66** species of hawks and harriers, including goshawks and sparrowhawks.

- **Young goshawks** first leave the nest at about 40 days old and start to fly at about 45 days. By 50 days or so they can hunt for themselves, and by 70 days they can manage without their parents.

- **The largest hawk** is the northern goshawk, which is up to 60 cm long and weighs as much as 1.3 kg.

- **Fledgling goshawks** 'play' as a way of practising their hunting skills.

- **At least 95%** of the northern harrier's diet is mice.

- **The smallest hawk** is the African little sparrowhawk, which is only about 25 cm long.

◀ *The sparrowhawk preys mostly on other birds, ranging in size from tits to pheasants.*

Rails and bustards

▼ *The great bustard, with its 2.5 m wingspan, lives on the plains, steppes and farmland of Europe and Asia, feeding mainly on insects.*

- **The weka** is a flightless rail that lives in New Zealand. Its diet includes seeds, fruit, mice, eggs and insects, and it also scavenges in rubbish bins.

- **Female great bustards** are much smaller and lighter than males, weighing only about 5 kg.

- **The world's smallest flightless bird**, the Inaccessible Island rail, weighs only 35 g – about the same as a small tomato. It lives on Inaccessible Island in the South Atlantic Ocean.

- **There are more than 130 species of rails** found all over the world, including many small islands. The family includes moorhens, coots and crakes, as well as rails.

- **The takahe**, a large flightless rail, is now extremely rare and lives only in South Island, New Zealand.

- **The 22 species of bustard** live in Africa, southern Europe, Asia and Australia.

- **Fights between Asian watercocks** (a type of rail) are staged for sport in some parts of Asia.

- **Coots** are the most aquatic of all the rails. They dive in search of plants and water insects to eat.

- **The female moorhen** makes a nest of dead leaves at the water's edge. The male helps incubate the 5–11 eggs.

★ **STAR FACT** ★
The great bustard of southern Europe and Asia is the world's heaviest flying bird. The male weighs up to 18 kg.

Prehistoric birds

- **The earliest known bird** is *Archaeopteryx*, which lived 155 million years ago. It had feathers like a modern bird but teeth like a reptile.

- *Ichthyornis* was a seabird with long, toothed jaws. It lived alongside dinosaurs in the Late Cretaceous period.

- **Although it could fly**, *Archaeopteryx* could not take off from the ground, and probably had to climb a tree before launching itself into the air.

- **Scientists believe** that birds evolved from lightly built dinosaurs such as *Compsognathus*, which ran on two legs.

◄ *Archaeopteryx had a wingspan of about 50 cm. Its name means 'ancient wing'.*

- **The dodo** stood 1 m tall and lived on the island of Mauritius. It became extinct in the 17th century.

- *Aepyornis*, a 3-m tall ostrich ancestor from Madagascar, probably became extinct in the 17th century.

- **The eggs** of Aepyornis, or elephant bird may have weighed as much as 10 kg – more than 9 times the weight of an ostrich egg today.

- **The tallest bird ever** was the moa (*Dinornis*) of New Zealand. It was a towering 3.5 m tall.

- **The great auk** first lived 2 million years ago. It became extinct in the mid 19th century after being overhunted for its fat, which was burned in oil lamps.

- **An early member** of the vulture family, *Argentavix* of South America had an amazing 7.3 m wingspan.

Waxwings and relatives

- **The waxwing** gets its name from the red markings like drops of wax at the tips of its wing feathers.

- **Palmchats** nest in palm trees. One nest may house 30 pairs of birds, each with its own tunnel entrance to the outside.

- **The silky flycatcher** feeds mostly on mistletoe berries, passing out the seeds.

Prominent crest

◄ *Bohemian waxwings will strip a bush clean of its berries before moving on.*

> ★ STAR FACT ★
> When courting, a male bohemian waxwing gives the female a gift – a berry or ant larva.

- **The bohemian waxwing** makes a nest of twigs, moss and grass, usually in a conifer tree. The female incubates 4–6 eggs, while the male keeps her fed.

- **Adult cedar waxwings** store berries in their crops, or throat pouches, and regurgitate them for their young.

- **The male silky flycatcher** builds a nest for his mate's eggs, and does most of the incubation.

- **Adult waxwings** eat mainly berries, but feed their young on insects for the first two weeks of their lives.

- **The single species of palmchat** is found on the islands of Haiti and the Dominican Republic in the Caribbean.

- **Cedar waxwings** have been seen sitting in rows on a branch passing a berry from one bird to the next until one of them swallows it!

True and harpy eagles

- **The most powerful of all eagles**, the South American harpy eagle hunts prey that may weigh more than itself, such as large monkeys and sloths.

- **The Philippine eagle** is one of the rarest of all birds of prey. Twenty years ago there were only about 200 birds. Now they are strictly protected, and there is a captive breeding programme to increase numbers.

- **The golden eagle** makes a bulky nest of sticks and branches that may measure as much as 2 m high and 1.5 m across often called the eyrie.

- **A harpy eagle** weighs over 8 kg, has a wingspan of more than 2 m, and talons the size of a bear's claws.

- **True eagles** are also known as booted eagles, because their legs are covered with feathers down to their toes.

- **Verreaux's eagle** lays 2 eggs, but the first chick to hatch usually kills the younger chick.

- **At up to 96 cm long**, the martial eagle is the largest African eagle. It feeds on mammals such as hyrax and young antelope, and on other

birds, including guineafowl and even storks.

- **A young martial eagle** is fed by its parents for about 60 days, by which time is has a full covering of feathers and is able to tear up prey for itself.

- **The golden eagle** usually has a hunting territory of about 260 sq km.

Hooked beak for tearing apart its prey

Large eyes – the eagle has excellent eyesight

Tapering wing feathers increase lift so the eagle can soar for long periods

Long curved talons

▶ *Golden eagles lay 2 eggs, but one chick usually dies. At first the mother keeps the surviving chick warm while the male finds food, but as the chick grows larger, both parents are kept busy supplying it with food.*

Turkeys and grouse

- **Male wild turkeys** of the USA, Mexico and Central America can weigh up to 8 kg.

- **At 87 cm long**, the western capercaillie is the biggest of the 17 species of grouse. The female is only 60 cm long.

▲ *Wild turkeys usually feed on the ground, but they are strong flyers over short distances.*

- **In winter**, the spruce grouse feeds mainly on the buds and needles of pine trees.

- **An adult turkey** has about 3500 feathers.

- **The 17 species of grouse** live in North America, Europe and northern Asia.

- **Wild turkeys** are not fussy eaters. They feed on seeds, nuts, berries, leaves, insects and other small creatures.

- **To attract females** and challenge rival males, the ruffed grouse makes a drumming sound with its wings.

- **At the start of the breeding season**, foot-stamping dances are performed by groups of male prairie chickens at their traditional display areas.

- **The ruffed grouse** lays 9–12 eggs. When the young hatch, the female shows them where to find food.

Mockingbirds and relatives

- **Mockingbirds** are so-called because they imitate the calls of other bird species – as many as 36 in all.

- **The alpine accentor** breeds high in the mountains, and has been seen nesting at 8000 m in the Himalayas.

- **As well as mockingbirds,** the 32 species in the family includes birds such as catbirds, thrashers and tremblers. The live in North and South America.

- **The brown trembler**, a resident of some Caribbean islands, gets its name from its habit of shaking its body from time to time.

- **The 13 accentor species** live in mountainous parts of northern Africa, Europe and Asia.

▶ *The northern mockingbird is the best mimic in its family, usually copying the sounds made by other bird species.*

- **'Mimic of many tongues'** is the meaning of the northern mockingbird's scientific name, *Mimus polyglottus*.

- **The grey catbird** lines its cup-shaped nest of sticks, leaves and grasses with pine needles and even hair. The female lays 3–5 eggs, and incubates them for 12–13 days.

- **The brown thrasher** scatters dead leaves with its beak as it searches on the ground for its insect prey.

- **The catbird** gets its name from its strange, catlike call.

Wrens and babblers

- **The white-necked rockfowl** (babbler family) makes a mud nest on the roof of caves. It sometimes builds onto old wasps' nests.

- **The cactus wren** builds its nest among the spines of the chola cactus. Few enemies will brave the spines to steal the wren's eggs or young.

- **At about 23 cm long**, the black-capped donacobious of South America is the largest of the wren family.

- **The only species** of the babbler family to live in North America is the wren-tit, while 256 species are found in Asia, Africa and Australasia.

- **The tuneful song** of the red-billed leiothrix (babbler family) makes it a popular cage bird in China.

- **Although common in west Africa**, the pale-breasted thrush-babbler is so good at hiding on the forest floor, where it searches for insects, that it is rarely seen.

- **A male wren** courts a mate by building up to 12 nests. The female chooses one in which to lay her eggs.

▶ *The cactus wren makes several decoy nests in different cactus plants to fool predators.*

- **The winter wren** usually lays 5–8 eggs, and incubates them for 14–17 days. The young stay in the nest for 20 days.

- **Brightly coloured patches** of bare skin on the head are a distinguishing feature of rockfowl (babbler family).

- **Most wrens** live in Europe, Asia, Africa and North America.

Caring for young

- **Many baby birds** are blind, naked and helpless when they hatch, and have to be cared for by their parents.

- **The young of ducks and geese** hatch with a covering of feathers, and can find food hours after hatching.

- **A young golden eagle** has grown feathers after 50 days and learned to fly after 70, but stays with its parents for another month while learning to hunt.

> ★ **STAR FACT** ★
> In a colony of thousands of terns, baby terns can recognize the call of their own parents.

- **A young bird** is known as a fledgling from the time it hatches until it is fully feathered and can fly.

- **A young pelican** feeds by putting its head deep into its parent's large beak and gobbling up any fish it finds.

- **A swan** carries its young on its back to keep them safe.

- **To obtain food** from its parent, a young herring gull has to peck at a red spot on the parent's beak. The adult gull then regurgitates food for the chick to eat.

- **Shearwaters** feed their young for 60 days, then stop. After a week the chicks get so hungry that they take to the air to find food for themselves.

- **In 3 weeks**, a new-born cuckoo gets 50 times heavier.

◀ *Bokmakierie shrike chicks are born blind, but can see by 4 days old.*

Ostriches and emus

- **The ostrich** is the largest of all birds alive today. It stands 2.5 m tall and weighs about 130 kg – more than twice as much as an average human.

- **The male emu** incubates his mate's clutch of eggs for 8 weeks, during which time he does not eat or drink. He lives on the stores of body fat that it has built up during the previous months.

- **In Southwest Asia**, the shells of ostrich eggs are believed to have magical powers, and are sometimes placed on the roofs of houses as protection from evil.

- **Ostriches don't really bury their heads** in the sand. But if a female is approached by an enemy while sitting on her nest on the ground, she will press her long neck flat on the ground, to appear less obvious.

- **The largest bird in Australia** is the emu, which measures 2 m tall and weighs as much as 45 kg. Like the ostrich, it cannot fly.

★ **STAR FACT** ★
The ostrich cannot fly, but is a very fast runner. It can speed along at 60 km/h – as fast as a racehorse.

- **An ostrich feather** was used as a symbol of justice in ancient Egypt.

- **Seeds, fruits, flowers and plant shoots** are the emu's main sources of food, but it also eats some insects and small animals.

- **The male ostrich** makes a shallow nest on the ground and mates with several females, all of whom lay their eggs in the nest. The chief female incubates the eggs during the day, and the male takes over at night.

- **Ostrich chicks** have many enemies, including jackals and hyenas, and only 15% are likely to survive until their first birthday.

The male has black feathers on its back; females and young birds have brown feathers

The long, flexible neck is bare skinned

Long, strong legs for running

▲ The ostrich lives in Africa in dry grassland areas, where it often has to run for long distances in search of food.

Migration

- **Migration** is generally the journey made twice a year between a summer breeding area, where food is plentiful, and a wintering area with a good climate.

- **Many migrating birds** have to build up fat stores to allow them to fly non-stop for many days without food.

- **A migrating bird** can fly across the Sahara Desert in 50–60 hours without stopping to 'refuel'.

- **Birds find their way** by observing landmarks, the patterns of stars and the position of the setting sun. They also use their sense of smell and monitor the Earth's magnetic field.

- **Most birds** that migrate long distances fly at night.

- **The snow goose** migrates nearly 5000 km south from Arctic Canada at an altitude of 9000 m.

- **Before migration was studied**, some people thought swallows simply spent the winter asleep in mud.

- **Even flightless birds migrate.** Emus make journeys on foot of 500 km or more, and penguins migrate in water.

- **Every year** at least 5 billion birds migrate from North to Central and South America.

- **The Arctic tern** spends the northern summer in the Arctic and migrates to the Antarctic for the southern summer, enjoying 24 hours of daylight in both places.

▼ *Geese migrate in huge flocks, but pairs stay together within the flock.*

Finches and relatives

- **The crossbill** gets its name from its crossed beak, specially shaped for extracting seeds from pine cones.

- **The beaks** of some crossbills cross to the left, while those of others cross to the right.

- **Canaries** were first domesticated in the early 16th century, from the island canary of the Canary Islands, the Azores and Madeira.

- **The male American goldfinch** brings

the female food while she incubates the 4–6 eggs.

- **The bullfinch** feeds on fruit buds in spring and it can pluck as many as 30 buds in a minute.

- **The kernels** of cherry stones and olive stones are a favourite food of the strong-beaked hawfinch.

- **The goldfinch** uses its slender beak like tweezers to take seeds from between the spines of a teasel head.

- **Finches are small birds**, ranging from 4-19 cm long and weighing up to 100 grams.

- **Siskins and goldfinches** have long been popular as cage birds, and are now rare in many areas.

▲ *Wild canaries have duller plumage than their bright yellow domestic relatives.*

★ STAR FACT ★
Although the hawfinch weighs only 50 g, its beak can exert a pressure of 45 kg.

Cranes and trumpeters

- **The whooping crane** is one of the world's most endangered birds, with only about 300 surviving in 1995.

- **The crowned crane**, which has a fine crest of yellow feathers, performs a spectacular courtship display that involves leaping 2 m into the air.

- **The 3 species of trumpeter** live in tropical rainforests. All make a loud trumpeting call – hence their name.

- **In China and Japan** the crane symbolizes long life and good luck.

- **At about 1.5 m long**, the Sarus crane of India, Southeast Asia and northern Australia is one of the largest members of the crane family.

▶ *The handsome crowned crane lives in Africa, usually around swamps and marshland.*

- **The limpkin** is a relative of the cranes and the only member of its family. It has a long, curved beak, which it uses to remove snails from their shells.

- **Trumpeters** spend most of their time on the ground in search of fruit, nuts and insects, but they roost in trees.

- **The sandhill crane** makes a nest of plant material on the ground. The female lays 2 eggs, which both parents help to incubate. Soon after hatching, the young leave the nest.

- **Siberian cranes** have been known to live more than 80 years – one captive male even fathered chicks at the age of 78!

- **The 14 or so species of crane** live all over the world, in North America, Africa, Europe, Asia and Australia.

Bowerbirds

- **Male bowerbirds** build bowers of twigs and other plant material to attract females. They decorate their creations with berries and shells, and some perform dances in front of their bowers.

- **The Vogelkop gardener bowerbird** builds a hutlike structure big enough for a person to crawl into.

- **Male bowerbirds' bowers** are not built as a place for the

◀ *The male spotted bowerbird spends much of its time looking after its bower.*

★ **STAR FACT** ★
The satin bowerbird decorates its bower with blue flowers, feathers, and even bottletops.

female to lay eggs and rear young. The females build their own, more practical nests.

- **The forests** of New Guinea and northern and eastern Australia are home to the 18 or so species of bowerbird.

- **At about 36 cm long**, the great grey bowerbird of northern Australia is the largest of the family.

- **Bowerbirds** feed on fruit, berries, seeds, insects and other small creatures.

- **A female bowerbird** cares for her 1–3 chicks alone.

- **The male regent bowerbird** paints its bower yellow using a mix of spit and the juice of crushed leaves.

- **Catbirds** are members of the bowerbird family. They get their name from their catlike calls.

Feathers

- **Feathers** are made of a protein called keratin. Human hair and nails are also made of keratin.

- **Feathers grow** at a rate of 1–13 mm a day.

- **The ruby-throated hummingbird** has only 940 feathers, while the whistling swan has 25,216.

- **A bird's feathers** are replaced once or twice a year in a process called 'moulting'.

- **Feathers** keep a bird warm, protect its skin, provide camouflage, and may also attract mates.

- **In most birds**, a third of the feathers are on the head.

- **The longest feathers ever known** were 10.59 m long, and belonged to an ornamental chicken.

- **The feathers** that cover a bird's body are called contour feathers. Down feathers underneath provide extra warmth.

- **The 7182 feathers** of a bald eagle weighed 677 g, more than twice as much as the bird's skeleton.

- **Birds** spend time every day 'preening' – cleaning and rearranging their feathers with their beaks.

▲ *The peacock has the most ornate feathers of any bird.*

▶ *The plumage of the little hummingbird gleams with iridescence.*

Antbirds and tapaculos

- **Antbirds** follow columns of army ants as they march over the forest floor, perching just above the ground to seize other insects as they flee from the ants.

- **The 230 or so species of antbird** live in Mexico, Central and South America.

- **The 30 species of tapaculos** are insect-eating birds that live in dry scrub and the cool mountain forests of South America.

- **Antbirds** mate for life.

- **During the courtship ritual** of the ocellated antbird, the male presents the female with an item of food.

- **Antbirds have white spots** on their back feathers, which they use to signal

> ★ **STAR FACT** ★
> An antbird rubs a mouthful of ants over its feathers to clean them. The formic acid from the ants kills any lice and mites in the feathers.

warnings to each other. They show the spots in particular patterns according to the message – like a sort of Morse code.

- **Antbird species** range from 10–38 cm long, and have differently shaped beaks to suit their food.

- **Some larger species of antbirds** have a special 'tooth' inside the beak that helps them chew food.

- **Most antbirds** do not fly much and have poorly developed wings, but their legs are strong, for running and perching.

◀ *Female antbirds are often brownish or greenish in colour. Males usually have dark grey plumage with white markings.*

Swallows and martins

- **There are about 80 species of swallows and martins** found all over the world. Most migrate between breeding grounds and wintering areas.

- **The sand martin** digs a 120 cm long nesting burrow in river banks.

- **Swallows** catch their insect food in the air as they fly.

- **Only discovered in 1968**, the white-eyed river martin spends the winter in reedbeds on Lake Boraphet in Thailand.

- **Purple martins** often nest in old woodpecker holes or in nest-boxes. The female incubates the 4–5 eggs

> ★ STAR FACT ★
> The ancient Romans used swallows as messengers to carry news of the winners of chariot races to neighbouring towns.

▼ *The house martin often lives near people, making its nest under the eaves of buildings or under bridges or other structures.*

alone, but the male helps feed the young.

- **There is an old saying** that the weather will be good when swallows fly high, but bad when swallows fly low. This is based on fact – in wet weather, insects tend to stay nearer the ground, so their predators – the swallows – do the same.

- **Adult swallows** will carry a mass of crushed insects, squashed in a ball in the throat, back to their young. A barn swallow may take 400 meals a day to its chicks.

- **Sand martins** breed in the northern hemisphere, migrating south in the winter in flocks of thousands.

- **In most swallow species** males and females are alike, but in the rare blue swallow the female has a short tail, while the male's is long and forked.

Snake and sea eagles

- **The bald eagle** performs an amazing courtship display, in which male and female lock their claws together and tumble through the air towards the ground.

- **The short-toed eagle** kills a snake with a bite to the back of the head, instantly severing the backbone.

- **The white-tailed sea eagle** snatches fish from the water in its powerful talons.

- **The bald eagle** was chosen as the national emblem of the USA in 1782, and appears on most of the gold and silver coins in the USA.

- **Spikes** on the underside of its toes help the African fish eagle hold

onto its fish prey. It also catches birds, terrapins and baby crocodiles.

- **Bald eagles** are not really bald. They have white feathers on their heads, which may make them appear bald from a distance.

- **The bateleur**, a snake eagle, may fly as much as 300 km a day in search of food.

- **Snake eagles** do eat snakes, and have short, strong toes ideal for tackling their writhing victims.

- **The name 'bateleur'** means 'tumbler' or 'tightrope walker' in French, and refers to the rocking, acrobatic movements that the bird makes in flight.

- **There are only about 40 pairs** of the Madagascar fish eagle left in the world.

◄ *Steller's sea eagle lives along Asia's coasts and rivers, preying mostly on salmon.*

Rainforest birds

- **Male and female eclectus parrots** of the Amazon rainforest have very different plumage. The male bird is mostly bright green, while the female is red with a blue underside.

- **The crowned eagle** lives in African rainforests, where it feeds on monkeys and other mammals such as mongooses and rats.

- **The king vulture** of South America is the only vulture to live in rainforest. As well as feeding on carrion, it also kills mammals and reptiles.

- **The sunbittern** lives along river banks in the rainforests of South America, feeding on frogs, insects and other creatures.

- **With its abundance** of flowers, leaves, fruits and insects all year round, a rainforest is the ideal home for many different kinds of birds.

- **The muscovy duck**, now familiar in farmyards and parks in many parts of the world, originally came from the rainforests of Central and South America.

- **Large, flightless cassowaries** live in the rainforests of New Guinea, where people hunt them to eat.

- **The spectacled eagle owl** of South America has rings of white feathers around its eyes. Its call resembles the hammering sound made by woodpeckers.

- **The rare Cassin's hawk eagle** lives in African rainforests, and hunts squirrels and other birds.

★ STAR FACT ★
The hoatzin builds its nest over rainforest rivers, so that if its chicks are threatened, they can drop into the water to escape.

Huge eagles nest at the tops of the highest rainforest trees

Macaws, parrots, toucans and many other species flutter through the rainforest canopy

The stunning, resplendent quetzal favours trees of the laurel family

▶ The tropical rainforest has more types of bird than anywhere else. Many of the birds in the canopy are amazingly colourful. Game birds and little insect eaters patrol the forest floor.

Larks and wagtails

- **The shore lark** has the widest distribution of any lark. Its habitats range from the icy Arctic to deserts.

- **The wagtail family** has about 60 species, most of which are small, insect-eating birds. They include pipits and longclaws.

- **The 75 species of lark** live in North America, parts of South America, Africa, Europe, Asia and Australia. The greatest number of species is found in Africa.

- **The female skylark** makes a shallow, grassy nest on the ground, and incubates 3–4 eggs.

- **The skylark** performs a beautiful song as it flutters up to a great height, hovers and descends again.

- **The thick-billed lark** has a larger, stronger beak than

> ★ STAR FACT ★
> The yellow-throated longclaw gets its name from the 5-cm long claw on each back toe.

most larks, and uses it to crush hard seeds and tough-shelled insects.

- **The shore or horned lark** is the only member of the family to live in the Americas.

- **The desert lark's coloration** varies according to where it lives – birds in areas of white sand have pale feathers, while those that live on dark laval sand are almost black.

- **Craneflies** are one of the favourite foods of the meadow pipit. Adults may feed their 3–5 chicks on craneflies for 2 weeks. The chicks develop in a nest of dry grass lined with hair.

◀ *The little pied wagtail bobs its tail up and down almost all the time as it searches for insects.*

Kingfishers

- **The common kingfisher** nests at the end of a 60-cm long tunnel that it excavates in a river bank. The female lays 4–8 eggs.

- **The tiny African pygmy kingfisher** dives not into water, like the common kingfisher, but into grass, where it snatches grasshoppers and beetles.

- **The 86 or so species of kingfisher** are found all over the world, except parts of the far north.

- **The giant kingfisher** of Africa and

◀ *The kingfisher fiercely defends the stretch of river bank where it feeds and nests.*

the Australian laughing kookaburra are the largest of the family, at about 45 cm long.

- **Common kingfishers** incubate their eggs for 19–21 days, and feed the young for up to 4 weeks.

- **The shovel-billed kingfisher** is armed with its own spade for digging in mud – it uses its large, heavy bill to dig up worms, shellfish and small reptiles.

- **A flash of iridescent turquoise feathers** streaking at high speed along a river bank indicates the presence of a common or European kingfisher.

- **In the forests of New Guinea**, the male paradise kingfisher shows off its very long tail feathers to females as part of its courtship display.

- **The laughing kookaburra** is named for its call, which sounds like noisy laughter. It makes its call to claim territory. Once one starts, others tend to join in!

- **In northern Australia**, termite mounds are adopted as nest sites by the buff-breasted kingfisher.

Thrushes and dippers

- **The wheatear** breeds in the Arctic, but in autumn flies some 3200 km to Africa, where it spends the winter.

- **The dipper** is the only type of songbird to live in and around water – it can swim underwater and even walk along streambeds as it searches for insect prey.

- **The familiar orange-red breast** of a robin indicates that the bird is at least 2 months old.

- **More than 300 species of thrush** are found nearly all over the world.

- **Best known for its beautiful song**, the nightingale sings during the day as well as at night.

- **The female blackbird** makes a cup-shaped nest of plant stems, grass, twigs and roots. The 4–5 eggs hatch after 11–17 days.

- **The 5 species of dipper** live in Europe, Asia and parts of North and South America.

- **The dome-shaped nests** of dippers usually have an entrance over running water.

- **The American robin** – the largest of the North American thrushes – lives both in cities and mountains.

- **Blackbirds** were taken to Australia and New Zealand in the 19th century, and their songs are now clearly different to blackbirds living in Europe.

◀ The European robin is Britain's national bird.

Sandpipers

- **Coasts and marshes** are the home of the 88 or so species of sandpiper, which include curlews, snipe and phalaropes. Most have long beaks and long legs.

- **The western curlew** plunges its long, curved beak into soft coastal mud to find worms and clams.

- **As it dives towards Earth**, air rushing through the outermost tail feathers of the European snipe makes a sound called 'drumming'.

◀ The curlew's long legs are ideal for wading through marshland.

- **Sandpipers** range in size from the eastern curlew, at about 66 cm long, to the least sandpiper, at 11 cm.

- **Once the dowitcher's 4 eggs** have hatched, feeding the chicks is the sole responsibility of the male.

- **Unusually for birds**, female phalaropes are more brightly coloured than males. The female lays several clutches of eggs, leaving the male parent of each clutch to do all the caring for the young.

- **The turnstone** is so-named because it turns over stones on the beach in search of shellfish and worms.

- **In the breeding season**, male ruffs grow amazing feathers around the head and neck, and dance In groups to attract females.

> ★ STAR FACT ★
> The eskimo curlew is one of the world's rarest birds. With only 50 or so birds left in the world, it is on the brink of extinction.

Large seabirds

- **The wandering albatross** has the longest wings of any bird – from tip to tip they are an incredible 3.4 m.

- **The white-tailed tropicbird** is noted for its amazing tail streamers, which measure up to 40 cm long.

- **The male frigatebird** has a bright red throat pouch that he inflates during courtship to attract females.

- **The wandering albatross** often flies 500 km in a day, soaring over the ocean in search of food.

- **The pirates of the bird world** are frigatebirds, which often chase other seabirds in the air and harass them into giving up their catches.

- **Frigatebird chicks** depend on their parents for longer than most birds. They start to fly at about 6 months, but continue to be fed until they are 1 year old.

- **The 5 species of frigatebird** fly over tropical areas of all oceans. They spend most of their lives in the air, rarely descending to land on water.

- **The 3 species of tropicbird** are all expert in the air and can dive into the sea to find prey, but cannot walk on land. With their legs set far back on their bodies, they can only drag themselves along.

- **The wandering albatross** can only breed every other year. It incubates its eggs for 11 weeks, and the chicks do not fly until they are about 40 weeks old.

▲ When courting a mate, the male frigatebird clatters his beak and flaps his wings, as well as inflating his red throat pouch into an eyecatching balloon. Also known as a 'man of war', the frigatebird is adept at stealing food and nest material from other birds in the colony. It builds its large nest in trees.

Long wings for gliding on the wind

★ **STAR FACT** ★

A wandering albatross chick may eat as much as 100 kg of food during the time it is being fed by its parents.

▶ Squid is the main food of the wandering albatross, but it will also snatch fish waste thrown from fishing boats. An expert glider, it can sail downwind from a height of about 15 m to just above the water's surface, before turning back into the wind to be blown upwards.

Sunbirds and relatives

- **The 115 or so species of sunbirds** live in tropical parts of Africa, Asia and Australia.

- **The Kauai o-o**, a honeyeater, was thought to be extinct, but in 1960 some birds were found, and there is now a very small protected population.

- **The flowerpecker family** contains about 58 species living in parts of Asia, Southeast Asia and Australia.

- **At about 23 cm long**, the Sao Tomé giant sunbird is the largest of its family. It uses its hooked beak to dig into the bark of trees for insects.

- **Sunbirds** use their long, slender beaks and tubular tongues to extract sweet liquid nectar from flowers.

- **Female sunbirds** make purse-shaped nests for their

> ★ STAR FACT ★
> The mistletoe bird (flowerpecker family) swallows mistletoe berries whole, digesting only the flesh and not the seeds.

2–3 eggs, which hatch after 13–15 days.

- **Honeyeaters** are the most important flower pollinators in Australia. The brushlike tip on the honeyeater's tongue helps it to extract flower nectar.

- **The crested berrypecker** (flowerpecker family) has a habit of rubbing its plumage with crushed flower petals.

- **The tui** (honeyeater family) of New Zealand is also known as the parson bird, because of the bib of white feathers at its throat.

▶ *Sunbirds feed from tropical flowers. They often hover as they do so, but cannot fly backwards like hummingbirds.*

Nests

- **The bald eagle** makes the biggest nest of any bird. It can be as large as 2.5 m across and 3.5 m deep – big enough for several people to hide inside!

- **The bee hummingbird's** nest is the smallest – only the size of a thimble.

- **The hammerkop**, a heronlike bird, makes a huge nest up to 2 m high and weighing 50 kg.

- **The hammerkop uses anything** from sticks to bits of bone and plastic to make its nest.

- **A cliff swallow's** nest is made up of about 1200 tiny balls of mud.

- **Nightjars** do not make a nest – they just lay their eggs on the ground.

- **The rufous-breasted castle builder** (woodcreeper family) makes a nest shaped like a dumb-bell, with two chambers – one for the chicks.

- **The turquoise-browed motmot** is a surprisingly efficient digger, excavating a 1.5-m long burrow in just 5 days.

- **The European bee-eater** nests underground to keep cool. While the surface temperature may reach 50°C, the bee-eater's nest remains a pleasant 25°C.

- **Hummingbirds and honeyeaters** use spiders' webs to hold their nests together.

▼ *A bald eagle's nest is used and enlarged year after year.*

Old World flycatchers

- **The spotted flycatcher** sits on a branch watching for insect prey, then darts out to catch it in mid-air – it has been seen catching 1 insect every 18 seconds.

- **The rufous-bellied niltava** lives and breeds in the Himalayas at altitudes of up to 2300 m.

- **The male pied flycatcher** may have two nests some distance apart, but he only helps rear the young in one of them.

- **There are 147 species of Old World flycatchers**. Some live in wooded parts of Europe, but they are more common in Asia, Africa and Australasia.

- **After a summer in Europe**, the red-breasted flycatcher flies to India and Southeast Asia for the winter.

- **The white-throated jungle flycatcher** is now very rare and lives only on two islands in the Philippines.

- **The female red-breasted flycatcher** makes a cup-shaped nest of moss, leaves, spiders' webs and plant down in which to lay her 5–6 eggs.

- **Male spotted flycatchers** bring all the food for their brood when they first hatch. Later, both parents feed the chicks.

- **Instead of catching all its food in the air**, the Australian flame robin often pounces onto its prey from a low perch.

- **In autumn and winter**, the pied flycatcher eats worms and berries as well as insects.

◄ *The spotted flycatcher lives in woodland, parks and gardens in Europe and parts of Asia and Africa.*

Ovenbirds and relatives

- **The nest** of the firewood-gatherer (ovenbird family) looks like a bonfire. A group of birds make the nest together and sleep in it during the winter.

- **The red-billed scythebill** (a woodcreeper) has a long, curved beak for delving deep into rainforest plants such as ferns and bromeliads to find insects.

- **Ovenbirds** live in the forests, mountains and semideserts of Mexico, Central and South America.

- **Woodcreepers** often nest in old woodpecker nests.

- **The common miner** (an ovenbird) digs a 3-m long burrow with a nest chamber at the end, where it raises its chicks and roosts for the rest of the year.

> ★ STAR FACT ★
> The rufous hornero's mud-and-straw nest is shaped like an old-fashioned clay oven.

- **Des Murs' wiretail** (an ovenbird) has only 6 tail feathers, 4 of which may be 3 times the length of the body.

- **The 50 or so species of woodcreeper** live in forests and woodland in Mexico, Central and South America.

- **Insects and spiders** hiding among the densely packed leaves of bromeliads may be extracted by the long, probing beak of the long-billed woodcreeper.

- **The campo miner** (an ovenbird) nests in a very particular place – an old armadillo burrow.

◄ *The rufous hornero is the national bird of Argentina.*

Polar and tundra birds

- **The willow ptarmigan** lives on the Arctic tundra. In winter it has white feathers that help to keep it hidden in the snow, but in summer it grows darker feathers again.

- **The ivory gull** of Arctic coasts and islands is the only all-white gull.

- **Adelie penguins** breed on coasts and islands around the Antarctic in huge colonies that return to the same site year after year.

- **Snowy owls** are among the fiercest Arctic birds. They soar over the tundra preying on other birds and small mammals such as lemmings.

- **Most birds leave Antarctica in winter**, but the southern black-backed gull stays all year round, feeding on fish, birds' eggs and carrion.

- **The emperor penguin** breeds in colder temperatures than any other bird. It survives temperatures of -40°C as it incubates its egg.

▲ In winter, the willow ptarmigan feeds mainly on the twigs and buds of dwarf willows.

- **The great skua** is the biggest flying bird in Antarctica, at up to 5 kg and 66 cm long.

- **Although only 10 cm long**, the little storm petrel may migrate 40,000 km a year between the poles.

- **The laysan albatross** breeds on central Pacific islands, but spends most of the year flying over the Arctic hunting for schools of fish to eat.

- **Tufted puffins** nest only on cliffs and islands in the Arctic North Pacific. One colony contained as many as 1 million nests.

Avocets and relatives

- **Young jacanas** often hide underneath floating leaves if danger threatens.

- **The 7 species of stilts and avocets** are all long-legged wading birds with long, slender beaks.

- **Female pheasant-tailed jacanas** mate with up to 10 males in one breeding season. The males incubate the eggs and care for the young.

- **If a male pheasant-tailed jacana** thinks his eggs are in danger, he may move them one at a time, holding them between its breast and throat.

- **The long, curved**

> ★ **STAR FACT** ★
> The American jacana or lilytrotter has extremely long toes and claws allowing it to walk on floating waterlily leaves.

beak of the pied avocet turns up at the end. The bird sweeps this strange tool through mud or shallow water to find worms and shrimps.

- **The black-winged stilt** has extremely long, bright pink legs that allow it to wade in deeper water than other stilts as it searches for worms and shellfish.

- **Jacanas** range in size from 16–53 cm long.

- **Avocets** nest in a hollow in the ground, lined with dead leaves. Both partners incubate the 3–5 eggs.

- **Young avocets** can run soon after hatching, and can fend for themselves after 6 weeks.

◀ The African jacana is common around lakes and marshes, where it feeds on insects, fish and water plants.

Lyrebirds and relatives

- **One of the biggest of all the songbirds**, the superb lyrebird has an extraordinary lyre-shaped tail, with feathers more than 50 cm long.

- **The rifleman**, one of the 3 species of New Zealand wren, lays eggs that are about 20% of her body weight. She and the male recruit helpers to bring food to their young.

- **The 2 species of scrub-bird** live in Australia, where they feed on insects, lizards and frogs.

- **In its loud song**, the lyrebird may imitate other birds, barking dogs, chainsaws and even passing trains.

- **The female lyrebird** builds a domed nest, usually close to the ground. Her 1 chick stays with her for 8 months or more.

- **The rufous scrub-bird** spends most of its time on the and rarely flies.

◄ *The lyrebird spends most of its life on the ground searching for insects.*

- **The 2 species of lyrebird** live in dense mountain forest in southeastern Australia.

- **Named after the small island** in Cook Strait where it lived, the Stephen Island wren was killed off by the lighthouse keeper's cat. It may have been the only flightless songbird.

- **A full-grown rufous scrub-bird** is 16–18 cm long and weighs about 30 g.

- **Young male superb lyrebirds** do not grow their lyre-shaped tails until they are 3 or 4 years old.

Eggs

- **All bird species** lays eggs.

- **The biggest egg** is the ostrich egg. At 1.5 kg, it is 30 times heavier than an average hen's egg.

- **Incubation** is the process of keeping eggs warm while they develop. It can take from 10–80 days.

- **The yellow yolk** in an egg provides food for the growing embryo. The white provides food and moisture.

- **Gannets stand on their eggs** to keep them warm!

- **The shell of an egg** contains 50–100 tiny pores per sq cm, allowing oxygen to seep into the egg and carbon dioxide does the same outwards

- **Egg yolks** are not always yellow. The common tern's yolk is deep red, and the gentoo penguin's a pinky red.

> ★ **STAR FACT** ★
> The bee hummingbird lays the smallest egg, at just 0.3 g. You could fit 4700 into 1 ostrich egg!

- **Eggshells** vary in thickness from 0.2 mm in the night heron's egg to 0.75 mm in the common murre's.

- **Not all eggs are oval** – those of owls and toucans are round, and auks lay pear-shaped eggs.

▲ *A bird's egg, though seemingly fragile, contains everything that the growing embryo inside needs to survive.*

Crows

- **Members of the crow family** live on all continents of the world, except Antarctica. There are about 117 species, including jackdaws, rooks, ravens, nutcrackers, choughs and jays, as well as common crows.

- **Bold and aggressive**, a typical crow is a big bird with a strong body and legs, and a powerful beak that can deal with nuts, seeds and even small prey.

- **At 66 cm long**, the raven is the largest of the crow family, and the largest of the songbird group of birds.

- **Crows** are thought to be among the most intelligent of all birds. Studies on ravens have shown that they are able to count up to five or six.

- **When food is plentiful**, nutcrackers hide nuts and pine seeds in holes in the ground, and are able to find them again months later.

- **There are many superstitions** about ravens – the arrival of a raven is said to be an evil omen and a sign of an imminent death.

- **A species of crow** that lives on the Pacific island of New Caledonia uses tools such as hooked twigs and sharp-ended stems to extract grubs from the crowns of palm trees.

- **Breeding pairs** of Australian white-winged choughs use a team of up to 8 other choughs to help them find food for their young.

- **Some crows in Japan** have learned how to get cars to crack nuts for them. They put the nuts in front of cars at traffic lights, wait for the cars to pass over them, and collect the kernels once the lights are red again!

★ **STAR FACT** ★

Magpies steal the eggs and young of other birds, as well as bright, shiny objects such as jewellery, which they hide in their nests.

▼ *The secret of the crows' success is their adaptability. They eat a wide range of foods and are intelligent enough to learn how to make use of new food sources. Shown here are: (1) the raven, (2) the rook, (3) the hooded crow,(4) the chough, (5) the jackdaw*

1

2

3

4

5

Old World sparrows

- **The house sparrow** originally came from Southwest Asia, but has spread throughout the world. It feeds mainly on seeds, but also eats some insects and is happy to eat scraps put out on bird tables.

- **Chestnut sparrows** drive other birds from their nests and use the nests themselves, instead of making their own.

- **The snow finch** lives high in mountain ranges and makes its nest on mountain ledges at altitudes of 5000 m.

- **All the house sparrows in the USA** are descended from a few birds that were released in Central Park, New York, in 1850.

▶ *There may now be as many as 150 million house sparrows in the USA.*

★ STAR FACT ★
Sparrows like to bathe and splash in water, and will even bathe in snow in winter.

- **House sparrows** generally have two broods a year of 4–7 eggs each.

- **The desert sparrow** makes a nest of dry grass and twigs, often in a wall, and lays 2–5 eggs.

- **Most sparrows** are about 14–18 cm long and have brownish or grey plumage.

- **The 40 or so species of Old World sparrow** live in Europe, Africa and parts of Asia, though some have been introduced elsewhere.

- **House sparrows** rarely nest away from human habitation.

Auks

- **The Atlantic puffin's colourful beak** is striped red, yellow and grey blue, and can hold 12 or more fish.

- **The ancient murrelet** is so-named because it develops fine white feathers on its head in the breeding season, said to look like the white hairs of an elderly person.

- **The common guillemot** nests on narrow cliff ledges. Its eggs are pointed, so that if they get knocked, they roll in a circle and do not fall off.

- **The guillemot** can dive in water to a depth of 180 m as it hunts for fish.

- **The auk family** includes 22 species of diving birds, including auks, guillemots, puffins and razorbills. They live in and around the North Pacific, Atlantic and Arctic oceans.

- **The common guillemot** is the largest of the auks, at about 45 cm long and 1 kg in weight. The least auklet is the smallest auk, at 16 cm long and 90 g.

- **Common guillemots** nest in colonies of thousands, with as many as 70 pairs occupying 1 sq m.

- **The little auk** nests in a cliff crevice and lays 1–2 eggs, which both parents incubate.

- **Auk eggs** are reputed to taste good, and have long been collected and eaten by humans.

▶ *The tufted puffin lives in the Arctic and North Pacific.*

★ STAR FACT ★
The puffin flies at up to 64 km/h, with its wings beating 300–400 times a minute.

Bee-eaters and relatives

- **The 5 species of tody** are all insect-eating birds that live in the Caribbean islands.

- **Bee-eaters catch a bee or wasp** and kill it by striking it against a branch. Before eating it, the bird rubs the insect against the branch to expel its venom.

- **The blue-crowned motmot** has 2 long tail feathers with racquet-shaped tips. As the bird sits watching for prey, it swings its tail like a clock's pendulum.

- **Motmots** range in size from the 19-cm long tody motmot to the 53-cm long upland motmot.

- **Motmots lay their eggs** in a chamber at the end of a burrow dug in an earth bank. Both parents incubate the eggs and feed the chicks.

> ★ **STAR FACT** ★
> A European bee-eater eats about 200 bees a day. Its summer diet is mainly bumblebees, and in winter it eats honeybees and dragonflies.

- **The 27 species of bee-eater** are colourful birds that live in southern Europe, Africa, Asia and Australia.

- **The European bee-eater** flies some 16,000 km between Europe, where it breeds, and Africa, where it overwinters.

- **Todies** nest in 30-cm long tunnels, which they dig with their beaks.

- **The 10 species of motmot** live only in forests from Mexico to northern Argentina.

◀ The white-fronted bee-eater lives in southern Africa.

Warblers

- **The willow warbler** is only 11 cm long, but flies all the way from northern Europe and Siberia to Africa to spend the winter – a distance of some 12,000 km.

- **The rarely seen grasshopper warbler** has an extraordinary whirring song and can 'throw its voice' like a ventriloquist.

▶ At 19 cm long, the great reed warbler is larger than most European warblers.

- **The warbler family** has more than 380 species. Most live in Europe, Africa, Asia and Australasia, but there are a few species in North and South America.

- **Most warblers** are 9–16 cm long, but the two largest – the South African grassbird and the Australian songlarks – are up to 23 cm long.

- **The Aldabra warbler**, discovered in 1967, lives only on a small part of Aldabra Island in the Indian Ocean. It has not been seen since 1983, so may well be extinct.

- **Insects** are the main food of most warblers, but they also eat some fruits, berries and seeds.

- **The marsh warbler** can mimic about 80 other species.

- **Chiffchaffs and willow warblers** look almost exactly alike, but their songs are quite different.

- **The blackcap** lays 4–6 eggs in a neat, cup-shaped nest. Both parents incubate them for 10–15 days.

- **The tailorbird** makes a cradlelike nest from two leaves sewn together with plant fibres or spiders' webs.

Pheasants and relatives

- **Domestic chickens** are descended from the red jungle fowl, which was first domesticated 5000 years ago. The jungle fowl still lives wild in Southeast Asia.

- **All 49 species of wild pheasant** are from Asia, except the Congo peafowl, which was first discovered in a Central African rainforest in 1936.

- **To attract females**, the male great argus pheasant dances and spreads out his enormously long wing feathers, like glittering fans.

- **The peacock's wonderful train** contains about 200 shimmering feathers, each one decorated with eyelike markings. When courting, he spreads the train and makes it 'shiver' to attract a female.

◀ *The peacock is a native of India, Sri Lanka and Pakistan, but it has been introduced in many areas throughout the world. Only the male has the spectacular tail, which does not reach its full glory until the bird is about 3 years old. It may continue to grow for another 2–3 years.*

★ **STAR FACT** ★
The crested argus has the largest, longest tail feathers of any bird, at up to 170 cm long and 12 cm wide.

- **The Himalayan monal pheasant** spends some of the year above the tree line, where it has to dig in the snow with its beak to find insects and other food.

- **The male pheasant** mates with several females, each of which lays up to 15 eggs in a shallow scrape on the ground. The females incubate the eggs and care for the young by themselves, with no help from the male.

- **Most pheasants** nest on the ground, but the 5 species of tragopan, which live in tropical forests in Asia, nest in trees, often taking over the old nests of other birds.

- **The common pheasant** comes from Asia, but is now common in Australia, North America and Europe, where it is shot for sport.

- **In ancient Rome**, peacocks were roasted and served in their feathers as a great delicacy.

▲ *The male pheasant is a beautiful bird with iridescent plumage on his head and bright red wattles. Originally from Asia, this pheasant has been successfully introduced in Europe and North America, where it is very common.*

Manakins and cotingas

- **Manakins** are small birds that live in Central and South America. There are about 57 species.

- **Female manakins** do all the nesting work alone – they build the nest, incubate the eggs and care for the young.

- **The largest of the cotingas** is the Amazonian umbrellabird, which gets its name from the crest of feathers that hangs over its head.

- **The three-wattled bellbird** (cotinga family) is best known for its extremely loud call, which resounds through its jungle home.

- **Two of the most colourful South American birds** are the Guianan cock of the rock, which is bright orange, and the Andean cock of the rock, which is red (both cotinga family species).

- **Cocks of the rock** perform remarkable courtship displays – up to 25 male birds leap and dance together, fanning their feathers and making loud calls.

- **The 65 or so cotinga species** live in the forests of Mexico, some Caribbean islands and Central and South America.

- **Fruit and insects** are the main foods of both manakins and cotingas.

- **The female cock of the rock** makes a nest of mud and plants attached to a rock or cave wall, and incubates her eggs alone.

- **In his courtship display**, the male wire-tailed manakin brushes the female's chin with his long, wirelike tail feathers.

◀ The little wire-tailed manakin lives in the lower levels of the Amazonian rainforest.

New World vultures

- **There are 7 species of New World vultures** in North and South America. Like Old World vultures, their diet includes carrion.

- **New World vultures** lay their eggs on the ground or on a cliff ledge. The parent birds feed their young on regurgitated food.

- **Unusually colourful** for a bird of prey, the king vulture has bright red, orange and yellow bare skin and wattles on its head.

- **The king vulture** has a particularly good sense of smell, and can find carrion even in dense rainforest.

- **The turkey vulture** does not make a nest, but lays its 1–3 eggs on a cliff ledge or in a cave. Both parents help to incubate the eggs for up to 41 days.

- **Black vulture chicks** are looked after by both parents. They do not fly until they are 11 weeks old.

- **Vultures can go for weeks without food**. When they do find carrion, they eat as much as possible.

- **King vultures** have stronger beaks than other New World vultures, and are able to tear apart large animals.

- **The last wild California condors** were captured for captive breeding. By 1998 there were 170 birds, 50 of which were released into the wild.

- **The largest of all birds of prey** is the Andean condor, with a wingspan of more than 3 m.

◀ The Andean condor soars for hundreds of kilometres over the Andes mountains, searching for food such as dead deer.

Shearwaters and petrels

- **The shearwater's legs** are placed far back on its body, making it an expert swimmer, but preventing it from standing up properly. It moves awkwardly on land and has to launch itself from a tree into the air.

- **Unlike most birds**, shearwaters and petrels have a good sense of smell. They have long, tube-shaped nostrils on the tops of their beaks.

- **Shearwaters and petrels** are not tuneful birds, and at night the colonies make a very loud, harsh noise.

- **The 56 or more species** in the shearwater family include petrels, fulmars and prions. They range from the Antarctic to the Arctic.

- **Largest of the shearwater family** are the giant petrels, which at 99 cm long are almost the size of albatrosses.

▶ *Manx shearwaters nest in colonies of thousands of birds on offshore islands or isolated cliff tops.*

- **Fish and squid** are the main food of shearwaters, but giant petrels also feed on carrion, and can rip apart whales and seals with their powerful beaks.

- **The manx shearwater** lays 1 egg in a burrow. The male and female take turns at incubating it and feeding one another.

- **Young shearwaters** are fed on a rich mixture of regurgitated fish and squid, and may put on weight so quickly that they are soon heavier than their parents.

- **Prions** feed on tiny plankton, which they filter from the water through comblike structures at the sides of their beaks.

★ STAR FACT ★
To defend themselves, shearwaters can spit out food and fish oil to a distance of 1 m.

Cassowaries and kiwis

- **There are 3 species of kiwi**, found only in New Zealand. All are flightless birds that live in burrows.

- **The female dwarf cassowary**, or moruk, is an extremely dangerous bird and will attack anything that comes near its nest with its 10-cm long claws.

- **The 3 species of cassowary** live in rainforests in New Zealand and northeastern Australia.

★ STAR FACT ★
A kiwi lays the largest eggs for its size of any bird – each egg weighs 25% of its body weight. Females lay up to 100 in a lifetime.

- **Largest of its family is the brown kiwi**, which is about 55 cm long and weighs up to 3.5 kg.

- **Only the kiwi has nostrils** at the end of its beak.

- **The kiwi** is the national symbol of New Zealand, appearing on stamps, coins and banknotes.

- **Cassowaries in Australia** are known to eat the fruits of 75 different types of tree.

- **The female cassowary** mates with several males, laying 6–8 eggs each time. The males care for the young.

- **About 1200 years ago** there were probably 12 million kiwis in New Zealand. Today there are only 70,000.

◀ *The kiwi detects worms, insects and spiders using its sense of smell.*

Storks

- **In tropical areas**, storks' nests perched high on buildings can get very warm, so parents cool their young by regurgitating a shower of water over them.

- **The huge beak** of the whale-billed stork, or shoebill, is 23 cm long and 10 cm wide. It uses it to catch lungfish, young crocodiles and turtles.

- **The white stork** has long been a symbol of fertility in Europe. Parents used to tell their children that new babies were brought by a stork.

- **The 17 species of stork** live in North and South America, Europe, Africa, Asia and Australia.

- **Marabou storks** often scavenge on rubbish tips.

- **The openbill stork's beak** meets only at the tip. This helps it to hold its favourite food – large snails.

- **The tail feathers** of marabou storks were once used to trim hats and dresses.

- **When the wood stork's partly open beak** touches a fish under water, it snaps shut in 25 milliseconds – one of the fastest reactions of any animal.

- **Male and female white storks** take turns to incubate their clutch of 3–5 eggs. When the partners change shifts, they perform a special bill-clattering display.

- **The adjutant stork** is named after the adjutant army officer, because of its stiff, military-style walk.

▼ The saddlebill stork of southern Africa is easily recognized by its large red, yellow and black bill.

Gulls and relatives

- **The great skua** is a pirate – it chases other birds and forces them to give up their prey in mid air.

- **The snowy sheathbill** scavenges for food on Antarctic research bases, and also steals eggs and chicks from penguin colonies.

- **There are about 48 species of gull** found on shores and islands all over the world.

- **Arctic glaucous and ivory gulls** sometimes feed on the faeces of marine mammals.

- **At up to 79 cm long**, the great black-backed gull is the giant of the group. The little gull is one of the smallest, at 28 cm long.

- **The Arctic explorer** James Clark Ross discovered Ross's gull in the 19th-century.

- **Skuas**, also called jaegers usually lay 2 eggs in a shallow, moss-lined nest on the ground. Both parents incubate the eggs and feed the young, which can fend for themselves by about 7 weeks old.

- **The kittiwake** spends much more time at sea than other gulls, and usually only comes to land in the breeding season. It has very short legs and rarely walks.

- **Herring gulls** have learned that they can find food in seaside towns, and many now nest on roofs instead of cliff ledges.

- **The south polar skua** lays 2 eggs, but the first chick to hatch usually kills the second.

▲ Gulls eat a wide range of food, including fish, shellfish, the young of other seabirds and waste from fishing boats.

Jacamars and relatives

- **Jacamars nest in tunnels** made in the ground or in termite mounds. They lay 2–4 eggs, which they incubate for 20–23 days.

- **Brightly coloured barbets** live in tropical forests and woodlands in Africa, Asia and South America.

- **At 30 cm long**, the great jacamar is the largest of the 17 species of jacamar. Its beak alone is almost 5 cm long.

- **The white-fronted nunbird** (puffbird family) digs a nesting burrow about 1 m long. The bird lays its eggs in a chamber at the end of the burrow.

- **Biggest of the 75 species of barbet** is the

▶ *The crested barbet of southern Africa usually searches for food on the ground.*

toucan barbet, at 20 cm long. It lives in mountain forests in the northern part of South America.

- **The double-toothed barbet** lays 3–4 eggs, usually in a tree hole. Both parents incubate the eggs and care for the young.

- **A jacamar** snaps up an insect in the air, then returns to its perch and bangs the insect against a branch to kill it before eating it.

- **There are about 33 species of puffbird** living in Mexico and Central and South America.

- **Barbet pairs** sing together to keep their relationship close. One bird starts to sing, then stops, and the other bird continues the song within a fraction of a second.

Drongos and relatives

- **The huia**, a species of wattlebird, has not been seen since 1907 and is probably extinct. It was noted for having a different shaped beak in males and females – the male's was straight and strong, the female's slender and curved.

- **The greater racquet-tailed drongo** has two long, wirelike tail feathers with twisted tips that make a humming noise as the bird flies.

- **The pied currawong** (Australian butcherbird family) attacks other birds and takes their young from their nests.

- **The 25 species of Old World oriole** live in Europe and parts of Asia, Africa and Australia. They are mainly tree-dwellers, feeding on insects and fruit.

- **There are 2 surviving species** of the wattlebird family – the kokako and the wattlebird, both of which live in New Zealand and rarely fly.

- **The golden oriole** makes a neat, cup-shaped nest that it binds to two supporting twigs. It lays 3–4 eggs.

- **Australia and New Guinea** are home to the 10 species of insect-eating bell-magpies.

- **Australian mud-nesters** work together to build nests of mud on the branches of trees.

- **The figbird** (oriole family) is a forest fruit-eater, but is now also common in towns.

- **Wood swallows**, found in Australasia and Southeast Asia, feed mostly on insects, but also drink nectar.

◀ *A common bird in southern Africa, the fork-tailed drongo has distinctive bright red eyes.*

Ibises and relatives

- **The ibis** was a symbol of the god Thoth in ancient Egypt, and appears in many paintings and carvings. Mummified ibises have also been discovered – as many as 500,000 in one tomb.

- **The spoonbill's beak** has a spoon-shaped tip that it uses to search shallow water for fish and small creatures.

- **At 1.4 m long** and weighing about 4 kg, the greater flamingo is the largest of the 5 species of flamingo.

- **The flamingo feeds** by forcing mud and water through bristly plates at each side of its beak with its tongue. Tiny creatures, algae and other food particles are trapped and swallowed.

- **Until their beaks have developed fully**, young flamingos feed on a 'milky' substance from their parents' throats.

- **The 31 species of ibis and spoonbill** live in North and South America, southern Europe, Asia, Africa and Australia, often in wetlands.

- **The glossy ibis** makes its nest in a reedbed or tree, and lays 3–4 eggs. The female does most of the incubation, but the male helps to rear the young.

- **Young flamingos** have grey feathers at first. Adult birds get their pink colour from pigments in the algae that they eat.

- **The greater flamingo** has a wingspan of 140–165 cm.

▲ The ancient Egyptian moon god Thoth was sometimes shown in paintings as an ibis, or as a human figure with the head of an ibis.

Beak for filtering food from water

Long neck allows the bird to feed in deep water

▶ The greater flamingo lives in huge flocks around lakes and deltas in Europe, Asia, parts of Africa, the Caribbean and Central America. It can live to be at least 50 years old.

Rheas and tinamous

- **The largest bird in South America** is the greater rhea, which stands 1.5 m tall and weighs up to 25 kg.

- **The 45 or so species of tinamou** all live in South America.

- **Most tinamous can fly**, if only for short distances, but they tend to run or hide rather than take to the air.

- **Female tinamous** lay eggs in the nests of more than one male. Males incubate the eggs and feed the chicks.

- **Rheas** feed mostly on plants, but will also eat insects and even lizards when they can.

- **Tinamous generally eat fruit**, seeds and other plant matter, but some species also gobble up insects.

- **Rheas live in flocks** of between 5–50 birds.

- **Rhea feathers** are used to make feather dusters, for sale mainly in the USA and Japan.

- **If threatened**, a rhea lies flat on the ground with its head stretched out in an attempt to hide.

◀ Flocks of rheas live on the pampas grasslands and in open woodland in southeastern South America.

Gannets and boobies

- **The gannet plunges 30 m or so** through the air and dives into the water to catch prey such as herring and mackerel.

- **A specially strengthened skull** helps cushion the impact of the gannet's high-speed dive into water.

- **Boobies** were given their common name because they were so easy for sailors to catch and kill.

- **The male blue-footed booby** attracts a mate by dancing and holding up his brightly coloured feet as it struts about.

- **When a gannet** comes to take its turn incubating the egg, it presents its mate with a piece of seaweed, which is added to the nest.

- **There are 3 species of gannet and 6 species of booby**. Boobies generally live in tropical and subtropical areas, while gannets live in cooler, temperate parts of the world.

- **The gannet** usually lays just 1 egg, which both partners help to incubate for 43–45 days. They feed their chick with regurgitated food for up to 13 weeks.

- **Young gannets and boobies** are kept warm on their mother's feet for their first few weeks.

- **Boobies** spend most of their time at sea, only landing to breed and rear their young.

- **At up to 86 cm long** and with a wingspan of 152 cm, the masked booby is the largest of the boobies.

◀ Blue-footed boobies usually feed close to the seashore, while red-footed boobies venture further out to sea.

Pelicans

- **The great white pelican** catches about 1.2 kg of fish a day in its large throat pouch.

- **The brown pelican** dives from a height of 15 m above the water to catch fish below the surface.

- **Great white pelican breeding colonies** may number as many as 30,000 pairs of birds.

◀ A great white pelican comes in to land on the water.

- **There are 7 species of pelican**. Most live and feed around fresh water, but the brown pelican is a seabird.

- **One of the largest pelicans** is the Australian pelican, which is up to 180 cm long and weighs about 15 kg.

- **The white pelican** lays 1–2 eggs in a nest mound on the ground. Both parents help to incubate the eggs and care for the young.

- **Pelican chicks** are able to stand at 3 weeks old and can fly at 7–10 weeks old.

- **In heraldry**, a pelican is often shown pecking its breast to feed its young on its blood. This myth may come from the bird's habit of resting its beak on its breast.

- **White pelicans work as a group** to herd fish into a shoal by swimming in a horseshoe formation. Then they scoop up pouchfuls of fish with their large beaks.

- **When flying**, a pelican flaps its wings 1.3 times a second.

Buzzards, kites and osprey

- **Bees and wasps**, their larvae and even their nests are the main food of honey buzzards, which remove the stings from adult insects before eating them.

- **The snail kite's hook-tipped beak** is perfectly shaped for extracting the soft flesh of snails from their shells.

- **One of the most common of all birds of prey** is the black kite, which lives throughout most of Europe, Africa, Asia and Australia.

- **Osprey parents** stop feeding their young when it is time for them to leave the nest.

- **When fishing**, the osprey plunges into water feet first and grasps its slithery prey with its spine-covered feet.

- **The red kite** often takes over the old nest of a raven.

- **The rough-legged buzzard** is common over open tundra in the far north. It preys on rodents and rabbits.

- **A buzzard can spot a rabbit** popping up out of its burrow from more than 3 km away.

- **Male ospreys** feed the whole family once the chicks have hatched.

◀ The osprey's body measures 55–58 cm long, and it has an impressive 1.6-m wingspan. The females are slightly larger than the males.

> ★ **STAR FACT** ★
> The osprey was described by Aristotle as early as 350 BC in his Natural History.

Toucans and honeyguides

- **At 61 cm long**, the toco toucan is the largest toucan. Its colourful beak alone is up to 20 cm long.

- **Although a toucan's beak is large**, it is not heavy. The beak is made of a lightweight material with a honeycomb structure.

- **The black-throated honeyguide** likes to feed on bees and their larvae. When it finds a bees' nest, it leads another creature, such as a honey badger, to the nest and waits while the animal breaks into the nest to feed on the honey. The honeyguide then has its share.

- **There are about 40 species of toucan**. They live in Mexico, Central and South America.

- **Toucans feed mostly on fruit,** which they pluck from

Beak is about 20 cm long and 7.5 cm deep at the base.

Strong claws for perching

▶ The black-throated honeyguide is usually a quiet little bird, but it chatters noisily when it wants to attract a helper, such as a honey badger, to a bees' nest, so it can have a share of the honey.

★ **STAR FACT** ★
Honeyguides are the only birds that are able to feed on the wax from bees' nests, as well as on the insects themselves.

branches with their long beaks. They also eat some insects and small animals such as lizards.

- **Toucans** usually nest in tree holes. The female lays 2–4 eggs, and the male helps with the incubation, which takes about 15 days.

- **There are about 15 species of honeyguide**. Most live in forests and woodlands in Africa, but there are a few species resident in Asia.

- **Many honeyguides** lay their eggs in the nests of other birds, such as woodpeckers. When they hatch, the young honeyguides kill the young of the host bird.

- **Toucans are noisy creatures** – their loud squawks can be heard nearly 1 km away.

◀ The toco toucan of Brazil is the largest and best-known of the toucans. It sometimes perches on a branch near another bird's nest to steal the eggs or chicks. Intimidated by the toucan's great beak, the parent bird will not generally attack. When it sleeps, the toucan turns its head to rest its long beak along its back, and folds its tail over its head.

Woodpeckers

- **The woodpecker feeds** by drilling into tree bark with its sharp beak and then inserting its long tongue into the hole to pick out insects living beneath the bark.

- **Woodpeckers drum** on tree trunks with their beaks to signal their ownership of territory or their readiness to mate. The greater spotted woodpecker has been timed making 20 strikes a second.

- **The 200 or so species of woodpecker** live all over the world, except in Antarctica and the far north.

- **The imperial woodpecker**, at 55 cm long, is the biggest of its family. The little scaled piculet, by contrast, is only 8 cm long.

- **Woodpeckers** nest in holes in trees. They may use a hole from a previous year, or dig out a new one for their 2–12 eggs.

- **The woodpecker's tongue** is well-adapted for catching insects. It is so long that the woodpecker can stick it out beyond the tip of its beak, and its sticky coating easily mops up its prey.

- **The sapsucker** (woodpecker family) feeds on sweet, sugary sap. It bores a hole in a tree and laps up the sap that oozes out.

- **As well as insects**, the great spotted woodpecker eats the eggs and young of other birds.

- **A woodpecker** may eat up as many as 1000 ants in one feeding session.

- **During autumn**, the acorn woodpecker of North America bores as many as 400 holes in tree trunks and puts an acorn in each one, to store for the winter.

◀ *This great spotted woodpecker is sharing a feeder with a siskin. It lives in Europe, parts of Asia and North Africa.*

Grassland birds

> ★ **STAR FACT** ★
> A fast walker, the long-legged secretary bird of the African grasslands may travel 30 km a day in search of snakes, insects and birds.

- **The yellow-billed oxpecker** of the African grasslands sits on buffaloes' backs, pulling ticks from their skin.

- **Flocks of 1 million or more red-billed quelea** are seen moving like vast clouds over southern Africa.

- **The grasslands of South America** are home to the red-legged seriema, a long-legged, fast-running bird that eats anything it can find, including snakes.

- **Unlike most hornbills**, the southern ground hornbill of southern Africa spends most of its time on the ground.

- **One of the biggest creatures** on the South American pampas is the rhea, which feeds mainly on grass.

- **Cattle egrets** accompany large grassland mammals, feeding on the insects that live on or around them.

- **The crested oropendola** is a grassland bird of South America. It hunts insects and other small creatures.

- **North America's largest owl**, the great horned owl, includes other grassland birds such as quail in its diet.

- **The western meadowlark** makes a ground nest of grass and pine needles in prairie grasslands.

▼ *Secretary birds are often seen perching and nesting in acacia trees.*

Monarchs and relatives

● **Monarch flycatchers** feed mainly on insects, darting out to catch them in the air and then taking them back to a perch to eat.

● **The male African paradise flycatcher's tail feathers** are up to 20 cm long – much longer than its body.

● **Only 7 Chatham Island robins** (Australasian robin family) were thought to exist in 1976, but a breeding programme using the Chatham Island tit to foster eggs has helped increase the population.

● **There are about 90 species of monarch flycatchers**. They live

▲ *The paradise flycatcher makes a neat nest of plant roots held together with spiders' webs on a slender branch or twig.*

┌─────────────────────────────────────┐
│ **★ STAR FACT ★**   │
│ Fantails are so-named because they continually │
│ fan their long tails from side to side. │
└─────────────────────────────────────┘

in wooded areas in Africa, Southeast Asia, Australia and some Pacific islands.

● **The yellow-breasted boatbill**, a monarch flycatcher, has a broad beak with a hooked tip, which it uses to pick small insects off leaves.

● **Smallest of the Australasian robin family** is the rose robin, at 10 cm long and weighing only 10 g.

● **The black-naped blue monarch** lays 3–4 eggs in a nest of grass and bark bound together with spiders' webs. The nest is usually built on a forked branch.

● **In aboriginal folklore**, the willie wagtail (a fantail), was thought to be a gossipy bird that spread secrets.

● **The pied fantail's beak** is ringed with bristles that may help the bird to trap insect prey.

Megapodes and guans

● **The 12 species of megapodes** are ground-living birds found in Australia and some Pacific islands.

● **The mallee fowl** (a megapode) lays her eggs in a huge mound of rotting leaves and sand, which acts as an incubator. The mound can be up to 11 m across and 5 m high.

● **The male mallee fowl** checks the temperature of his nest mound with its beak and keeps it a constant 33°C by adding or removing material.

● **Mallee fowl chicks** must dig their way out of their nest mound, and are able to fly a few hours later.

● **To attract females**, as it flies the male crested guan flaps his wings briefly at more than twice the normal speed, making a whirring sound.

● **One megapode in Tonga** makes a nest of hot volcanic ash, which keeps its eggs warm.

● **The 45 species of guan and curassow** live from the southern USA to northern Argentina.

● **The great curassow** is 95 cm long and weighs 4.8 kg.

● **True to its name**, the nocturnal curassow comes out at night to sing and feed on fruit.

● **The plain chachalaca** (curassow family) lays 3 eggs in a nest made of sticks and lined with leaves and moss.

● **Now rare**, the white-winged guan lives in the Andean foothills, feeding on fruit, berries, leaves and insects.

▼ *The male mallee fowl keeps a constant watch on its nest.*

Owls

- **Owls** range is size from the least pygmy owl, at only 12–14 cm long, to the Eurasian eagle owl, at 71 cm.

- **The burrowing owl** nests in burrows in the ground, either digging its own with its strong claws, or taking over the burrows of animals such as prairie dogs.

- **The soft, fluffy edges of an owl's feathers** help to reduce flight noise, so it can hunt almost silently.

- **Female owls** are usually larger than males.

- **Owls swallow prey**, such as mice and insects, whole.

- **The female barn owl** lays 4–7 eggs, often in a tree hole.

- **The brown fish owl** has bare legs and feet – feathers would get clogged with fish scales.

- **The 151 or so species of owl** live in most parts of the world except the far north, New Zealand and Antarctica.

- **About 80 species of owl** hunt mostly at night.

- **Some Native Americans** believed that owls were the souls of people, and so should never be harmed.

▼ *Pel's fishing owl lives along riverbanks in parts of southern Africa.*

Buntings and tanagers

- **The little snow bunting** breeds in northern Greenland, further north than any other bird.

- **One tanager, the glossy flowerpiercer**, has a hooked, up-curved beak that it uses to pierce the bases of tubular flowers so it can feed on the nectar inside.

- **The 240 species in the tanager family** include flowerpiercers, honeycreepers and euphonias. All live in North and South America.

- **The male scarlet tanager** has bright red feathers in the breeding season, but in autumn his plumage changes to olive-green, similar to the female.

- **The western tanager** lines its nest of twigs and moss with fine roots and animal hair. The female incubates 3–5 eggs.

- **Some tanagers follow columns of army ants** in forests, and snap up the insects that flee the ants' path.

- **Seeds** are the main food of the dark-eyed junco (bunting family), although it does eat a few spiders.

- **The woodpecker finch** (a bunting) uses a fine twig or cactus spine as a tool to winkle out insects from holes.

- **The 13 species of finch** (bunting family) in the Galapagos Islands are probably all descended from the same ancestor, but have evolved different beak shapes and feeding habits depending on their environment.

- **The Galapagos finches** gave Charles Darwin important evidence for his theory of evolution.

◄ *The snow bunting spends summers in the Arctic, but flies south in winter.*

Hornbills

- **There are about 45 species of hornbill**, 25 in Africa and 20 in Southeast Asia. Most live among trees.

- **Hornbills range in size** from 38–165 cm. The largest of the family is the great Indian hornbill, and the smallest is the dwarf red-billed hornbill.

- **The eastern yellow-billed hornbill and the dwarf mongoose** have an unusual relationship – they help each other find food and watch out for predators.

- **The female great Indian hornbill** incubates her eggs in a tree hole, the entrance of which is walled up with chewed bark and mud. Through a slit-like opening in the wall, the male passes her food.

- **Hornbills keep the nest clean** by pushing any food waste and droppings out through the slit opening.

- **In parts of South Africa**, the southern ground hornbill is traditionally considered sacred, and is protected.

- **Fruit** is the main food of most hornbills, but the two ground hornbills catch and eat small animals.

- **All hornbills have large beaks**. In many species the beak is topped with a casque made of keratin and bone.

- **A male hornbill** may carry more than 60 small fruits at a time to his nest to regurgitate for its young.

- **Hornbills are the only birds** in which two neck vertebrae are fused, possibly to help support the beak's weight.

◀ *The 50-cm long yellow-billed hornbill lives in southern Africa.*

Bulbuls and relatives

- **The bearded greenbul** lives in African rainforests and has a beautiful whistling call that it uses to keep in touch with others of its species in the dense jungle.

- **Despite its small size**, the red-vented bulbul is an aggressive bird. In Asia, people sometimes bet on a male bird to win a fight against another male.

- **The yellow-vented bulbul** makes a nest of twigs, leaves and vine stems, often in a garden or on a balcony. Both parents incubate the 2–5 eggs and care for the young.

- **There are about 120 species of bulbul** found in Africa and southern Asia, usually in forests, although some bulbuls have adapted to built-up areas.

- **Bulbuls** range in

▲ *The fairy bluebird spends most of its time looking for ripe fruit, especially figs.*

size from 14–23 cm, and eat mainly insects and fruit.

- **The 2 species of fairy bluebirds** live in Asia, feeding on fruit, nectar and some insects.

- **Leafbirds** lay 2–3 eggs in a cup-shaped nest made in the trees.

- **The common iora** (a leafbird) scurries through trees searching the leaves for insects. It also sometimes eats mistletoe and other berries.

- **Male fairy bluebirds** have bright blue upperparts. Females are a dull greenish-blue with dark markings.

> ★ STAR FACT ★
> When courting, the male common iora fluffs up its feathers, leaps into the air and tumbles back to its perch again.

Old World vultures

- **There are about 15 species of Old World vultures** living in southern Europe, Africa and Asia.

- **Unlike most birds of prey**, the palm-nut vulture is mostly vegetarian. Its main food is the husk of the oil palm fruit, although it also eats fish, frogs and other small creatures.

- **The Egyptian vulture** steals birds' eggs. It cracks the eggs by dropping them on the ground or throwing stones at them.

- **Most vultures are scavengers** rather than hunters – they feed on the carcasses of dead animals.

- **The lack of feathers** on a vulture's head means that it does not have to do lots of preening after it has plunged its beak deep into a carcass to feed.

- **Different species of vulture** eat different parts of a body – bearded vultures even eat the bones.

- **In hot weather**, some vultures cool down by squirting urine onto their legs – which can't smell nice!

▶ *This Egyptian vulture is about to break open a thick-shelled ostrich egg with a stone so that it can eat the contents. The vulture also eats carrion – several birds may be seen circling above a dead or dying animal when they find one.*

★ STAR FACT ★
The bearded vulture drops bones from a great height to smash them. It then swallows the bone fragments, which are broken down by powerful acids in its stomach.

- **The female white-backed vulture** lays 1 egg in a large stick nest made high in a tree. She incubates the egg for 56 days, being fed by the male. Both parents feed and care for the chick.

- **The lappet-faced vulture** is the largest vulture in Africa – it measures about 1 m long and has a huge 2.8 m wingspan. It also has a bigger beak than any other bird of prey.

Hooked beak for pecking scraps of meat from bones

Stone raised to throw at egg to break it open

Herons and bitterns

- **There are about 60 species of heron and bittern.**

- **The largest of the heron family** is the goliath heron of Africa and southwest Asia – it measures 1.5 m long.

- **The loud booming call** made by the male bittern in the breeding season can be heard up to 5 km away.

- **The great blue heron** makes a platform nest of twigs,

▲ *The great egret catches fish and shellfish in shallow water.*

> ★ **STAR FACT** ★
> The green-backed heron of Japan tempts fish with bits of 'bait' such as bread or feathers.

often high in a tree. The 4 eggs take 25–29 days to hatch.

- **Special feathers** on the heron's breast and rump crumble into a powdery substance that the bird rubs into its plumage to help remove dirt and fish slime.

- **The white feathers of the great egret** were popular hat decorations in the late 1800s – more than 200,000 birds were killed for their feathers in a single year.

- **Like most herons,** the grey heron feeds on fish and frogs, which it catches with swift stabs of its beak.

- **Cattle egrets** nest in colonies – there may be more than 100 nests close together in one tree.

- **When hunting,** the black heron holds its wings over its head like a sunshade. This may help the bird spot fish, or the patch of shade may attract fish to the area.

Hummingbirds

- **The bee hummingbird** is not much bigger than a bumblebee and, at 6 cm long, is probably the smallest bird.

- **A hummingbird** hovers in front of flowers to collect nectar with its tongue, which has a brushlike tip.

- **When a bee hummingbird hovers,** it beats its wings 200 times a second.

- **The 320 or so species of hummingbird** live in North, Central and South America. Largest is the giant hummingbird, at about 20 cm long and weighing 20 g.

- **At 10.5 cm,** the beak of the sword-billed hummingbird is longer than the rest of its body.

- **Aztec kings** used to wear ceremonial cloaks made of hummingbird skins.

▲ *The tiny bee hummingbird lives on the island of Cuba in the Caribbean.*

- **Tiny ruby-throated hummingbirds** migrate each autumn from the USA across the Gulf of Mexico to Central America. Although only 9 cm long, the bird flies at a speed of about 44 km/h.

- **The female calliope hummingbird** lays 2 tiny eggs in a nest made of lichen, moss and spiders' webs. She incubates the eggs for 15 days, and feeds the young for about 20 days until they are able to fly and find food for themselves.

- **Hummingbirds** are the only birds able to fly backwards as well as forwards while they are hovering.

- **A hummingbird** must eat at least half its weight in food each day to fuel its energy needs.

Nuthatches and relatives

- **The red-breasted nuthatch** paints the entrance of its tree hole nest with sticky pine resin. This may stop insects and other creatures getting into the nest, but the birds also have to take care not to get their own feathers stuck.

- **The wallcreeper** is an expert climber and can clamber up steep cliffs and walls in its search for insect prey. It lives high in mountains such as the Alps and Himalayas.

- **The treecreeper** supports itself with its stiff tail feathers as it moves up tree trunks feeding on insects and spiders.

- **The 24 or so species of nuthatch** live in North America, Europe, North Africa, Asia and Australasia.

- **The European nuthatch's 6–9 eggs** hatch after 14–18 days.

- **Insects and spiders** are the main food of nuthatches, but in autumn the birds store nuts and seeds for the winter.

- **There are 7 species** of treecreeper, 7 species of Australian creeper and 2 species of Philippine creeper.

- **The largest nuthatch** is the giant nuthatch, at up to 20 cm long.

- **The Kabylie nuthatch** was only discovered in 1975, on an Algerian mountain.

▲ The common treecreeper lives in woodland, parks and gardens in Europe and Asia.

★ **STAR FACT** ★
Nuthatches are the only birds that can climb down trees head first, as well as up.

Finfoots and relatives

- **The sunbittern** gets its name from the rich red-orange markings on its wings.

- **The sungrebe** (finfoot family) has an unusual way of caring for its young. The male bird carries his chicks in two skin pouches beneath his wings while they complete their development, even flying with them.

- **The only species in its family**, the sunbittern lives in jungles and swamps in Central and South America.

- **The kagu** is a flightless bird that lives only on the Pacific island of New Caledonia.

- **Finfoots are aquatic birds** that feed in the water on fish, frogs and shellfish. There is one species each in Africa, Southeast Asia and Central and South America.

- **The 2 species of seriema** live in South America. They eat snakes, banging their heads on the ground to kill them.

- **Seriemas can fly**, but prefer to escape danger by running fast over the grassy plains where they live.

- **Much of the kagu's habitat** on the island of New Caledonia has been destroyed by nickel mining, and the bird is now very rare.

- **The sunbittern lays 2 eggs** in a tree nest made of leaves and plant stems. Both parents take turns to incubate the eggs and care for the chicks.

- **The sungrebe and finfoots** have lobed feet, which help them swim.

▶ A sunbittern shows off its beautiful plumage with its wings spread.

Desert birds

- **The little cinnamon quail-thrush** of Australia hides in a burrow during the day to escape the hot sun.

- **The verdin** lives in the deserts of Mexico and the southwest of the USA, where it makes its nest on a cactus plant.

- **With few trees and bushes to sit in**, desert birds spend most of their lives on the ground.

- **The mourning dove** is a desert bird of the southwestern USA. A fast flier, it often travels great distances to find food and water.

- **Turkey vultures** soar over the American desert searching for carrion to eat.

- **Insects** are a favourite food of many desert birds, but some catch small mammals and others eat seeds.

★ STAR FACT ★
Desert-living bird species are usually smaller than those found elsewhere in the world.

- **Most desert birds** are active at dawn and towards sunset, resting in shade for much of the day.

- **Owls, poorwills and nightjars** cool down in the desert heat by opening their mouths wide and fluttering their throats.

- **The roadrunner** reabsorbs water from its faeces before it excretes them.

◀ *The greater roadrunner lives in the western USA, where it preys on snakes as well as insects and mice.*

Mesites and relatives

- **Mesites** are thrushlike birds that search for insects on the forest floor. They do have wings, but rarely fly.

- **There were 3 species of mesite in Madagascar**, but two have not been seen for years and may be extinct.

- **The 15 species of buttonquail** live in parts of Europe, Africa, Asia, Australia and some Pacific islands, usually on grassland. Although they look like quails, they are not related.

◀ *The little buttonquail lives in southern Europe, Africa and parts of Asia. It is 13–15 cm long.*

- **Shy little birds**, buttonquails lurk among low-growing plants feeding on seeds and insects.

- **The female buttonquail** is larger than the male. She mates with several males and leaves each to incubate the clutch of eggs and rear the young.

- **Buttonquails** are sometimes known as hemipode, or half-footed, quails, because they lack rear toes.

- **The plains-wanderer** lives on the dry plains of central Australia. If in danger, it stays very still.

- **Plains-wanderers** are now rare because so much of the grassland where they live and feed has been cleared for agriculture. There may be fewer than 8000 left in the wild.

- **The female plains-wanderer** lays 4 eggs, usually in a nest made in a hollow in the ground, but it is the male that incubates the eggs and rears the young.

- **Buttonquail young** can fly 2 weeks after hatching, and start to breed when only 4–5 months old.

Cuckoos and hoatzin

- **The greater roadrunner**, a type of cuckoo, can move at a speed of 20 km/h or more on land.

- **The Eurasian cuckoo** is a 'brood parasite' – it lays its eggs in the nests of other birds.

- **Most birds take several minutes to lay an egg**, but the cuckoo lays one in just 9 seconds, so it can quickly take advantage of any brief absence of the host bird.

- **Of the 129 or so species of cuckoo**, only about 50 lay their eggs in other birds' nests.

- **The 60-cm long hoatzin** (there is only one species) lives in South America's rainforest.

- **Hoatzin chicks** leave the nest soon after hatching. Two little claws on each wing help them clamber about.

- **The 22 species of turaco** live only in Africa. Largest is the 90-cm long great blue turaco, weighing 1 kg.

- **Turacos** feed mostly on fruit, leaves and flowers, but also catch some insects in the breeding season.

- **Amazingly, the eggs of brood parasite cuckoos** vary in colour and markings according to the host they use. A Eurasian cuckoo's eggs may resemble those of reed warblers, garden warblers or redstarts.

- **The Australian koel** prefers fruit to the caterpillars and other creatures eaten by other cuckoos.

▲ *These flycatchers are busy feeding a cuckoo chick in their nest.*

Pittas and relatives

- **Bright red, green or yellow eyes** characterize the 15 colourful species of broadbill, which live in parts of tropical Africa and Southeast Asia.

- **The brightly coloured pittas** live in Africa, Southeast Asia and Australia. 'Pitta' is an Indian word meaning 'bird' – it was first used in the 1700s.

- **The 4 species of asity** are found only in Madagascar.

- **Most broadbills** feed on insects, which they catch in the air. Some also eat lizards and frogs.

- **The 24 or so species of pitta** range in size from 15–25 cm.

★ **STAR FACT** ★

Rainbow pittas put wallaby droppings in and around their nests to disguise their own smell and keep tree snakes away from their eggs.

- **The Indian pitta** makes a nest of moss and twigs. Both parents incubate the 4–6 eggs.

- **The wattled false sunbird** (asity family) gets its name from its long, sunbird-like beak. Like the sunbirds, it takes nectar from flowers.

- **The green broadbill** hangs its nest from a vine and covers it with lichen and spiders' webs.

- **Pittas are said to have the best sense of smell** of any songbird. This may help them find worms and snails in the dim light of the forest floor.

◀ *The hooded pitta (front) and red-bellied pitta live in tropical rainforests.*

Mousebirds and trogons

▶ The beautiful quetzal is becoming rare because much of its forest habitat in Central America has been destroyed.

- **The quetzal** is a species of trogon that lives in Central America. It was sacred to the ancient Maya and Aztec civilizations.

- **The male quetzal's beautiful tail feathers** are up to 1 m long.

- **Mousebirds** get their name from their habit of scurrying around on the ground like mice as they search for seeds and leaves to eat.

- **There are about 37 species of trogon** living in the forests and woodlands of Central America, the Caribbean islands and parts of Africa and Asia.

- **Trogons range in size** from the black-throated trogon, at 23 cm long, to the slightly larger resplendent quetzal, at 33 cm long not including the tail feathers.

- **The 6 species of mousebird** are all small, dull-coloured birds of about 10 cm in length. They live in Africa south of the Sahara.

- **Mousebirds are plant eaters**, feeding on a variety of leaves, buds, flowers and fruits.

- **Trogons nest in tree holes** or in old termite mounds or wasps' nests. Both parents incubate the 2 –4 eggs for 17–19 days, and both care for the young.

- **Insects** are the main food of the trogons, but some also eat fruit and catch creatures such as lizards.

> ★ **STAR FACT** ★
> The monetary unit of Guatemala is known as the quetzal, after the resplendent quetzal – the country's national bird.

Wood warblers and icterids

- **The crested oropendola**, an icterid, weaves a hanging nest that may be up to 1 m long. The birds nest in colonies, and there may be as many as 100 large hanging nests in one tree.

- **Like the cuckoo**, the female brown-headed cowbird lays her eggs in the nests of other birds. She may lay as many as 40 eggs a year.

- **Kirtland's warbler** has very specialized breeding needs – it nests only around jack pine trees that are up to about 6 m tall.

- **The 114 species of wood warbler** live in North, Central and South America.

▶ The yellow warbler can be found from chilly Alaska to tropical South America.

- **The bobolink** breeds in southern Canada and the USA and migrates to South America for the winter – the longest migration journey of any icterid.

- **Great-tailed grackles** (icterid family) are big, noisy birds that scavenge on rubbish as well as feeding on insects, grain and fruit. They are common in towns and villages.

- **The Baltimore oriole** is the state bird of Baltimore, USA. A song named after the bird was written by Hoagy Carmichael in the 1930s.

- **Male icterids** are generally much larger than females. The male great-tailed grackle is as much as 60% heavier than the female.

- **The yellow warbler** lays 4–5 eggs in a nest of bark and plant fibres made in a tree.

- **Largest of the 92 species of icterid** is the olive oropendola, at 52 cm long.

Vireos and relatives

- **Plantcutters** get their name from their large, serrated beaks, used to chop leaves from plants.

- **The 3 species of plantcutter** live in southern South America. The birds are 17–20 cm long.

- **The sharpbill** of Central and South America picks tiny insects and spiders from leaves.

- **The 43 species of vireo** live in North, Central and South America, and range in size from 10–16 cm.

- **The black-capped vireo** usually attaches its nest to a forked twig. Both parents incubate the 3–5 eggs and feed the young.

- **Red-eyed vireo chicks** are naked and helpless when they hatch, but open their eyes after 4–5 days, and leave the nest after 12 days.

- **Insects** such as caterpillars and aphids are the main foods of vireos, but some species also eat fruit.

- **Vireos** take about a week to make their nest. The female makes a cup-shape of spiders' webs and silkworm threads around her body, and then adds plant material such as grass and moss to the nest.

- **When vireos were first named** in the 1800s, people thought they heard the word 'vireo', meaning 'I am green', in the birds' song. In fact most virous are green.

- **The brown-headed cowbird** often lays its eggs in the nests of vireos, which sometimes throw out the cowbird's eggs.

◀ The red-eyed vireo breeds in North America in the summer.

Endangered birds

- **More than 80 species of parrot**, such as the hyacinth macaw, are in danger of extinction or are very rare.

- **At least 1000 bird species** now face extinction – 30 or so became extinct in the 1900s.

- **The Hawaiian mamo** (Hawaiian honeycreeper family) became extinct in 1899, partly because more than 80,000 birds were killed to make a cloak for King Kamehameha I.

- **There are only about 600** black-faced spoonbills left.

★ **STAR FACT** ★
The bald eagle was threatened by the harmful effects of DDT on its eggs, but has recovered since the pesticide was banned in 1972.

- **The Fiji petrel** was first discovered on the island of Gau Fiji in 1855, and was not seen again until 1984. Numbers are thought to be low.

- **Possibly less than 1000** red siskins remain in the wild – it has been a popular cage-bird since the mid 1800s.

- **The Floreana mockingbird** disappeared from one of the Galapagos Islands because rats were introduced.

- **The short-tailed albatross** has long been exploited for its feathers, and has been extremely rare since 1930.

- **In New Zealand**, Hutton's shearwater is preyed on by introduced stoats, while deer trample its burrows.

◀ The hyacinth macaw has suffered from illegal hunting for the pet trade and from habitat destruction. It is now bred in captivity.

1000 THINGS YOU SHOULD KNOW ABOUT

WILD ANIMALS

KEY

- Mammals
- Birds
- Reptiles and amphibians
- Sea creatures
- Insects, spiders and creepy crawlies
- How animals live

The monkey group

- **Monkeys** belong to a group of mammals called primates, along with apes, humans, lemurs and lorises.

- **Monkeys** live mostly in trees, and their hands have fingers and their feet have toes for gripping branches. Most monkeys also have tails.

- **There are 150 species** of monkey, and they live in tropical forests in Asia, Africa and the Americas.

- **The biggest Old World monkeys** are the mandrills from West Africa. A large male weighs up to 40 kg. The female is barely half this size.

◄ *Baboons such as the Hamadryas (sacred) baboon are large, doglike monkeys which are well adapted to living on the ground in African bush country.*

- **The largest New World monkeys** (from the Americas) are woolly spider monkeys, also called muriquis. A full-grown male can weigh up to 12 kg.

- **One of the fastest** members of the monkey group is the patas monkey of West Africa. It can gallop on its four long legs, faster than most people can run.

- **The proboscis** monkey gets its name from its huge nose (proboscis is another word for nose).

- **Bald uakaris** of the Amazon really are bald, with almost no hair on the face. The fur on the rest of the body varies according to where they live, giving local names such as white, red and golden uakari.

- **A female** and male titi monkey are rarely apart. They even sing together with tails intertwined.

> ★ **STAR FACT** ★
> One of the rarest monkeys is the golden lion tamarin, with just 1000 left.

Rays

- **Rays** are a huge group of over 300 species of fish, which includes skates, stingrays, electric rays, manta rays, eagle rays and guitar fish.

- **Many rays** have flat, almost diamond-shaped bodies, with pectoral fins elongated into broad wings. Guitar fish have longer, more shark-like bodies.

- **A ray's gills** are slot-like openings beneath its fins.

- **Rays have no bones.** Instead, like sharks, they are cartilaginous fish – their body framework is made of rubbery cartilage (you have this in your nose and ears).

- **Rays live mostly** on the ocean floor, feeding on seabed creatures such as oysters, clams and other shellfish.

- **Manta rays** live near the surface and feed on plankton.

- **The Atlantic manta ray** is the biggest ray, often over 7 m wide and 6 m long.

- **Stingrays** get their name from their whiplike tail with its poisonous barbs. A sting from a stingray can make humans very ill.

▲ *Manta rays often bask near the surface of the oceans, with the tips of their pectoral fins poking out of the water.*

- **Electric rays** are tropical rays able to give off a powerful electric charge to defend themselves against attackers.

- **The black torpedo ray** can put out a 220 volt shock – as much as a household electric socket.

Lizards

- **Lizards** are a group of 3800 scaly-skinned reptiles, varying from a few centimetres long to the 3 m-long Komodo dragon.

- **Lizards cannot** control their own body heat, and so rely on sunshine for warmth. This is why they live in warm climates and bask in the sun for hours each day.

- **Lizards move** in many ways – running, scampering and slithering. Some can glide. Unlike mammals, their limbs stick out sideways rather than downwards.

- **Most lizards** lay eggs, although a few give birth to live young. But unlike birds or mammals, a mother lizard does not nurture (look after) her young.

- **Most lizards** are meat-eaters, feeding on insects and other small creatures.

> **★ STAR FACT ★**
> The Basilisk lizard is also known as the Jesus Christ lizard because it can walk on water.

- **The glass lizard** has no legs. Its tail may break off and lie wriggling as a decoy if it is attacked. It later grows another one.

- **The Australian frilled lizard** has a ruff around its neck. To put off attackers, it can puff out its ruff to make itself look bigger.

- **Horned lizards** can squirt a jet of blood from their eyes almost as far as 1 m to put off attackers.

- **The Komodo dragon** of Sumatra is the biggest lizard, weighing up to 150 kg or more. It can catch deer and pigs and swallow them whole.

▶ Lizards have four legs and a long tail. In most lizards, the back legs are much stronger than the front, and are used to drive the animal forwards in a kind of writhing motion.

Life on the seashore

- **Seashores** contain a huge variety of creatures which can adapt to the constant change from wet to dry as the tide rolls in and out.

- **Crabs, shellfish** and other creatures of rocky shores have tough shells to protect them from pounding waves and the sun's drying heat.

- **Anemones, starfish** and shellfish such as barnacles have powerful suckers for holding on to rocks.

- **Limpets** are the best rock clingers and can only be prised away if caught by surprise.

- **Anemones** may live on a hermit crab's shell, feeding on its leftovers but protecting it with their stinging tentacles.

▲ Crabs, lugworms, sandhoppers, shellfish and many other creatures live on seashores. Many birds come to feed on them.

- **Rock pools** are water left behind among the rocks as the tide goes out. They get very warm and salty.

- **Rock pool creatures** include shrimps, hermit crabs, anemones and fish such as blennies and gobies.

- **Sandy shores** are home to burrowing creatures such as crabs, razor clams, lugworms, sea cucumbers and burrowing anemones.

- **Sandhoppers** are tiny shelled creatures that live along the tide line, feeding on seaweed.

- **Beadlet anemones** look like blobs of jelly on rocks when the tide is out. But when the water returns, they open a ring of flower-like tentacles to feed.

Raptors – birds of prey

▲ *The bald eagle eats fish, snatching them from rivers.*

- **There are** about 300 species of raptors (birds of prey). The group includes eagles, hawks, harriers, kestrels, falcons, goshawks, buzzards and vultures.

- **Most birds of prey** are hunters that feed on other birds, fish and small mammals.

- **Most birds of prey** are strong fliers, with sharp eyes, powerful talons (claws) and a hooked beak.

- **Birds of prey lay** only one or two eggs at a time. This makes them vulnerable to human egg collectors .

- **Eagles and vultures (including condors)** are the biggest members of the raptor group, with wing spans of 2.5 m or more.

- **The Everglades or snail kite** has a diet of water snails, hooking them out of the shell with its extra-curved beak.

- **There are two kinds of hawks.** Accipiters, like the goshawk, catch their prey by lying in wait on perches. Buteos, like the kestrel and buzzards, hover in the air.

- **The wedge-tailed eagle** is Australia's largest raptor.

- **In the Middle Ages**, merlins and falcons were trained to fly from a falconer's wrist to catch birds and animals.

> ★ **STAR FACT** ★
> The peregrine falcon can reach speeds of
> 350 km/h when stooping (diving) on prey.

Frogs and toads

- **Frogs and toads** are amphibians – creatures that live both on land and in the water.

- **There are about 3500 species** of frog and toad. Most live near water, but some live in trees and others live underground.

- **Frogs** are mostly smaller and better jumpers. Toads are bigger, with thicker, wartier skin which holds on to moisture and allows them to live on land longer.

- **Frogs and toads** are meat-eaters. They catch fast-moving insects by darting out their long, sticky tongues.

- **Frogs and toads begin life** as fish-like tadpoles, hatching in the water from huge clutches of eggs called spawn.

- **After 7 to 10 weeks**, tadpoles grow legs and lungs and develop into frogs ready to leave the water.

- **In midwife toads**, the male looks after the eggs, not

◄ *Frogs are superb jumpers, with long back legs to propel them into the air. Most also have suckers on their fingers to help them land securely on slippery surfaces.*

the female – winding strings of eggs around his back legs and carrying them about until they hatch.

- **The male Darwin's frog** swallows the eggs and keeps them in his throat until they hatch – and pop out of his mouth.

- **The goliath frog** of West Africa is the largest frog – at over 25 cm long. The biggest toad is the cane toad of Queensland, Australia – one weighed 2.6 kg and measured 50 cm in length with its legs outstretched.

- **The arrow-poison frogs** that live in the tropical rainforests of Central America get their name because natives tip their arrows with deadly poison from glands in the frogs' skin. Many arrow-poison frogs are very colourful.

Bat wings and flight

- **Bats** are the only true flying mammals. Their wings are made of leathery skin.

- **The inner part** of a bat's wing, nearest the body, is held out by the long, slim arm and hand bones.

- **The outer part** of a bat's wing, nearest the wing tip, is held out by the even longer, slimmer bones of the second to fifth fingers.

- **The bat's thumb** (first finger) has a claw that the bat uses to hang from trees and rocks, clamber and climb, and comb or groom its fur.

- **The bat's main power for flight** comes from the pectoral muscles in its chest, which pull the wing powerfully on the down-stroke, to keep the bat up in the air and moving forwards.

- **Bats are not blind** – their eyesight is as good as that of most humans.

- **Frog-eating bats** can tell edible frogs from poisonous ones by the frogs' mating calls.

▶ A bat's wing membrane is called the patagium. It is made of stretchy fibres sandwiched between two layers of skin.

- **A colony** of 100 vampire bats can drink blood from 25 cows or 14,000 chickens in just one night.

- **False vampire bats** are bats that do not suck blood, but feed on small creatures such as other bats and rats. The greater false vampire bat of Southeast Asia is one of the biggest bats.

- **Most bats sleep** or roost during the day, hanging upside down in caves, attics and other dark places.

Animal senses

- **Animals** sense the world in a variety of ways, including by sight, hearing, touch, smell and taste. Many animals have senses that humans do not have.

- **Sea creatures** rely on smell and taste, detecting tiny particles drifting in the water. For balance they often rely on simple balance organs called statocysts.

- **Sharks** have a better sense of smell than any other kind of fish. They can detect one part of animal blood in 100 million parts of water.

◀ The slow loris is nocturnal, and its enormous eyes help it jump safely through forests in the darkness.

- **For land animals**, sight is usually the most important sense. Hunting animals often have very sharp eyesight. Eagles, for instance, can see a rabbit moving from as far as 5 km away.

- **Owls** can hear sounds ten times softer than any human can.

- **Male gypsy moths** can smell a mate over 11 km away.

- **Pit vipers** have special sensory pits (holes) on their heads which can pinpoint heat. This lets them track warm-blooded prey such as mice in pitch darkness.

- **The forked tongues** of snakes and lizards are used to taste the air and detect prey.

- **Cats' eyes** absorb 50% more light than human eyes, so they can see very well in the dark.

★ **STAR FACT** ★
Many butterflies can smell with special sense organs in their feet.

Lion prides

- **A group or pride of lions** is a settled unit which remains unchanged over the years.

- **There are usually** from 3 to 6 lionesses (female lions) in a pride, plus their offspring.

- **In regions** where prey is plentiful, there may be more than 10 lionesses in a pride.

- **When food** is scarce, or during times of drought, prides tend to be smaller, perhaps only 2 or 3 lionesses and young.

- **Lionesses** tend to stay in the pride where they were born. Sometimes a young female may be lured away by a young adult male, when he tries to establish a new pride.

- **Male lions** may be solitary, or band into small groups called coalitions.

★ **STAR FACT** ★
A male lion can drag along a 300 kg zebra – it would take at least six men to do this.

The mane can be blonde, but gets darker with age

▲ The male lion's mane is not present when he is young. It starts growing when he is about 2 or 3 years old, and is fully grown by the time he is 5. Its condition shows his health. The mane tends to becomes straggly and sparse in older males.

◀ Lion cubs in a pride tend to be born at the same time, so are the same age.

Cubs have very big paws for their size

▲ Lionesses (female lions) are slightly smaller than males, with an average weight of 120 kg. The lionesses in a pride are usually related – sisters, aunts, nieces and cousins. They often suckle each other's cubs.

- **Male lions** tend to hold and defend a large area called a territory. They mark the boundaries with urine spray, scent smears and scratch marks, and roar as they patrol the boundaries to make sure other males do not invade.

- **The male lions** join each pride in their territory for a time. The chief male usually mates with the females but a secondary male may do this too.

- **After staying with a pride** for a time, the male or males move on to another pride in their territory, and do the same there. So for part of the time, a pride consists of females and young only, without males.

- **A young male** must prove his strength and fitness by threatening other males, and perhaps getting into a real fight, to take over their territory. Males which cannot establish a territory cannot usually mate with females.

Wading birds

- **Herons** are large wading birds that hunt for fish in shallow lakes and rivers. There are about 60 species.

- **When hunting**, a heron stands alone in the water, often on one leg, apparently asleep. Then it makes a lightning dart with its long beak to spear a fish or frog.

- **Herons** usually nest in colonies called heronries. They build loose stick-nests in trees.

- **Storks** are very large black-and-white water birds with long necks and legs. There are 17 species of stork.

- **The white stork** lives in Eurasia in the summer, and then migrates to Africa, India and southern China in the winter.

- **White storks** build twig-nests on roofs, and some people think they bring luck to the house they nest on.

- **Flamingos** are large pink wading birds which live in huge colonies on tropical lakes.

- **Spoonbills and ibises** are wading birds whose bills are sensitive enough to let them feel their prey moving in the water.

- **There are 28 species** of spoonbill and ibis.

- **The spoonbill's name** comes from its spoon-shaped bill, which it swings through the water to scoop up fish.

◀ Egrets are large wading birds that live in marshy areas, feeding on fish and insects.

Beetles

- **At least 250,000** species of beetle have been identified. They live everywhere on Earth, apart from in the oceans.

- **Unlike other insects**, adult beetles have a pair of thick, hard, front wings called elytra. These form an armour-like casing over the beetle's body.

- **The goliath beetle** of Africa is the heaviest flying insect, weighing over 100 grams and growing to as much as 13 cm long.

- **Dung beetles** roll away the dung of grazing animals to lay their eggs on. Fresh dung from one elephant may contain 7000 beetles – they will clear the dung away in little more than a day.

- **A click beetle** can jump 30 cm into the air.

★ STAR FACT ★
The Arctic beetle can survive in temperatures below -60°C.

- **The bombardier beetle** shoots attackers with jets of burning chemicals from the tip of its abdomen.

- **The rove beetle** can zoom across water on a liquid given off by glands on its abdomen.

- **The leaf-eating beetle** can clamp on to leaves using the suction of a layer of oil.

- **Stag beetles** have huge jaws which look like a stag's antlers.

Elytra (hard front wings)

▶ The jewel beetles of tropical South America get their name from the brilliant rainbow colours of their elytra (front wings).

Surviving the winter

- **Some animals** cope with the cold and lack of food in winter by going into a kind of deep sleep called hibernation.

- **During hibernation**, an animal's body temperature drops and its heart rate and breathing slow, so it needs little energy to survive.

- **Small mammals** such as bats, squirrels, hamsters, hedgehogs and chipmunks hibernate. So do birds such as nighthawks and swifts.

- **Reptiles** such as lizards and snakes go into torpor whenever the temperature gets too low. This is a similar state to hibernation.

◀ Many mammals survive cold winters by hibernating. Some, like this Arctic fox, will sleep for a few days at a time when there is little food to be found.

- **Butterflies and other insects** go into a kind of suspended animation called diapause in winter.

- **The pika** (a small lagomorph) makes haystacks from grass in summer to provide food for the winter.

- **Beavers** collect branches in autumn and store them next to their lodges so they can feed on the bark during the winter.

- **Bears** go to sleep during winter, but not all scientists agree that they go into true hibernation.

- **Squirrels** bury stores of nuts in autumn to feed on during winter. They seem to have remarkable memories, as they can find most stores when they need them.

> ★ STAR FACT ★
> Macaque monkeys in Japan keep warm in winter by bathing in hot volcanic springs.

Beaver lodges

▶ In North America, beavers were once hunted so much that they were almost wiped out. They are protected by law in some places.

- **Beavers** are large rodents with flat, paddle-like tails, whose closest relatives are squirrels, including chipmunks. They live in northern America and northern Eurasia.

- **The beaver's home** is called a lodge. It is usually occupied by a beaver family, a female, male and their offspring of various ages.

- **Most lodges** are like mini-islands, strongly made of branches, stones and mud, in a lake.

- **A typical lodge** has only a few underwater tunnels as entrances, to keep out beaver predators such as wolves, pumas and bobcats.

- **Beaver lodges** keep a beaver family so warm that in cold weather steam can often be seen rising from the ventilation hole near the top.

- **The lodge** is maintained and repaired by all members of the family, including the offspring.

- **The chief lodge-builder** is the adult female beaver, with the adult male as the assistant.

- **In winter**, the beavers plaster the outside of their lodge with mud.

- **Some lodges** measure more than 5 metres across and 4 metres high.

- **The mountain beaver** is a different species and lives in a tunnel.

Jellyfish

- **Jellyfish** are sea creatures with bell-shaped, jelly-like bodies, and long stinging tentacles.

- **Biologists** call jellyfish medusa, after the mythical Greek goddess Medusa, who had wriggling snakes for hair.

- **Jellyfish** belong to a large group of sea creatures called cnidarians, which also includes corals and anemones.

- **Unlike anemones**, jellyfish float about freely, moving by squeezing water out from beneath their body. When a jellyfish stops squeezing, it slowly sinks.

- **A jellyfish's tentacles** are covered with stinging cells called nematocysts, which are used to catch fish and for protection. The stinging cells explode when touched, driving tiny poisonous threads into the victim.

- **Jellyfish vary in size** from a few millimetres to over 2 m.

> ★ **STAR FACT** ★
> The box jellyfish has the world's most deadly poison. It can kill a human in 30 seconds.

- **The bell of one giant jellyfish** measured 2.29 m across. Its tentacles were over 36 m long.

- **The Portuguese man-of-war** is not a true jellyfish, but a collection of hundreds of tiny animals called polyps which live together under a gas-filled float.

- **The purple jellyfish** can be red, yellow or purple.

▼ *Jellyfish are among the world's most ancient animals.*

The variety of otters

- **Otters** are small-to-medium hunting mammals in the mustelid family, related to weasels.

- **There are 12 species of otters**, which live naturally on all continents except Australia and Antarctica.

- **Otters** hunt fish, mostly at night, but they also eat crayfish and crabs, clams and frogs.

- **Nearly all otters** live close to water and are excellent swimmers and divers.

- **The smallest otter** is the Oriental short-clawed otter, which is about 70 cm in total length and weighs around 4 kg.

- **Otters hunt fish**, mostly at night, but they also eat crayfish and crabs, clams and frogs.

- **Otters** usually live in burrows called holts, in the banks of rivers or lakes.

- **Three species of otters** live in Africa – the spot-necked otter, Eurasian river otter (only in the north) and Cape clawless otter.

- **The marine otter** of western South America has the local name of the chingungo.

- **The otter** with the most restricted range is probably the Southern river otter, found only in Argentina.

◄ *Sea otters are protected by law.*

Farm animals

- **Cattle** are descended from a creature called the wild auroch, which was tamed 9000 years ago. There are now over 200 breeds of domestic cow.

- **Female cows** reared for milk, butter and cheese production are called dairy cows. They give birth to a calf each year, and after it is born they provide milk twice a day.

- **A typical dairy cow** gives 16 litres of milk a day, or almost 6000 litres a year.

- **Male cattle** are reared mainly for their meat, called beef. Beef breeds are usually heftier than dairy ones.

- **Sheep** were first domesticated over 10,000 years ago. There are now more than 700 million sheep in the world, and 800 different breeds.

◄ *Female cattle are called cows, and males are called bulls. The young are calves. Female calves are also called heifers.*

- **Hairy sheep** are kept for their milk and meat (lamb and mutton). Woolly sheep are kept for their wool.

- **Hens lay** one or two eggs a day – about 350 a year.

- **To keep hens laying**, their eggs must be taken from them every day. Otherwise the hens will try to nest so they can hatch them.

- **Turkeys** may have got their name from the mistaken idea that they came from Turkey.

> ★ **STAR FACT** ★
> When a cow chews the cud, the cud is food regurgitated from one of its four stomachs.

Colours and markings

▲ *A zebra's stripes may seem to make it easy to see, but when it is moving the stripes actually blur its outline and confuse predators.*

- **Protective colouring** helps an animal hide from its enemies or warns them away.

- **Camouflage** is when an animal is coloured to blend in with its surroundings, making it hard to see.

- **Ground-nesting birds** like the nightjar are mottled brown, making them hard to spot among fallen leaves.

- **The fur** of wild pig and tapir babies is striped and spotted to make them hard to see in dappled jungle light.

- **Squid** can change their colour to blend in with new surroundings.

- **Disruptive colouring** distorts an animal's body so that its real shape is disguised.

- **Bright colours** often warn predators that an animal is poisonous or tastes bad. For example, ladybirds are bright red and the cinnabar moth's caterpillars are black and yellow because they taste nasty.

- **Some creatures mimic** the colours of poisonous ones to warn predators off. Harmless hoverflies, for instance, look just like wasps.

- **Some animals frighten off** predators with colouring that makes them look much bigger. Peacock butterflies have big eyespots on their wings.

- **Courting animals**, especially male birds like the peacock, are often brightly coloured to attract mates.

Crocodiles and alligators

- **Crocodiles**, alligators, caimans and gharials are large reptiles that together form the group known as crocodilians. There are 14 species of crocodile, 7 alligators and caimans, and 1 gharial.

- **Crocodilian species** lived alongside the dinosaurs 200 million years ago, and they are the nearest we have to living dinosaurs today.

- **Crocodilians are hunters** that lie in wait for animals coming to drink at the water's edge. When crocodilians seize a victim they drag it into the water, stun it with a blow from their tail, then drown it.

- **Like all reptiles**, crocodilians get their energy from the sun. Typically, they bask in the sun on a sandbar or the river bank in the morning, then slip into the river at midday to cool off.

- **Crocodiles live** in tropical rivers and swamps. At over 5 m long, saltwater crocodiles are the world's largest reptiles – one grew to over 8 m long.

- **Crocodiles are often said** to cry after eating their victims. In fact only saltwater crocodiles cry, and they do it to get rid of salt, not because they are sorry.

- **Crocodiles have thinner snouts** than alligators, and a fourth tooth on the lower jaw which is visible when the crocodile's mouth is shut.

- **The female Nile crocodile** lays her eggs in nests which she digs in sandy river banks, afterwards covering the eggs in sand to keep them at a steady temperature. When the babies hatch they make loud piping calls. The mother then digs them out and carries them one by one in her mouth to the river.

- **Alligators** are found both in the Florida Everglades in the United States and in the Yangtze River in China.

▼ *Crocodiles often lurk in rivers, with just their eyes and nostrils visible above the water.*

> ★ **STAR FACT** ★
> Crocodilians often swallow stones to help them stay underwater for long periods. Without this ballast, they might tip over.

▶ *Crocodiles are huge reptiles with powerful bodies, scaly skin and great snapping jaws. When a crocodile opens its jaws, it reveals a flash of bright scarlet tongue and throat, as well as rows of very sharp teeth. The bright colour is thought to terrify potential victims.*

A crocodile will often kill its victims with a swipe from its strong tail

The skin on its back has ridges formed by dozens of tiny bones called osteoderms

The crocodile's eyes and nostrils are raised so it can see and breathe while floating under water

The skin on its belly is smooth and was once prized as a material for shoes and handbags

Webbed feet help the crocodile walk on swampy ground

Bears

- **Bears belong to the** *Carnivora* group of mammals, along with dogs, foxes, weasels, otters and cats.

- **The bear family is called** *Ursidae,* and bears are sometimes known as ursids.

- **There are eight species of bears.** Most live north of the Equator, in all kinds of environments.

- **Two species of bear** live south of the Equator – the spectacled bear in South America and the sun bear in Southeast Asia.

◀ *The polar bear has a white coat to camouflage it against the Arctic snow when it is hunting seals. Sometimes, only its black nose gives it away.*

★ STAR FACT ★
Bears and humans are the only animals to walk on the soles of their feet.

- **Although bears** are the largest meat-eating land animals, they also eat many other foods, including fruits, nuts, leaves, roots, shoots, bark and sap.

- **Polar bears** are the most carnivorous of bears, although if meat is scarce, they have been seen to eat berries, lichens and even seaweed.

- **Bears do not hug** their prey to death, as is sometimes thought. Instead, they kill their victims with a powerful cuff from their front paws, or with their teeth.

- **The grizzly bear** is actually a type of brown bear with white tips to the hairs of its fur.

- **The Asiatic black bear** spends up to half of its time in trees, and the curved yellowish-white patch on its chest gives it the local name of moon bear.

Bees and wasps

▲ *Honey bees and bumble bees feed on pollen. They make honey from flower nectar to feed their young.*

- **Bees and wasps** are narrow-waisted insects (usually with hairy bodies). Many suck nectar from flowers.

- **There are 22,000 species of bee.** Some, like leaf-cutter bees, live alone. But most, like honey bees and bumble bees, live in vast colonies.

- **Honey bees** live in hives, either in hollow trees or in man-made beehive boxes. The inside of the hive is a honeycomb made up of hundreds of six-sided cells.

- **A honey bee colony** has a queen (the female bee that lays the eggs), tens of thousands of female worker bees, and a few hundred male drones.

- **Worker bees** collect nectar and pollen from flowers.

- **Each worker bee** makes ten trips a day and visits 1000 flowers each trip. It takes 65,000 trips to 65 million flowers to make 1 kg of honey.

- **Honey bees** tell others where to find flowers rich in pollen or nectar by flying in a special dance-like pattern.

- **Wasps** do not make honey, but feed on nectar, fruit juice or tiny creatures. Many species have a nasty sting in their tail.

- **Paper wasps build** huge papier maché nests the size of footballs, containing 15,000 or more cells.

- **Paper wasps make** papier maché for their nest by chewing wood and mixing it with their spit.

Communication

- **Crows** use at least 300 different croaks to communicate with each other. But crows from one area cannot understand crows from another.

- **When two howler monkey** troops meet, the males scream at each other until one troop gives way.

- **The male orang-utan** burps to warn other males to keep away.

- **Dogs** communicate through barks, yelps, whines, growls and howls.

- **Many insects** communicate through the smell of chemicals called pheromones, which are released from special glands.

◀ Lone wolves often howl at dusk or in the night to signal their ownership of a particular territory and to warn off rival wolves.

- **Tropical tree ant** species use ten different pheromones, combining them with different movements to send 50 different kinds of message.

- **A gorilla** named Coco was trained so that she could use over 1000 different signs to communicate, each sign meaning different words. She called her pet cat 'Soft good cat cat', and herself 'Fine animal gorilla'.

- **Female glow worms** communicate with males by making a series of flashes.

- **Many birds** are mimics and can imitate a whole variety of different sounds, including the human voice and machines like telephones.

> ★ STAR FACT ★
> Using sign language, Coco the gorilla took an IQ test and got a score of 95.

Parrots and budgerigars

▲ The blue-and-yellow macaw of the Amazon rainforest has been trapped so much for the pet trade, it is now quite rare.

- **The official name** of the parrot group is the order *Psittaciformes*.

- **The parrot group** is divided into three – true parrots, cockatoos and lories.

- **Most parrots** are colourful birds with curved bills for eating fruits and seeds and for cracking nuts. They are very noisy and they live mostly in tropical rainforests.

- **Parrots have** feet with two toes pointing forwards and two facing backwards, allowing them to grip branches well and also to hold and manipulate food.

- **Half of all parrot species**, including macaws, green Amazon parrots and parakeets, live in Latin America.

- **Australia and New Guinea** are home to parrots called cockatoos (which have feathered crests on their heads), as well as to lories and lorikeets.

- **The budgerigar** is a small parakeet from central Australia which is very popular as a pet.

- **Parrots** are well known for their mimicry of human voices. Some have a repertoire of 300 words or more.

- **Many parrots** imitate the sounds of other animals, like dogs and cats, and machine noises such as telephone rings and chainsaws.

- **An African grey parrot** called Alex was trained by scientist Irene Pepperberg to identify at least 50 different objects. Alex could ask for each of these objects in English – and also refuse them.

Flightless birds

▶ Ostriches live on the grasslands of Africa and nest in holes scooped out of the ground. The male scoops out the hole and leads several females to it to lay their eggs.

★ **STAR FACT** ★
The biggest bird ever is now extinct – the flightless elephant bird of Madagascar was truly elephantine, growing up to 4.5 m tall (taller than two grown men).

Bony crest

◀ The cassowary lives in the forests of tropical Australia and New Guinea. It has a crest which it uses like a crash helmet as it charges through the undergrowth.

Two toes with very sharp toenails

◀The emu of Australia is the world's second largest bird, growing up to 1.7 m tall and weighing up to 45 kg.

- **The major group** of flightless birds is known as the ratites and contains the largest of all birds – the ostrich, emus, rheas and cassowaries.

- **Ratites** always walk or run everywhere, only using their small wings for balance, show or shade.

- **There is a single species** each of the ostrich in Africa and the emu in Australia, but 2 species of rhea in South America, and three species of cassowary in Southeast Asia and Australia.

- **Other groups of birds** which are totally flightless include the penguins of the southern oceans and the kiwis of New Zealand.

- **Some types of tinamous** in South America (which resemble partridges), and some members of the rail group (types of waterbirds), are also flightless.

- **Ostriches** have only two toes on each foot – unlike the rheas of South America, which have three.

- **The male emu** is one of the bird world's most attentive fathers, caring for his chicks for 6 months.

- **The rare kakapo parrot** of New Zealand could fly once, but it lost the power of flight because it had no natural predators – until Europeans introduced dogs and cats to New Zealand.

- **The dodo** was a flightless bird that once lived on islands such as Mauritius in the Indian Ocean. It was wiped out in the 17th century when its eggs were eaten by pigs and monkeys imported by Europeans.

- **The emu** of Australia is the best swimmer of any flightless bird. Ostriches can swim well, too.

◀ Ostriches have soft downy plumage, but their head, neck and legs are almost bare.

The dog family

- **The dog family** is a large group of four-legged, long-nosed, meat-eating animals. It includes dogs, wolves, foxes, jackals and coyotes.

- **All kinds of dog** have long canine teeth for piercing and tearing their prey (canine means 'dog').

- **When hunting**, dogs rely mainly on their good sense of smell and acute hearing.

- **There are 35 species** in the dog family, *Canidae*.

- **The canids** include nine species of wolf and wild dog, 21 species of foxes, four species of jackals and the domestic dog.

- **All breeds of domestic dog**, from huge Great Danes and wolfhounds to tiny chihuahuas, belong to one species, *Canis familiaris*.

- **Domestic dogs** probably descended from the grey wolf more than 10,000 years ago.

- **Some members of the dog family** can interbreed with each other.

- **Interbred dogs have their own names**. The cross (hybrid) between a domestic dog and a coyote is called a coydog.

- **The domestic dog** cross with a dingo is known as the dingo-dog or pariah-dog, and is common in Southeast Asia.

▶ Most wolves are grey wolves – either the timber wolf of cold forest regions, or the tundra wolf of the Arctic plains.

Poisonous insects

- **Insects** are small, but many have nasty poisons to protect themselves.

- **Most poisonous insects** are brightly coloured – including many caterpillars, wasps and cardinal beetles–to warn potential enemies off.

- **Ants, bees and wasps** have stings in their tails which they use to inject poison to defend themselves or paralyse prey.

- **Bee and wasp stings** have barbed ends to keep the sting in long enough to inject the poison. Honey bees cannot pull the barb out from human skins, and so tear themselves away and die.

- **Velvet ants** are not really ants at all, but wingless wasps with such a nasty sting that they are called 'cow killers'.

- **Ladybirds** make nasty chemicals in their knees.

- **When attacked**, swallowtail caterpillars whip out a smelly forked gland from a pocket behind their head and hit their attacker with it.

▲ Wasps poison their victims with the sharp sting in their tail.

- **The lubber grasshopper** is slow moving, but when attacked it oozes a foul-smelling froth from its mouth and thorax.

- **It is not only insects** that are poisonous, but some spiders. The black widow spider is the deadliest of all, with a bite that can kill a human. The funnel-web spider and many bird-eating spiders are also poisonous.

Swimming birds

- **The fastest** and most skilled underwater swimmers among the birds are the penguins.

- **Many other sea birds** also swim well underwater, including guillemots, razorbills, divers, cormorants and darters or anhingas.

- **Divers (also called loons)** use their powerful legs and large webbed feet to reach depths of 75 m.

- **Penguins** do not really use their wings as oars, to 'row' through the water, but as wing-flippers which they flap up and down, like a flying bird.

- **Penguins** have coats waterproofed with oil, and thick fat under the skin, so they can survive underwater in temperatures below freezing, when fresh water would have turned to ice.

> ★ **STAR FACT** ★
> The male emperor penguin keeps the female's egg warm on his feet until it hatches.

▲ *Penguins are sociable birds that live in large colonies.*

- **A penguin** uses its webbed feet to steer and to brake quickly after swimming fast.

- **The emperor penguin** is the biggest swimming bird, at up to 1.2 m tall and weighing over 40 kg.

- **The most widespread** expert bird swimmer is the great cormorant, living in almost all watery habitats.

- **When crossing the ice**, Adélie penguins steer by the sun. They lose their way when the sun goes down.

Iguanas

- **Iguanas** are large lizards that live around the Pacific and in the Americas.

- **Larger iguanas** are the only vegetarian lizards. Unlike other lizards, most eat fruit, flowers and leaves, rather than insects.

- **The common iguana** lives high up in trees, but lays its eggs in a hole in the ground.

- **Common iguanas** will jump 6 m or more out of the trees to the ground if they are disturbed.

- **The rhinoceros iguana** of the West Indies gets its name from the pointed scales on its snout.

- **The marine iguana** of the Galapagos Islands is the only lizard that spends much of its life in the sea.

- **Marine iguanas** keep their eggs warm ready for hatching in the mouth of volcanoes, risking death to put them there.

- **When in the water**, a marine iguana may dive for 15 minutes or more, pushing itself along with its tail.

- **Although marine iguanas** cannot breathe underwater, their heart rate slows so that they use less oxygen.

- **The chuckwalla** inflates its body with air to wedge itself in a rock crack if it is in danger.

◄ *Before each dive into water, marine iguanas warm themselves in the sun to gain energy.*

Crabs and lobsters

- **Crabs and lobsters** are part of an enormous group of creatures called crustaceans.

- **Most crabs and lobsters** have their own shell, but hermit crabs live inside the discarded shells of other creatures.

- **Crabs and lobsters** are decapods, which means they have ten legs – although the first pair are often strong pincers which are used to hold and tear food.

- **For spotting prey**, crabs and lobsters have two pairs of antennae on their heads and a pair of eyes on stalks.

- **One of a lobster's claws** usually has blunt knobs for crushing victims. The other has sharp teeth for cutting.

- **Male fiddler crabs** have one giant pincer which they waggle to attract a mate.

- **Robber crabs** have claws on their legs which they use to climb up trees to escape from predators.

- **The giant Japanese** spider crab can grow to measure 3 m across between the tips of its outstretched pincers.

- **When American spiny** lobsters migrate, they cling to each others' tails in a long line, marching for hundreds of kilometres along the seabed.

- **Sponge crabs** hide under sponges which they cut to fit. The sponge then grows at the same rate as the crab and keeps it covered.

▼ Lobsters are dark green or blue when alive and only turn red when cooked.

Life in the desert

▲ Deserts like this are among the world's toughest environments for animals to survive.

- **In the Sahara desert**, a large antelope called the addax survives without waterholes because it gets all its water from its food.

- **Many small animals** cope with the desert heat by resting in burrows or sheltering under stones during the day. They come out to feed only at night.

- **Desert animals** include many insects, spiders, scorpions, lizards and snakes.

- **The dwarf puff adder** hides from the sun by burying itself in the sand until only its eyes show.

- **The fennec fox** and the antelope jack rabbit both lose heat through their ears. This way they keep cool.

- **The kangaroo rats** of California's Death Valley save water by eating their own droppings.

- **The Mojave squirrel** survives through long droughts by sleeping five or six days a week.

- **Swarms of desert locusts** can cover an area as big as 5000 square kilometres.

- **Sand grouse** fly hundreds of kilometres every night to reach watering holes.

> ★ **STAR FACT** ★
> The African fringe-toed lizard dances to keep cool, lifting each foot in turn off the hot sand.

Finding a mate

- **Humans** are among the few animals that mate at any time of year. Most animals come into heat (are ready to mate) only at certain times.

- **Spring** is a common mating time. The warmer weather and longer hours of daylight may trigger the production of sperm in males and eggs in females.

- **Some mammals**, such as bats, bears and deer, have only one mating time a year. Others, such as rabbits, have many.

- **Many large mammals** pair for a short time, but a few (including beavers and wolves) pair for life. Some males (including lions and seals) have lots of mates.

- **To attract a mate**, many animals put on courtship displays such as a special colours, songs and dances.

◀ *Prairie dogs live in families called coteries, each made up of a male and several wives.*

- **The male capercaillies** (turkey-like birds) of Scotland attract a mate with a clicks and rattles then a pop and a hiss.

- **Great crested grebes** perform dramatic dances in the water and present water plants to one another.

- **Male bower birds** paint their nests blue with berry juice and line them with blue shells and flowers to attract a mate.

- **Male birds of paradise** flash their bright feathers while strutting and dancing to attract a mate.

- **The male tern** catches a fish as a gift for the female. The male dancefly brings a dead insect which the female eats while mating.

Life in tropical grasslands

- **Tropical grasslands** are home to vast herds of grazing animals such as antelope and buffalo – and to the lions, cheetahs and other big cats that prey on them.

- **There are few places** to hide on the grasslands, so most grassland animals are fast runners with long legs.

▼ *With their long necks, giraffes can feed on the high branches of the thorn trees that dot the savannah grasslands of Africa.*

★ **STAR FACT** ★
Cheetahs are the fastest runners in the world, reaching 110 km/h in short bursts.

- **Pronghorn** can manage 67 km/h for 16 km.

- **There are more** than 60 species of antelope on the grasslands of Africa and southern Asia.

- **The springbok** gets its name from its habit of springing 3 m straight up in the air.

- **Grazing animals** are divided into perrisodactyls and artiodactyls, according to how many toes they have.

- **Perrisodactyls** have an odd number of toes on each foot. They include horses, rhinos and tapirs.

- **Artiodactyls** have an even number of toes. They include camels buffaloes, deer, antelope and cattle.

- **A century ago in South Africa**, herds of small antelopes called springboks could be as large as 10 million strong and hundreds of kilometres long.

Elephant life

- **There are three kinds of elephant** – the African forest elephant (Central and West Africa), the African savanna elephant (East and South Africa) and the Asian elephant, which lives in India and Southeast Asia.

- **African elephants** are the largest land animals, growing as tall as 4 m and weighing more than 6000 kg.

- **Asian elephants** are not as large as African elephants, and have smaller ears and tusks. They also have one 'finger' on the tip of their trunk, while African elephants have two.

- **The African forest elephant** tends to have straighter tusks than its savanna relative, and these point almost stright down to the ground rather than curving upwards and outwards

- **Elephants** are very intelligent animals, with the biggest brain of all land animals. They also have very good memories.

- **Female elephants**, called cows, live with their calves and younger bulls (males) in herds of 20 to 30 animals. Older bulls usually live alone.

- **Once a year**, bull elephants go into a state called musth (said 'must'), when male hormones make them very wild and dangerous.

- **Elephants** usually live for about 70 years.

- **When an elephant dies**, its companions seem to mourn and cry.

▼ On dry areas, herds may travel vast distances to find food, with the bigger elephants protecting the little ones between their legs.

★ STAR FACT ★
Elephants use their trunks like snorkels when crossing deep rivers.

▼ When the leader of the herd senses danger, she lifts her trunk and sniffs the air – then warns the others by using her trunk to give a loud blast called a trumpet. If an intruder comes too close, she will roll down her trunk, throw back her ears, lower her head and charge at up to 50 km/h.

Camelids

- **The camelids** are a group of large, plant-eating, hoofed mammals (ungulates).

- **Camelid** body features include a long, craning neck, a compact body and very long legs.

- **There are only** six species in the camelid group, two in the Old World and four in the New World.

- **The Old World species** are the single-humped dromedary or Arabian camel of Africa and the Middle East, and the two-humped Bactrian camel of Central Asia.

- **The New World species** are the llama, vicuna, alpaca and guanaco.

▶ The Arabian camel has been the 'ship of the desert', transporting people and baggage, for thousands of years.

- **Old World camels** are the biggest desert mammals and they have adapted in many ways to help them live in extremely dry conditions.

- **An Old World camel's** hump is made of fat, but the camel's body can break the fat down into food and water when these are scarce.

- **A camelid's feet** have two joined toes to stop it sinking into soft ground.

- **Of the New World camelids**, only the guanaco and vicuna are through to be truly wild.

★ STAR FACT ★
Camels have by far the worst-smelling breath in the entire animal kingdom.

Eating food

▲ Bears are omnivores, eating fish and other meat, although they will eat berries, leaves and almost anything when hungry.

- **Herbivores** are animals that usually eat only plants.

- **Carnivores** are animals that eat animal flesh (meat).

- **Omnivores** eat plants and animals. Many primates such as monkeys, apes and humans are omnivorous.

- **Insectivores** eat insects. Some, such as bats and shrews, have teeth for breaking through insects' shells. Others, such as anteaters, have long, sticky tongues for licking up ants and termites, but few or no teeth.

- **Herbivores** such as cattle, elephants and horses either graze (eat grass) or browse (eat mainly leaves, bark and the buds of bushes and trees).

- **Herbivores** have tough, crowned teeth to cope with their plant food.

- **Carnivores** have pointed canine teeth for tearing meat.

- **Some carnivores**, such as hyenas, do not hunt and instead feed on carrion (the remains of dead animals).

- **Herbivores** eat for much of the time. However, because meat is very nourishing, carnivores eat only occasionally and tend to rest after each meal.

- **Every living thing** is part of a food chain, in which it feeds on the living thing before it in the chain and is in turn eaten by the living thing next to it in the chain.

The dolphin family

- **Dolphins** are sea creatures that belong to the same family as whales – the cetaceans.

- **Dolphins are mammals**, not fish. They are warm-blooded, and mothers feed their young on milk.

- **There are about** 32 kinds or species in the main dolphin family, called the Delphinidae.

- **Dolphins usually live** in groups of 20 to 100 animals.

- **Dolphins look after** each other. Often, they will support an injured companion on the surface.

- **Dolphins communicate** with high-pitched clicks called phonations. Some clicks are higher than any other animal noise and humans cannot hear them.

- **Dolphins use sound** to find things and can identify different objects even when blindfolded.

> ★ STAR FACT ★
> Dolphins are usually friendly, but careless humans may be injured by them.

▲ Dolphins are among the most intelligent of the animals, along with humans and chimpanzees.

- **Dolphins can be trained** to jump through hoops, toss balls, or 'walk' backwards through the water.

- **Bottle-nosed dolphins** get their name from their short beaks (which make them look like they are smiling). They are very friendly and often swim near boats.

Game birds

- **'Game birds'** were named because they were mainly birds hunted for sport – and for cooking afterwards.

- **There are more than 280 species** of game birds, including pheasants, grouse, partridges, quails, turkeys, peafowl, curassows and megapodes.

- **The official name** for the game bird group is the order Galliformes.

- **Game birds** spend most of the time strutting along the ground looking for seeds. They fly only in emergencies, and a few cannot fly at all.

- **In contrast to the showy males,** many hen (female) game birds have dull brown plumage that helps them to hide, nest and rear chicks in their woodland and moorland homes.

- **In the breeding season,** cock (male) game birds strut and puff up their plumage to attract a mate.

- **Courting male game birds** draw attention to themselves by cackles, whistles and screams.

- **Some male game birds** gather at traditional sites called leks, to compete and show off.

- **The western capercaille,** a type of grouse, eats almost nothing but pine needles during the winter.

- **Peacocks** were once used to reward treasure-seeking explorers.

◀ The peacock (the male peafowl) of India and Sri Lanka is the most spectacular of all pheasants. When courting the drab peahen, the peacock throws up his tail feathers to create a gigantic turquoise fan.

Marsupial babies

- **In most marsupials,** the babies develop inside the mother for only about one-third of the time which other mammal babies take to develop.

- **The largest kangaroo,** the red, has a pregnancy (gestation period) of 33 days. In a placental mammal of the same size, this would be 8–10 months.

- **After birth,** the baby red kangaroo remains attached to the milk teat permanently for about 3 months.

- **Three months after birth,** the young red kangaroo detaches from its mother's teat, but it still remains in the pouch for another 3 months.

- **From 6 to 8 months,** the young kangaroo begins to leave the mother's pouch.

- **From about 8 months,** the young red kangaroo rarely returns to the pouch, but it still pokes its head in to feed on mother's milk.

▲ Koalas drink very little water, and their name comes from an Aboriginal word for 'no drink'.

- **The juvenile red kangaroo** is fully weaned and independent of its mother by one year of age.

- **The female koala** is pregnant for 35 days.

- **A baby koala** eats soft droppings produced by its mother, to take in helpful microbes.

- **A young koala** spends 6-7 months in its mother's pouch and another 5–6 months riding on her back.

Inside the pouch, the baby sucks on its mother's teat

◄ When they are first born, kangaroos are naked and look like tiny jellybabies – just a few centimetres long, with two tiny arms. But straight away they have to haul themselves up through the fur on their mother's belly and into her pouch. Here the baby kangaroo (called a joey) lives and grows for 6 to 8 months, sucking on teats inside the pouch. Only when it is quite large and covered in fur will it pop out of the pouch to live by itself.

Newborn kangaroo climbing up its mother's belly

Entrance to pouch

Young kangaroo or 'joey'.

Newborn kangaroo

Mother kangaroo's birth canal

Which animals migrate?

- **Animal groups known to migrate** include numerous mammals and birds, reptiles such as sea turtles, and fish like salmon and eels.

- **Certain kinds** of insects like locusts and butterflies, crustaceans such as spiny lobsters, and even worms in the sea, are also known to migrate.

- **Some migrations** are daily, some are monthly or tidal, some are seasonal, and some are permanent.

- **Nearly all of the great whales** migrate, between the cool or polar seas where food abounds in summer, to nutrient-poor subtropical or tropical seas in winter.

- **Starlings** migrate every day from the country to their roosts in the city.

- **One knot** (a kind of small bird) took just 8 days to fly 5600 km, from Britain to West Africa.

- **Barheaded geese** migrate right over the top of the Himalayan mountains, flying as high as 8000 m.

- **Monarch butterflies** migrate 4000 km every year.

▶ In summer, moose spend most of the time alone. But in winter they gather and trample areas of snow (called yards) to help each other get at the grass beneath.

- **Monarchs breed on migration**, so no single butterfly makes the whole journey.

- **Predators often gather** at migration 'funnels' or 'bottlenecks' to feast. Birds of prey collect near the Strait of Gibraltar to catch small birds heading between West Europe and West Africa.

Eels

- **Eels** are long, slimy fish that look like snakes.

- **Baby eels** are called elvers.

- **Some eels** live in rivers, but most live in the sea, including moray eels and conger eels.

- **Moray eels** are huge and live in tropical waters, hunting fish, squid and cuttlefish.

- **Gulper eels** can live more than 7500 m down in the Atlantic Ocean. Their mouths are huge to help them catch food in the dark, deep water – so big that they can swallow fish larger than themselves whole.

- **Every autumn**, some European common eels migrate more than 7000 km, from the Baltic Sea in Europe to the Sargasso Sea near the West Indies to lay their eggs.

- **Migrating eels** are thought to find their way partly by

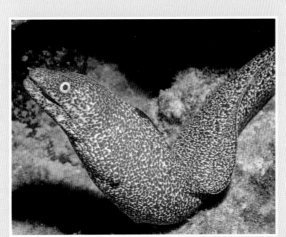

◀ Moray eels are fearsome predators that can grow to as long as 3 m. They hide in rock crevices during the day and come out at night to hunt.

detecting weak electric currents created by the movement of the water.

- **When European eels** hatch in the Sargasso Sea they are carried northeast by the ocean current, developing as they go into tiny transparent eels called glass eels.

- **The electric eels** of South America can produce an electric shock of over 500 volts – enough to knock over an adult human.

- **Garden eels** live in colonies on the seabed, poking out from holes in the sand to catch food drifting by. Their colonies look like gardens of weird plants.

The mammal groups

- **There are about 21 main subgroups** of mammals, called orders.

- **By far the biggest subgroup** of mammals is the rodents, Rodentia, including rats, mice, squirrels and cavies. It has more than 1700 species – about two-thirds of all types of mammals.

- **The next-largest subgroup** of mammals is the bats, *Chiroptera*, with almost 1000 species.

- **The smallest order (subgroup)** of mammals is called *Tublidentata*, with one species, the aardvark.

- **Another very small subgroup** of mammals is the colugos or flying lemurs, *Dermoptera*. There are just 2 species, both in Southeast Asia.

- **Most mammals keep** their body temperatures at around 37°C, although the three-toed sloth's temperature varies from 24.4°C to 40°C.

- ***Ungulata* or hoofed mammals** number about 245 species and include horses, rhinos, pigs, deer, cattle,

▲ *Pigs are even-toed or 'cloven-hoof' ungulate mammals.*
sheep, goats, gazelles and antelopes.

- **The flesh-eating** mammals, Carnivora, gain much attention but number only about 250 species.

- **The sea-cows,** *Sirenia*, make up another very small mammal order. There are only four species.

- **The mammals most** similar to the 'original' first mammals are thought to be tree-shrews (19 species).

Ocean fish

◄ *Flying fish beat their tails so fast they are able to 'fly' away from predators.*

- **Nearly 75%** of all fish live in the seas and oceans.

- **The biggest,** fastest swimming fish, such as swordfish and marlin, live near the surface of the open ocean, far from land. They often migrate vast distances to spawn (lay their eggs) or find food.

- **Many smaller fish** live deeper down, including seabed-dwellers like eels and flatfish (such as plaice, turbot and flounders).

- **Flatfish start life** as normal-shaped fish. As they grow older, one eye slowly slides around the head to join

the other. The pattern of scales also changes so that one side is the top and one side is the bottom.

- **Plaice** lie on the seabed on their left side, while turbot lie on their right side. Some flounders lie on their left and some on their right.

- **The upper side of a flatfish** is usually camouflaged to help it blend in with the sea floor.

- **In the temperate waters** of the Atlantic there are rich fishing grounds for fish such as herring.

- **The swordfish** can swim at up to 80 km/h. It uses its long spike to stab squid.

- **The bluefin tuna** can grow to as long as 3 m and weigh more than 500 kg. It is also a fast swimmer – one crossed the Atlantic in 199 days.

> ★ **STAR FACT** ★
> Flying fish can glide over the sea for 400 m
> and soar up to 6 m above the waves.

Grasshoppers and crickets

- **Grasshoppers** are plant-eating insects related to crickets, locusts and katydids.

- **Grasshoppers belong** to two main families – short-horned, which includes locusts, and long-horned, which includes katydids and crickets.

- **Short-horned grasshoppers** have ears on the side of their body. Long-horned grasshoppers have ears in their knees.

- **Grasshoppers** have powerful back legs, which allow them to jump huge distances.

- **Some grasshoppers** can leap more than 3 m.

- **Grasshoppers sing** by rubbing their hind legs across their closed forewings.

- **A grasshopper's singing** is called stridulation.

- **Crickets chirrup** faster the warmer it is.

- **If you count** the number of chirrups a snowy tree cricket gives in 15 seconds, then add 40, you get the temperature in degrees Fahrenheit.

> ★ STAR FACT ★
> A frightened lubber grasshopper oozes a horrible smelling froth from its mouth.

▼ *The spikes on the long-horned grasshopper's back legs are what make the chirruping sound as it rubs them against its forewings.*

Life in the mountains

- **Mountains** are cold, windy places where only certain animals can survive – including agile hunters such as pumas and snow leopards, and nimble grazers such as mountain goats, yaks, ibex and chamois.

- **The world's highest-living** mammal is the yak, a type of wild cattle which can survive more than 6000 m up in the Himalayas of Tibet.

- **Mountain goats** have hooves with sharp edges that dig into cracks in the rock, and hollow soles that act like suction pads.

- **In winter**, the mountain goat's pelage (coat) turns white, making it hard to spot against the snow.

- **The Himalayan snowcock** nests higher than almost any other bird – often above 4000 m in the Himalayas.

▲ *Sheep like these dall sheep are well equipped for life in the mountains, with their thick woolly coats and nimble feet.*

- **The Alpine chough** has been seen flying at 8200 m up on Everest.

- **Lammergeiers** are the vultures of the African and southern European mountains. They break tough bones, when feeding, by dropping them from a great height on to stones and then eating the marrow.

- **The Andean condor** of the South American Andes is a gigantic scavenger which can carry off deer and sheep. It is said to dive from the skies like a fighter plane (see also vultures).

- **The puma**, or mountain lion, can jump well over 5 m up on to a rock ledge – that is like you jumping into an upstairs window.

- **The snow leopard** of the Himalayan mountains is now one of the rarest of all the big cats, because it has been hunted almost to extinction for its beautiful fur coat.

Life in the oceans

▲ *Many kinds of fish and other sea creatures live in the sunlit zone near the surface of the oceans.*

- **Oceans** cover 70% of the Earth and they are the largest single animal habitat.

- **Scientists** divide the ocean into two main environments – the pelagic (which is the water itself), and the benthic (which is the seabed).

- **Most benthic animals** live in shallow waters around the continents. They include worms, clams, crabs and lobsters, as well as bottom-feeding fish.

- **Scientists** call the sunny surface waters the euphotic zone. This extends down 150 m and it is where billions of plankton (microscopic animals and plants) live.

- **Green plant plankton** (algae) in the oceans produce 30% of the world's vegetable matter each year.

- **Animal plankton** include shrimps and jellyfish.

- **The surface waters** are also home to squid, fish and mammals such as whales.

- **Below the surface zon**e, down to about 2000 m, is the twilight bathyal zone. Here there is too little light for plants to grow, but many hunting fish and squid live.

- **Below 2000 m** is the dark abyssal zone, where only weird fish like gulper eels and anglerfish live (see strange sea creatures).

- **The Sargasso** is a vast area where seaweed grows thick. It is a rich home for barnacles and other sea creatures.

Corals and anemones

- **Sea anemones** are tiny, meat-eating animals that look a bit like flowers. They cling to rocks and catch tiny prey with their tentacles (see life on the seashore).

- **Coral reefs** are the undersea equivalent of rainforests, teeming with fish and other sea life. The reefs are built by tiny, sea-anemone-like animals called polyps.

- **Coral polyps** live all their lives in just one place, either fixed to a rock or to dead polyps.

- **When coral polyps** die, their cup-shaped skeletons become hard coral.

- **Coral reefs** are long ridges, mounds, towers and other shapes made from billions of coral polyps and their skeletons.

- **Fringing reefs** are shallow coral reefs that stretch out

▼ *Sea anemones look like flowers with petals, but they are actually carnivorous animals with their ring of tentacles.*

from the seashore.

- **Barrier reefs** form a long, underwater wall a little way offshore.

- **The Great Barrier Reef** off eastern Australia is the longest reef in the world, stretching over 2000 km.

- **Coral atolls** are ring-shaped islands that formed from fringing reefs around an old volcano (which has long since sunk beneath the waves).

- **Coral reefs** take millions of years to form – the Great Barrier Reef is 18 million years old, for example. By drilling a core into ancient corals, and analysing the minerals and growth rate, scientists can read history back for millions of years.

Butterflies

- **Butterflies** are insects with four large wings that feed either on the nectar of flowers or on fruit.

- **Together with moths**, butterflies make up the scientific order Lepidoptera – the word means 'scaly wings'. There are more than 165,000 species of Lepidoptera – 20,000 butterflies and 145,000 moths.

- **Many butterflies** are brightly coloured and fly by day. They have slim, hairless bodies and club-shaped antennae (feelers).

- **The biggest butterfly** is the Queen Alexandra's birdwing of New Guinea, with 25 cm-wide wings. The smallest is the Western pygmy blue.

- **Butterflies** can only fly if their wing muscles are warm. To warm up, they bask in the sun so their wings soak up energy like solar panels.

- **The monarch butterfly** is such a strong flier it can cross the Atlantic Ocean.

- **The shimmering blue wings** of the South American morpho butterfly are very beautiful – in the 19th century millions of the butterflies were caught and made into brooches.

- **Most female butterflies** live only a few days, so they have to mate and lay eggs quickly. Most males court them with elaborate flying displays.

- **Butterflies** taste with their tarsi (feet). Females 'stamp' on leaves to see if they are ripe enough for egg laying.

- **Every butterfly's caterpillar** has its own chosen food plants – different from the flowers the adult feeds on.

▲ Every species of butterfly has its own wing pattern, just like humans have their own fingerprint.

1. Egg – eggs are laid on plants that will provide food when the caterpillars hatch

2. Larva – when the caterpillar hatches, it begins eating and growing straight away

3. Pupa – butterfly caterpillars develop hard cases and hang from a stem or leaf

4. Metamorphosis – it takes a few days to a year for the pupa to turn into an adult

5. Imago – the adult's new wings are damp and crumpled, but soon dry in the sun

◀ Few insects change as much as butterflies do during their lives. Butterflies start off as an egg, then hatch into a long, wiggly larva called a caterpillar, which eats leaves greedily and grows rapidly. When it is big enough, the caterpillar makes itself a case, which can be either a cocoon or a chrysalis. Inside, it metamorphoses (changes) into an adult, then breaks out, dries its new wings and flies away.

★ **STAR FACT** ★
Butterflies fly like no other insects, flapping their wings like birds.

Octopuses and squid

- **Octopuses and squid** belong to a family of molluscs called cephalopods.

- **Octopuses** are sea creatures with a round, soft, boneless body, three hearts and eight long arms called tentacles.

- **An octopus's tentacles** are covered with suckers that allow it to grip rocks and prey.

- **Octopuses** have two large eyes, similar to humans, and a beaklike mouth.

- **When in danger** an octopus may send out a cloud of inky black fluid. Sometimes the ink cloud is the same shape as the octopus and may fool a predator into chasing the cloud.

> ★ **STAR FACT** ★
> The 30 cm-long blue-ringed octopus's poison is so deadly that it kills more people than sharks.

- **Some octopuses** can change colour dramatically to startle a predator or blend in with its background.

- **The smallest octopus** is just 2.5 cm across. The biggest measures 6 m from tentacle tip to tentacle tip.

- **A squid** has eight arms and two tentacles and swims by forcing a jet of water out of its body.

- **Giant squid** in the Pacific can grow to 18 m or more long.

◄ *Most of the hundreds of species of octopus live on the beds of shallow seas around the world. Octopuses are quite intelligent creatures.*

Life on the grasslands

▲ *Until they were wiped out by European settlers, vast herds of bison (buffalo) roamed the North American prairies.*

- **Grasslands** form in temperate (moderate temperature) regions where there is too little rainfall for forests, but enough to allow grass to grow.

- **Temperate grasslands** include the prairies of North America, the pampas of South America, the veld of South Africa, and the vast steppes of Eurasia.

- **There is little cover** on grasslands, so many grassland animals have very good eyesight and large ears to detect predators from afar.

- **Some grassland animals** escape from predators by speed. These include jack rabbits, deer, pronghorn antelopes, wild asses and flightless birds like the emu.

- **Some animals**, such as mice and prairie dogs, escape by hiding underground in burrows.

- **Some birds** hide by building their nests in bushes. These include meadowlarks, quails and blackbirds.

- **The main predators** are dogs like the coyote and fox.

- **The North American** prairies have a small wild cat called the bobcat.

- **Prairie dogs** live in huge underground colonies called towns. One contained 400 million animals and covered over 60,000 square kilometres.

- **When they meet**, prairie dogs kiss each other to find out whether they are from the same group.

Birds of the sea

▲ Seagulls catch small fish, steal eggs and young from other birds, scavenge on waste – and sometimes fly inland to find worms.

- **Two main groups** of true sea birds are albatrosses and petrels, and the gulls, auks and waders.

- **The albatross and petrel** group is called the Procellariiformes.

> ★ STAR FACT ★
> Herring gulls watch ducks diving for fish and then steal it when the ducks resurface.

- The *Procellariiformes* includes more than 100 species of albatrosses, fulmars, shearwaters and petrels.

- **Wilson's storm petrel,** small and black with a white rump, is one of the world's most common birds.

- **The gull and auk group** is called *Charadriiformes*.

- **The *Charadriiformes*** includes almost 350 gulls, skuas, terns, skimmers, puffins, auks and auklets.

- **Skuas** are such good acrobats that they can catch the disgorged meal of another bird in mid-air.

- **The great skua** often pounces on seagulls, drowns them, and then steals their chicks.

- **The least auklet** has a beak-tail length of 15 cm, hardly larger than most sparrows.

Giraffe families

- **Giraffes** have a very lengthy family life compared to most other hoofed mammals (ungulates).

- **During breeding time**, rival male giraffes rub their necks together and swing them from side to side, occasionally hitting the opponent with the side of the head. This contest is called neck-fighting.

- **The dominant male** in an area, who wins the necking contest, mates with all or most of the females.

- **A female giraffe** gives birth about 15 months after mating – one of the longest pregnancies of any mammal.

- **The female giraffe gives birth** away from the main group, in a secluded thicket or clump of trees.

▲ A young giraffe stays near its mother for up to 20 months, until it finally achieves independence.

- **When first born,** a baby giraffe is very wobbly on its legs and cannot stand up for about 20 minutes.

- **A mother giraffe** does not rejoin the group with her baby until it is about 10 to 20 days old.

- **The young giraffe stays near** its mother, being fed and protected by her, for at least 12 months.

- **The juvenile giraffe** finally becomes independent of its mother about 15 to 20 months after birth.

- **A giraffe's coat** is patched in brown on cream, and each giraffe has its own unique pattern. Reticulated giraffes of East Africa have triangular patches, but the South African Cape giraffes have blotchy markings.

The whale group

- **Whales**, dolphins and porpoises are large mammals belonging to the order (group), *Cetacea*, which took to the sea more than 40 million years ago.

- **Nearly all cetaceans** live in seas and oceans. Only a few kinds of dolphins stay in fresh water, although a few others can swim there temporarily.

- **Like all mammals**, cetaceans have lungs rather than gills, and breathe air. This means they must come to the surface every few minutes, although some can stay down for an hour or more. A sperm whale can hold its breath for over 2 hours.

- **Whales breathe** through blowholes on top of their head. When a whale breathes out, it spouts out water vapour and mucus. When it breathes in, it sucks in about 2000 litres of air in a couple of seconds.

▶ Killer whales or orcas are big deep-sea predators, growing to as long as 9 m and weighing up to 10 tonnes. They feed on fish, seals, penguins and dolphins.

Dorsal fin

To swim, whales flap their fluke (tail) up and down

▲ Humpback whales live together in groups called pods and keep in touch with their own 'dialect' of noises.

- **Like land mammals**, mother whales feed their babies with their own milk. Whale milk is so rich that babies grow incredibly fast. Blue whale babies are over 7 m long when they are born and gain an extra 100 kg or so a day for about 7 months.

- **There are 12 kinds or species** of great or baleen whales, and about 71 species of toothed whales (including dolphins and porpoises).

- **The 6 subgroups** of toothed whale are the sperm whales, the little-known beaked whales, the beluga (white whale) and narwhal, the dolphins, the porpoises, and the river dolphins.

> ★ **STAR FACT** ★
> Male humpbacks make elaborate 'songs' lasting 20 minutes or more – perhaps to woo females.

- **The three subgroups** of great whales are the rorquals (such as the blue, fin, sei, minke and humpback), the right whales (including the bowhead), and the single species of gray whale

- **Rorqual have grooves** or pleats on their throats, which allow the chin and throat to expand hugely as the whale gulps in mouthfuls of water.

- **Recently, scientists have realized** that what was thought to be one species of rorqual, Bryde's whale (pronounced 'Broodah's'), is in fact two species — the Bryde's whale and the pygmy Bryde's whale.

Watching birds

- **The scientific study of birds** is called ornithology.

- **Some ornithologists** are professional scientists who are concerned with birds full-time.

- **Millions of people** watch birds as a hobby or pastime, for pleasure – it is one of the world's most popular spare-time activities.

- **'Birders'** are people who develop greater enthusiasm for travelling to the best places, and spending more time and money, than casual bird-watchers.

- **'Twitchers' are extremely keen** on spotting rare or exotic species, and ticking them in a book or list.

- **One of the commonest ways** of encouraging birds, to watch and enjoy them, is by a bird-feeder.

▲ Most birds flap their wings to fly. Even birds that spend much of their time gliding have to flap their wings to take off and land.

- **A small sheltered place** for watching birds, which blends into the surroundings, is called a hide.

- **Birders have many** specialities such as photography, or recording bird song with a dish-like microphone.

- **A good 'birding' telescope** magnifies 25 to 35 times.

> ★ STAR FACT ★
> Experts catch birds with mist nets – very fine, small-mesh nets that birds do not notice.

Life in rivers and lakes

- **Rivers,** lakes and other freshwater habitats are home to all sorts of fish, including bream and trout.

- **Fast-flowing** streams are preferred by fish such as trout and grayling. Slow-flowing rivers and lakes are home to tench, rudd and carp.

▲ Upland lakes like these are home to many fish, including char, powan and bullhead. Fish such as brown trout swim in the streams that tumble down into the lake.

- **Some fish** feed on floating plant matter, while others take insects from the surface of the water.

- **Common bream** and barbel hunt on the riverbed, eating insect larvae, worms and molluscs.

- **Perch** and pike are predators of lakes and slow-flowing rivers.

- **Pike** are the sharks of the river – deadly hunters that lurk among weeds waiting for unwary fish, or even rats and birds. Pike can weigh as much as 30 kg.

- **Mammals of rivers** and lakes include voles, water rats and otters.

- **Birds of rivers** and lakes include birds that dive for fish (such as kingfishers), small wading birds (such as redshanks, avocets and curlews), large wading birds (such as herons, storks and flamingos), and waterfowl (such as ducks, swans and geese).

- **Insects** include dragonflies and water boatmen.

- **Amphibians** include frogs and newts.

Cobras and vipers

◀ *When on the defensive, a cobra rears up and spreads the skin of its neck in a hood to make it look bigger. This often gives victims a chance to hit it away.*

- **Two kinds of poisonous** snake are dangerous to humans – vipers and elapids such as cobras and mambas.

- **Elapids** have their venom (poison) in short front fangs. A viper's fangs are so long that they usually have to be folded away.

- **The hamadryad cobra** of Southeast Asia is the world's largest poisonous snake, growing to over 5 m.

- **In India**, cobras kill more than 7000 people every year. The bite of a king cobra can kill an elephant in 4 hours. The marine cobra lives in the sea and its venom is 100 times more deadly.

- **Snake charmers** use the spectacled cobra, playing to it so that it follows the pipe as if about to strike – but the snake's fangs have been removed to make it safe.

- **A spitting cobra** squirts venom into its attacker's eyes, and is accurate at 2 m or more. The venom is not deadly, but it blinds the victim and is very painful.

- **The black mamba** of Africa can race along at 25 km/h with its head raised and its tongue flickering.

- **A viper's venom** kills its victims by making their blood clot. Viper venom has been used to treat haemophiliacs (people whose blood does not clot well).

- **The pit vipers** of the Americas hunt their warm-blooded victims using heat-sensitive pits on the side

> ★ STAR FACT ★
> Fer-de-lance snakes have 60 to 80 babies, each of which is deadly poisonous.

The horse family

- **Horses** are big, four-legged, hooved animals, now bred mainly for human use.

- **Male horses** are stallions, females are mares, babies are foals, and young males are colts.

- **The only wild horse** is the Przewalski of central Asia.

- **The mustangs** (wild horses) of the USA are descended from tame horses.

- **Tame horses** are of three main kinds –

▲ *All horses, wild and tame, may be descended from the prehistoric Merychippus (see evolution).*

light horses for riding (such as Morgans and Arabs), heavy horses for pulling ploughs and wagons (such as Percherons and Suffolk Punches), and ponies (such as Shetlands).

- **Most racehorses** and hunting horses are thoroughbred (pure) Arab horses descended from just three stallions that lived around 1700 – Darley Arabian, Godolphin Barb and Byerly Turk.

- **Lippizaners** are beautiful white horses, the best-known of which are trained to jump and dance at the Spanish Riding School in Vienna.

- **The shire horse** is probably the largest horse, bred after King Henry VIII had all horses under 1.5 m destroyed.

- **You can tell** a horse's age by counting its teeth – a 1 year-old has six pairs, a 5-year-old has twelve.

- **Quarter horses** are agile horses used by cowhands for cutting out (sorting cows from the herd). They got their name from running quarter-mile races.

Seal and sea lion family

- **Seals,** fur seals, sea lions and walruses are aquatic mammals that belong to the order (main group) called *Pinnipedia*, which means 'flipper-feet'.

- **Pinnipeds** live mainly in water and are agile swimmers, but waddle awkwardly on land.

- **All pinnipeds** have ears, but only sea lions and fur seals have ear flaps – seals lack them.

> **★ STAR FACT ★**
> The 4 m-long leopard seal of Antarctica feeds on penguins and even other seals.

- **There are about 34 kinds** or species of pinnipeds: 19 true (haired or earless) seals; 13 eared seals (including sea lions and fur seals); and the walrus.

- **Only sea lions** can move their back flippers under their bodies to 'hump' on land.

- **The back flippers of a seal** trail behind on land and the seal must wriggle or slide along.

- **When seals** come ashore to breed, they live for weeks in vast colonies called rookeries.

- **Sometimes hunters kill** seal pups for their fur, or to keep their numbers down to protect fisheries.

- **There** are freshwater seals in Lake Baikal in Russia.

◀ *Seal pups (babies) like this one grow a thick, furry coat.*

Moths

- **Like butterflies,** moths belong to the insect group Lepidoptera.

- **Most moths** have fat, hairy bodies, and feathery or thread-like antennae.

- **Many moths** fly at dusk or at night. By day, they rest on tree trunks and in leaf litter, where their drab colour makes them hard for predators such as birds to spot. However, there are also many brightly coloured day-flying moths.

- **Tiger moths** give out high-pitched clicks to warn that they taste bad and so escape being eaten.

- **The biggest moths** are the Hercules moth and the bent wing ghost moth of Asia, with wingspans of over 25 cm.

- **Night-flying moths** shiver their wings to warm them up for flight.

- **Hawk moths** are powerful fliers and migrate long distances. The oleander hawk moth flies from tropical Africa to far northern Europe in summer.

- **The caterpillars** of small moths live in seeds, fruit, stems and leaves, eating them from the inside.

- **The caterpillars** of big moths feed on leaves from the outside, chewing chunks out of them.

- **When threatened,** the caterpillar of the puss moth rears up and thrusts its whip-like tail forward, and squirts a jet of formic acid from its head end.

▼ *Hawk moths have very long tongues for sucking nectar from flowers. They often hover like hummingbirds as they are feeding.*

Breeding birds

- **Birds show all kinds of breeding methods**, from a single lifelong pair 'mated for life', to one adult having several partners.

- **One male** mating with several females is called polygyny, while one female mating with several males is polyandry.

- **Each kind or species** of bird lays eggs of a slightly different size, shape, colour and pattern.

- **The number of eggs** laid varies hugely. Hornbills lay just one egg a year, hens can lay around 350 a year.

- **Most birds** build nests to lay their eggs in – usually bowl-shaped and made from twigs, grasses and leaves.

- **The biggest ground nest** is that of the Australian mallee fowl, which builds a mound of soil 5 m across, with egg-chambers filled with rotting vegetation to keep the eggs warm.

- **Flamingos** build mud nests that look like upturned sandcastles poking out of the water.

- **The great treeswift** lays its single egg in a nest the size of an eggcup.

- **Some birds lay** a second clutch of eggs if the first is destroyed.

▶ *After they lay their eggs, most birds sit on them to keep them warm until they are ready to hatch. This is called incubation.*

Defence

- **Animals** have different ways of escaping predators – most mammals run away, while birds take to the air.

- **Some animals** use camouflage to hide (see colours and markings). Many small animals hide in burrows.

- **Turtles** and tortoises hide inside their hard shells.

▼ *Meerkats stand on their hind legs and give a shrill call to alert other meerkats to danger.*

- **Armadillos** curl up inside their bendy body armour.

- **The spiky-skinned armadillo** lizard of South Africa curls up and stuffs its tail in its mouth.

- **Hedgehogs**, porcupines and echidnas are protected by sharp quills (spines).

- **Skunks** and the stinkpot turtle give off foul smells.

- **Plovers** pretend to be injured to lure hunters away from their young.

- **Many animals** defend themselves by frightening their enemies. Some, such as peacock butterflies, flash big eye-markings. Others, such as porcupine fish and great horned owls, blow themselves up much bigger.

- **Other animals** send out warning signals. Kangaroo rats and rabbits thump their feet. Birds shriek.

The ape family

- **Apes** are our closest relatives in the animal world. The great apes are gorillas, chimpanzees and the orang-utan. Gibbons are called lesser apes.

- **Like us**, apes have long arms, and fingers and toes for gripping. They are clever and can use sticks and stones as tools.

- **There are 20 kinds** or species of apes, divided into two groups, the lesser and greater apes.

- **The lesser apes** are the gibbons, with about 14 species, all from the mainland and various islands of Southeast Asia.

- **The greater apes** include two species each of gorillas and chimpanzees, all from Africa, and two species of orang-utans, which live only in Southeast Asia.

- **Gorillas** are the biggest of all the apes, weighing twice as much as an adult human, while most types of gibbons weigh only 5 to 8 kg

- ◄ Gorillas climb trees only to sleep at night or to pull down branches to make a one-night nest on the ground. They usually walk on all fours.

- **The two gorilla species** are both from Africa – western gorillas, and eastern gorillas (which include the mountain gorillas).

- **Mountain gorillas** live in the mountains of Rwanda and Uganda. They are very rare, with only about 500 of them.

- **Recent studies of genes,** coupled with observations in the wild, show that what was thought to be one orang-utan species, is really two species – the Bornean and the Sumatran orang-utans.

- **Chimpanzees are our closest** living relatives, as shown by studies of genes, body chemicals and fossils. They and ourselves branched from a common chimp-like ancestor in Africa, some time between 10 and 7 million years ago.

▶ Gorillas live in troops (groups) of a dozen or so. They travel through the forests searching for food led by a mature male, called a silverback because of the silver hairs on his back. Gorillas like to groom each other and cuddle when they rest in the afternoon.

An adult male has a crest of hair on his head

Gorillas have no hair on their face or chest, and their palms and soles are also bare

Baby gorillas are carried by their mother until they are 3 years old

Hoofed giants

- **Rhinos and hippos** are both big hoofed mammals, and though they seem similar in many ways, they have lots of differences.

- **Rhinos** are more closely related to horses, zebras and tapirs, having an odd number of toes on each foot (perissodactyl).

- **Hippos** are more closely related to pigs, camels and deer, having an even number of toes on each foot (the group called artiodactyl).

- **There are only two kinds** or species of hippo, both in Africa, but five species of rhino across parts of Africa, South Asia and Southeast Asia.

> ★ **STAR FACT** ★
> The African white rhinoceros's horn can grow to over 1.5 m long.

◄ *The African black rhino is almost extinct in the wild. Between 2 –3 thousand are left on nature reserves. Some gamekeepers have tried cutting off their horns to make them less of a target for poachers.*

- **The five species of rhinos** are the Sumatran, Javan, Indian (Asian), black or square-lipped, and white or hook-lipped rhinos.

- **Powdered rhino horn** is believed by some to be a love potion, leading to mass slaughter. All species are now threatened.

- **The two species of hippo** are the common or river hippo, and the smaller and rarer pygmy hippo.

- **The common hippo** has the biggest mouth of any land animal.

- **A pygmy hippo** weighs only 200-300 kg, which is between one-fifth and one-tenth of the weight of its larger cousin.

Salmon

▲ *Salmon returning to their spawning ground make mighty leaps up raging torrents. The journey can take months.*

- **Salmon** are river and sea fish caught or farmed in huge quantities for food.

- **All salmon** are born in rivers and lakes far inland, then swim down river and out to sea.

- **Adult salmon** spend anything from 6 months to 7 years in the oceans, before returning to rivers and swimming upstream to spawn (lay their eggs).

- **More than five salmon species**, including the sockeye and the chinook, spawn in North American rivers running into the North Pacific.

- **Cherry salmon** spawn in eastern Asian rivers, and amago salmon spawn in Japanese rivers.

- **Atlantic salmon** spawn in rivers in northern Europe and eastern Canada.

- **Spawning salmon** return to the same stream they were born in, up to 3000 km inland.

- **To reach their spawning grounds**, salmon have to swim upstream against strong currents, often leaping as high as 5 m to clear waterfalls.

- **When salmon reach their spawning grounds**, they mate. The female lays up to 20,000 eggs.

- **After spawning**, the weakened salmon head down river again, but few make it as far as the sea.

Turtles and tortoises

- **Turtles and tortoises** are reptiles that live inside hard, armoured shells. Together with terrapins, they make up a group called the chelonians.

- **Turtles** live in the sea, freshwater, or on land, tortoises live on land, and terrapins live in water.

- **The shield on the back of a chelonian** is called a carapace. Its flat belly armour is called a plastron.

- **Most turtles and tortoises** eat plants and tiny animals. They have no teeth, just jaws with very sharp edges.

- **Tortoises** live mostly in hot, dry regions and will hibernate in winter if brought to a cold country.

- **Turtles and tortoises** live to a great age. One giant tortoise found in 1766 in Mauritius lived 152 years.

> ★ STAR FACT ★
> Giant tortoises were once kept on ships to provide fresh meat on long voyages.

- **The giant tortoise** grows to as long as 1.5 m.

- **The leatherback turtle** grows to as long as 2.5 m and weighs more than 800 kg.

- **Every three years**, green turtles gather together to swim thousands of kilometres to Ascension Island in the mid-Atlantic, where they lay their eggs ashore by moonlight at the highest tide. They bury the eggs in the sand, to be incubated by the heat of the sun.

▶ Tortoises are very slow moving and placid.

Hoofed mammals

- **Giraffe, antelopes,** gazelles, deer, cattle, sheep, goats, camels, hippos and pigs all belong to the huge group of hoofed mammals called artiodactyls – those with an even number of toes on each foot.

- **Many artiodactyls** are ruminants. They chew food a second time (chewing the cud), after first partially digesting it in a special stomach chamber.

▲ Reindeer cope with harsh winters by finding lichen to eat under the snow – perhaps by smell.

- **Most antelope and gazelle** species live in herds in Africa, and many are very fast yet graceful runners.

- **Antelopes and gazelles** have horns, not antlers. Horns are not shed yearly — they last a lifetime.

- **Antelopes and gazelles** are mainly mammals of open country, savanna and bush; most are grazers.

- **Most deer species** live in wooded areas and are browsers (leaf-eaters) rather than grazers.

- **There are 45 species** in the deer family, *Cervidae*.

- **The *Bovidae* family** has 145 species of antelopes, gazelles, cows, bison, buffalo, sheep and goats.

- **Unlike most deer**, where only males have antlers, in antelopes and gazelles both sexes have horns.

> ★ STAR FACT ★
> There are more domesticated species of artiodactyls than any other mammal group.

Evolution

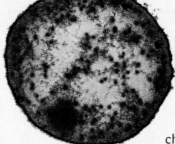

▶ All life on Earth may have evolved almost 4 billion years ago from organisms like this archaebacteria. Archaebacteria thrive in extreme conditions such as those on the early Earth. This one came from under the Antarctic ice. Others thrive in scorching undersea volcanic vents.

- **Charles Darwin's** Theory of Evolution, first published in 1859, showed how all species of plant and animal adapt and develop over millions of years.

- **Darwin's theory** depended on the fact that no two living things are alike.

- **Some animals** start life with characteristics that give them a better chance of surviving to pass the characteristics on to their offspring.

- **Other animals**' characteristics mean that they are less likely to survive.

- **Over many generations** and thousands of years, better-adapted animals and plants survive and flourish, while others die out or find a new home.

- **Fossil discoveries** since Darwin's time have supported his theory, and lines of evolution can be traced for thousands of species.

- **Fossils** also show that evolution is not always as slow and steady as Darwin thought. Some scientists believe change comes in rapid bursts, separated by long slow periods when little changes.

▶ One of the horse's earliest ancestors, Hyracotherium, appeared about 45 mya. It was a small woodland creature which browsed on leaves. When the woods began to disappear and grasslands became more widespread, it paid to be faster to escape predators. The modern horse, Equus, is the latest result of this evolutionary adaptation.

Other scientists believe that bursts of rapid change interrupt periods of long steady change.

- **For the first 3 billion years** of Earth's history, the only life forms were microscopic, single-celled, marine (sea) organisms such as bacteria and amoeba. Sponges and jellyfish, the first multi-celled creatures, appeared by 700 million years ago (mya).

- **About 600 mya**, evolution speeded up dramatically in what is called the Precambrian explosion. Thousands of different organisms appeared within a very short space of time, including the first proper animals with bones and shells.

- **After the Precambrian**, life evolved rapidly. Fish developed, then insects and then, about 380 mya, amphibians – the first large creatures to crawl on land. About 340 mya, reptiles evolved – the first large creatures to live entirely on land.

- **Dinosaurs** developed from these early reptiles about 220 mya and dominated the Earth for 160 million years. Birds also evolved from the reptiles, and cynodonts furry, mammal-like creatures.

Hyracotherium

Mesohippus

Parahippus

Merychippus

Pliohippus

Longer neck for grazing

Longer legs for running

Equus

What are insects?

◀ Insects were the first creatures to live on land – nearly a quarter of a billion years before the first dinosaurs – and the first to fly.

● **Insects may be tiny**, but there are more of them than all the other animals put together – over 1 million known species.

● **They range from tiny flies** to huge beetles, and they are found everywhere there is land.

● **Insects** have six legs and a body divided into three sections – which is why they are called insects ('in sections'). The sections are the head, thorax (middle) and abdomen.

● **An insect's body** is encased in such a tough shell (its exoskeleton) that there is no need for bones.

● **Insects grow** by getting rid of their old exoskeleton and replacing it with a bigger one. This is called moulting.

● **Insects change dramatically** as they grow. Butterflies, moths, and beetles undergo metamorphosis (see butterflies). Grasshoppers and mayflies begin as wingless nymphs, then gradually grow wings with each moult. Silverfish and springtails simply get bigger with each moult.

● **Insects' eyes** are called compound because they are made up of many lenses – from six (worker ants) to more than 30,000 (dragonflies).

● **Insects have two antennae** (feelers) on their heads.

● **Insects do not have lungs**. Instead, they breathe through holes in their sides called spiracles, linked to their body through tubes called tracheae.

● **The world's longest insect** is the giant stick insect of Indonesia, which can grow to 33 cm long.

The woodpecker group

● **Woodpeckers** and their relatives form a large main group, or order, of birds called the *Piciformes*.

● **In addition to woodpeckers**, the *Piciformes* group include toucans, toucanets, barbets, tinkerbirds, jacamars, honeyguides, puffbirds, wrynecks, piculets, sapsuckers and flickers.

● **Members of the *Piciformes*** all have two toes on one foot pointing forwards and two pointing backwards.

● **There are more than** 370 species of Piciformes.

● **Gila woodpeckers** escape the desert heat by nesting inside giant saguaro cacti (where it can be 30°C cooler).

● **A tinkerbird's** 'tink' call sounds like someone hitting or hammering metal – as in the old trade of mending pots and pans, called tinkering.

★ STAR FACT ★
The swallow-winged puffbird has such long wings, it can be mistaken for a bat in flight.

▲ The toucan's giant beak is full of air holes, so it is not heavy enough to overbalance the bird. Toucans eat mainly small fruit.

● **Honeyguides** lead not only other animals to bees' nests, but also people, who break the nest so the bird can join a feast.

● **When toucans sleep**, they turn their heads around and lay their bills down their backs.

● **Flickers** are named after the way they flick and spread out their wings and tail when confronting rivals.

Rabbits

▶ Rabbits and hares look like rodents but they belong to another group of mammals called lagomorphs or 'leaping shapes'.

- **The common or European rabbit** probably orginated from Spain and (or) North Africa, and is the ancestor of all today's pet rabbits.

- **Rabbits** have been kept in captivity since the time of Ancient Greece and Rome, more than 2000 years ago, mainly for cooking and eating.

- **The Romans** helped to spread the wild rabbit through Europe, as a convenient source of fresh meat.

- **Selective breeding** of wild European rabbits, to produce different colour forms, began in the Middle Ages, probably by monks in monasteries.

- **Wild rabbits** reached Britain during the Norman invasion, from 1066.

- **A painting** by the artist Titian, from 1530, shows a white rabbit — the first good evidence of rabbit selective breeding.

- **In the late 1500s**, natural history writer Scaliger recorded black, grey, yellow, white and spotted forms of domesticated rabbits.

- **In the 1800s** many poor Europeans still regarded the rabbit as their main meaty meal of the week.

- **The breeding of fancy rabbits**, with very long coats, began in the middle of the 19th century.

- **Today's rabbits** are bred for meat, wool (Angoras), skin (pelt), fancy breeds for display, and as pets.

▶ Rats and mice have long thin tails, pointed noses and beady black eyes.

Waterfowl

- **Ducks, geese and swans** are known as waterfowl, and they all live on or near freshwater.

- **The scientific name** of the waterfowl group is the order Anseriformes, and the whole group contains about 150 species.

- **Waterfowl** can float for hours and have webbed feet for swimming and diving with grace and power.

- **On land**, most waterfowl waddle awkwardly, since their legs are set far back under the

◀ Canada geese breed in the far north of Canada and Alaska, and migrate south to warmer regions in the autumn.

body, more efficient for swimming than walking.

- **Three South American** types of waterfowl are called screamers, after their clanging, piercing calls which have led to local names such as 'mahooka'.

- **Screamers** differ in several ways from other waterfowl – they have turkey-shaped bodies, narrow rather than broad beaks, and partly webbed feet.

- **Ducks** tend to have shorter necks and wings, and flatter bills, than geese or swans.

- **Male ducks** are called drakes, the females are ducks, and the babies are called ducklings.

- **Diving ducks** (such as the pochard, tufted duck and the scoter) dive for food such as roots, shellfish and insects on the river bed.

- **Dabbling ducks** (such as the mallard, widgeon, gadwall and the teal) dabble – they sift water through their beaks for food.

Coral reef fish

- **Many fish species** live in warm seas around coral reefs.
- **Butterfly fish** and angelfish have slender, oval bodies and are also popular as aquarium fish.
- **Male triggerfish** boost their colour to attract females.
- **Cuckoo wrasse** are all born female, but big females change sex when they are between 7 and 13 years old.
- **Cleaner fish** are the health clinics of the oceans. Larger fish such as groupers queue up for cleaner fish to go over them, nibbling away pests and dead skin.
- **The banded coral shrimp** cleans up pests in the same way as cleaner fish do, from fish such as moray eels.
- **The sabre-toothed blenny** looks so like a cleaner fish that it can nip in close to big fish but then take a bite out of them.

> ★ STAR FACT ★
> Cleaner fish will go to work inside
> a shark's mouth.

▲ *Coral reefs are home to many brilliantly coloured fish.*

- **Cheilinus** is a carnivorous fish of coral reefs which changes colour to mimic harmless plant-eating fish, such as parrotfish and goatfish.
- **The regal tang** starts out life mostly bright yellow and gradually turns a vivid royal blue as the fish matures.

Ants and termites

- **Ants** are a vast group of insects related to bees and wasps. Most ants have a tiny waist and are wingless.
- **Ants** are the main insects in tropical forests, living in colonies of anything from 20 to millions.
- **Ant** colonies are all female. Most species have one or several queens which lay the eggs. Hundreds of soldier ants guard the queen, while smaller workers build the nest and care for the young.
- **Males** only enter the nest to mate with young queens, then die.
- **Wood ants** squirt acid from their abdomen to kill enemies.
- **Army ants** march in huge swarms, eating small creatures they meet.

▲ *African termites use mud and saliva to build amazing nests more than 12 m high, housing over 5 million termites.*

- **Groups of army ants** cut any large prey they catch into pieces which they carry back to the nest. Army ants can carry 50 times their own weight.
- **Ants** known as slavemakers raid the nests of other ants and steal their young to raise as slaves.
- **Termite** colonies are even more complex than ant ones. They have a large king and queen who mate, as well as soldiers to guard them and workers to do the work.
- **Termite nests** are mounds built like cities with many chambers – including a fungus garden.

Birds 'without feet'

- **Swifts and hummingbirds** are on the wing so much that their feet have become weak, giving their group the name *Apodiformes*, meaning 'footless ones'.

- **There are more than 420** members of the *Apodiformes*, including swiftlets, needle-tails, racquet-tails, sicklebills, coquettes and hillstars.

- **Swifts** are well-named as among the fastest fliers – spine-tailed swifts have been timed at 240 km/h.

- **Most swifts use** their short, gaping bills to catch insects on the wing.

- **Great dusky swifts** nest and roost behind waterfalls, and have to fly through the water to get in and out.

- **Swifts and hummingbirds** have a specialized 'elbow' that allows the wing extra twist for aerial acrobatics.

> ★ STAR FACT ★
> Some hummingbirds defend 'their' flowers from other birds, bats and even butterflies.

▲ Hummingbirds have long bills to suck nectar from flowers.

- **The Andean hillstar** (a hummingbird) allows its body temperature to fall at dusk, a condition called torpor, to save energy during the cold mountain night.

- **Hummingbirds** are named, not after their calls or songs, but after the hum of their fast-beating wings.

- **Needle-tails** have spiny ends to their tail feathers.

Prosimians

- **Prosimians include lemurs**, bushbabies and galagos, pottos, lorises and tarsiers.

- **Prosimians** are members of the primate group, with apes and monkeys.

- **There are about 85 kinds** or species of prosimians, found naturally in only Africa and Asia.

- **Most lemurs** are active at night and live in trees, but

▲ Ring-tailed lemurs get their name from their black-ringed tail which they raise to show where they are.

one of the most common types, the ring-tailed lemur, lives mostly on the ground in groups.

- **Most lemurs** eat fruit, leaves, insects and small birds.

- **The potto** is a slow-moving, cautious, careful, nocturnal climber in the tropical forests of West Africa. It eats gum and sap, fruits and berries, and the occasional insect or other small animal.

- **A potto can** 'freeze' and stay completely still, to escape notice, for more than two hours.

- **Bushbabies** are the fast-jumping, long-leaping acrobats of the prosimian group. They get their name because their calls sound like a human baby crying.

- **Bushbabies** are nocturnal animals and their big eyes and ears help them see and hear in the dark.

- **The eight species of tarsiers** from the Philippines and Southeast Asia are tiny, huge-eyed prosimians with very long fingers. A tarsier can turn its head around in a half-circle to look directly backwards.

Pythons and boas

- **Constrictors** are snakes that squeeze their victims to death, rather than poisoning them. They include pythons, boas and anacondas.

- **A constrictor** does not crush its victim. Instead, it winds itself around, gradually tightening its coils until the victim suffocates.

- **Constrictors usually swallow** victims whole, then spend days digesting them. They have special jaws that allow their mouths to open very wide. A large meal can be seen as a lump moving down the body.

- **Pythons** are big snakes that live in Asia, Indonesia and Africa. In captivity, reticulated pythons grow to 9 m. Boas and anacondas are the big constrictors of South America.

- **Boas** capture their prey by lying in wait, hiding motionless under trees and waiting for victims to pass by. But like all snakes, they can go for many weeks without eating.

- **Like many snakes**, most constrictors begin life as eggs. Unusually for snakes, female pythons look after their eggs until they hatch by coiling around them. Even more unusually, Indian and green tree pythons actually keep their eggs warm by shivering.

- **Female boas** do not lay eggs, giving birth to live young.

- **Boas** have tiny remnants of back legs, called spurs, which males use to tickle females during mating.

- **Anacondas** spend much of their lives in swampy ground or shallow water, lying in wait for victims to come and drink. One anaconda was seen to swallow a 2 m-long caiman (a kind of crocodile).

- **When frightened**, the royal python of Africa coils itself into a tight ball, which is why it is sometimes called the ball python. Rubber boas do the same, but hide their heads and stick their tails out aggressively to fool attackers.

▲ *Pythons are tropical snakes that live in moist forests in Asia and Africa. They are the world's biggest snakes, rivalled only by giant anacondas. Pythons are one long tube of muscle, well able to squeeze even big victims to death. They usually eat animals about the size of domestic cats, but occasionally they go for really big meals such as wild pigs and deer.*

★ STAR FACT ★
A 4 to 5 m-long African rock python was once seen to swallow an entire 60 kg impala (a kind of antelope) whole – horns and all.

Snails and slugs

- **Snails and slugs** are small, squidgy, slimy, soft-bodied crawling creatures. They belong to a huge group of animals called molluscs which have no skeleton. Squid and oysters are also molluscs.

- **Snails and slugs** are gastropods, a group that also includes whelks and winkles.

- **Gastropod** means 'stomach foot', because these animals seem to slide along on their stomachs.

- **Most gastropods** live in the sea. They include limpets which stick firmly to seashore rocks.

> ★ **STAR FACT** ★
> Snails are a great delicacy in France, where they are called *escargot*.

◄ *Garden snails have a shell which they seal themselves into in dry weather, making a kind of trapdoor to save moisture. They have eyes on their horns.*

- **Most land snails and slugs** ooze a trail of sticky slime to help them move along the ground.

- **Garden snails** are often hermaphrodites, which means they have both male and female sex organs.

- **The great grey slugs** of western Europe court by circling each other for over an hour on a branch, then launching themselves into the air to hang from a long trail of mucus. They mate for between 7 to 24 hours.

- **Among the largest gastropods** are the tropical tritons, whose 45–cm shells are sometimes used as warhorns. Conches are another big kind of gastropod.

- **Some cone snails** in the Pacific and Indian oceans have teeth that can inject a poison which can actually kill people.

Life in tropical rainforests

- **Tropical rainforests** are the richest and most diverse of all animal habitats.

- **Most animals** in tropical rainforests live in the canopy (treetops), and are either agile climbers or can fly.

- **Canopy animals** include flying creatures such as bats, birds and insects, and climbers such as monkeys, sloths, lizards and snakes.

▲ *Year-round rainfall and warm temperatures make rainforests incredibly lush, with a rich variety of plant life.*

- **Many rainforest creatures** can glide through the treetops – these include gliding geckos and other lizards, flying squirrels and even flying frogs.

- **Some tree frogs** live in the cups of rainwater held by plants growing high up in trees.

- **Antelopes, deer, hogs, tapir** and many different kinds of rodent (see rabbits and rats) roam the forest floor, hunting for seeds, roots, leaves and fruit.

- **Beside rivers** in Southeast Asian rainforests, there may be rhinoceroses, crocodiles and even elephants.

- **Millions of insect species** live in rainforests, including butterflies, moths, bees, termites and ants. There are also many spiders.

- **Rainforest butterflies and moths** are often big or vividly coloured, including the shimmering blue morpho of Brazil and the birdwing butterflies.

- **Rainforest birds** can be vividly coloured too, and include parrots, toucans and birds of paradise.

Sharks

- **Sharks** are the most fearsome predatory fish of the seas, with 375 species, living mostly in warm seas.

- **Sharks** have a skeleton made of rubbery cartilage – most other kinds of fish have bony skeletons.

- **The world's biggest fish** is the whale shark, which can grow to well over 12 m long. Unlike other sharks, the whale shark and the basking shark (at 9 m long) mostly eat plankton and are completely harmless.

★ STAR FACT ★
Great white sharks are the biggest meat-eating sharks, growing to over 7 m long.

- **A shark's main weapons are its teeth** – they are powerful enough to bite through plate steel.

- **Sharks** put so much strain on their teeth that they always have three or four spare rows of teeth in reserve.

- **Nurse sharks** grow a new set of teeth every 8 days.

- **Up to 20 people** die from recorded shark attacks each year.

- **The killing machine** of the shark world is the great white shark, responsible for most attacks on humans.

- **Hammerhead sharks** can also be dangerous . They have T-shaped heads, with eyes and nostrils at the end of the T.

◀ A shark's torpedo-shaped body makes it a very fast swimmer.

Prehistoric reptiles

- **Dinosaurs** were reptiles that dominated life on land from about 220 million to 65 million years ago, when all of them mysteriously became extinct.

- **Although modern reptiles** walk with bent legs splayed out, dinosaurs had straight legs under their bodies – this meant they could run fast or grow heavy.

- **Some dinosaurs** ran on their back two legs, as birds do. Others had four sturdy legs like an elephant's.

- **Dinosaurs** are split into two groups according to their hipbones – saurischians had reptile-like hips and ornithischians had birdlike hips.

- **Saurischians** were either swift, two-legged predators called theropods, or hefty four-legged herbivores called sauropods.

- **Theropods** had acute eyesight, fearsome claws and sharp teeth. They included *Tyrannosaurus rex*, one of the biggest hunting animals to ever live on land – over 15 m long, 5 m tall and more than 7 tonnes.

- **Sauropods** had massive bodies, long tails, and necks.

- **The sauropod** *Brachiosaurus* was over 23 m long, weighed 80 tonnes and towered 12 m into the air. It was one of the biggest creature ever to live on land.

- **Most dinosaurs** are known from fossilized bones, but fossilized eggs, footprints and droppings have also been found. In 1913, mummified hadrosaur skin was found.

- **Some scientists** think the dinosaurs died out after a huge meteor struck Earth off Mexico, creating a cloud that blocked the sun's light and heat.

▶ Dinosaur means 'terrible lizard', and they came in all shapes and sizes. This is a plant-eating sauropod called Diplodocus.

Panda life

▶ Giant pandas are big, chubby animals. When they stand on their hind legs they are as tall as a man. But they have a poor digestive system, and to sustain their huge bulk, they have to eat for most hours of the day — up to five times longer than other members of their carnivore group, such as the cats.

Pandas hold the bamboo in their front paws while they are chewing

Giant pandas eat only certain kinds of bamboo

- **Giant pandas** live in the bamboo forests of western China and Tibet, mainly in the provinces of Sichuan (which has most pandas, about four-fifths of the total), Shaanxi (most of the rest) and Gansu.

- **Giant pandas live at** relatively high altitudes, between 1200 and 3500 m above sea level, in mixed woodland where the bamboo grows as dense thickets between the hillside trees.

- **Giant pandas are among the rarest species** of large mammals, and their habitat has been cut back by the loss of forests for wood and farmland.

- **In the wild**, giant pandas give birth to one or two cubs. If there are two, usually the mother tries to rear only

one. The cub is very tiny and the mother has to give up eating to look after it for the first 10-20 days. The cub stays with its mother for 18 months.

- **One reason** that giant pandas are now so rare, and perhaps always have been quite rare, is because they breed so slowly. A female has a cub only once every 2 or 3 years.

- **The giant panda** plays an important part in local folklore and legend. It has many regional names including Pixiu and Mo (Ancient Chinese), Baixiong ('white bear') and Daxiongmao ('giant bear-cat').

- **Today's giant pandas** are split into about 25 separate populations, covering some 15,000 sq km of mixed and bamboo-rich forest.

- **One of the major problems** in panda conservation is to link the very fragmented and spread-out populations, by safe corridors of woodland. Otherwise the small groups will become inbred due to lack of genetic variety.

- **The only other panda** is the red panda, which looks a little like a raccoon. People once thought that both the red and giant pandas were related to raccoons, even though giant pandas look more like bears.

- **DNA tests** have shown that red pandas are closer relatives of raccoons, but giant pandas are closer to bears and now included in the bear family.

▶ No one quite knows the purpose of the giant panda's black eye patches. When these animals were first brought to Europe in 1869, by French priest Père Armand David, many people believed they were hoaxes— that the dark eye patches and ears had been painted onto the fur.

> **! NEWS FLASH !**
> Giant panda eggs, sperm and tissues are deep-frozen, to help save them in the future.

Flies

▶ Flies have only one pair of proper wings. The hind wings are small stumps called halteres which help a fly balance in flight.

- **Flies** are one of the biggest groups of insects, common nearly everywhere – there are over 90,000 species.

- **Unlike other insects**, flies have only one pair of proper wings.

- **Flies** include bluebottles, black flies, gnats, horseflies, midges, mosquitoes and tsetse flies.

- **A house fly** flies at over 7 km/h – equal to flying 350,000 times its own length in an hour. If a jumbo jet flew at the same speed relative to its length for an hour, it would get almost right around the world.

- **Alaskan flies** can stand being frozen at temperatures of -60°C and still survive.

- **Flies suck up** their food – typically sap from rotting plants and fruit. Houseflies often suck liquids from manure. Blowflies drink from rotting meat.

- **The larvae** (young) of flies are called maggots, and they are tiny, white, wriggling tube-shapes.

- **Flies resemble** or mimic many other kinds of insects. There are wasp flies, beetle flies, ant flies and moth flies.

- **Many species** of fly are carriers of dangerous diseases. When a fly bites or makes contact, it can infect people with some of the germs it carries – especially the flies that suck blood. Mosquitoes spread malaria, and tsetse flies spread sleeping sickness.

> ★ **STAR FACT** ★
> The buzzing of a fly is the sound of its wings beating. Midges beat their wings 1000 times a second.

Perching birds

- **More than half** of all types of birds – over 5000 species – belong to the perching bird group.

- **The perching bird group** is also known as the passerines or *Passeriformes*.

- **The main common feature** of the passerines is that they have feet with three toes pointing forwards and one backwards, to help them cling to a perch.

- **Most perching birds** build neat, small, cup-shaped nests, usually hidden in dense foliage.

- **Most perching birds sing well,** which means they produce sequences of pleasing musical notes.

- **Songbirds**, such as thrushes, warblers and nightingales, are perching birds with especially attractive songs.

- **Usually only male songbirds** sing – and mainly in the mating season, to warn off rivals and attract females.

- **Perching birds** are regarded by experts as the most highly evolved of all birds, with the most complicated, adaptable and 'intelligent' behaviour.

▲ Starlings often gather on overhead cables ready to migrate.

- **The red-billed quelea** of Africa is the world's most abundant bird. There are more than 1500 million of these 'feathered locusts'.

- **The foot of a perching bird** is designed so that the toes clamp around the perch under the bird's weight, with little need for muscle power.

Spiders

- **Spiders** are small scurrying creatures which, unlike insects, have eight legs not six, and bodies with two parts not three.

- **Spiders** belong to a group of 70,000 creatures called arachnids, which also includes scorpions, mites and ticks.

- **Spiders** live in nooks and crannies almost everywhere in the world, especially where there is plenty of vegetation to feed tiny creatures.

- **Spiders are hunters** and most of them feed mainly on insects. Despite their name, bird-eating spiders rarely eat birds, preferring lizards and small rodents such as mice.

▲ *Like all arachnids, spiders have eight legs, plus two 'arms' called pedipalps and a pair of fangs called chelicerae. They also have eight simple eyes.*

★ **STAR FACT** ★
Female black widow spiders eat their mates after mating.

- **Spiders have eight eyes**, but most have poor eyesight and hunt by feeling vibrations with their legs.

- **Many spiders** catch their prey by weaving silken nets called webs. Some webs are simple tubes in holes. Others, called orb webs, are elaborate and round. Spiders' webs are sticky to trap insects.

- **The Australian trapdoor** spider ambushes its prey from a burrow with a camouflaged entrance flap.

- **Most spiders** have a poisonous bite which they use to stun or kill their prey. Tarantulas and sun spiders crush their victims with their powerful jaws.

- **The bite of black widow** and red-back funnel-web spiders is so poisonous that it can kill humans.

Cockles and mussels

- **Cockles and mussels** belong to a group of molluscs called bivalves, which includes oysters, clams, scallops and razorshells.

- **Bivalve** means 'having two valves', and all these creatures have two halves to their shells, joined by a hinge that opens rather like that of a locket.

- **Most bivalves** feed by filtering food out from the water through a tube called a siphon.

- **Cockles** burrow in sand and mud on the seashore. Mussels cling to rocks and breakwaters between the high and low tide marks.

- **Oysters** and some other molluscs line their shells with a hard, shiny, silvery white substance called nacre.

- **When a lump of grit** gets into an oyster shell, it is gradually covered in a ball of nacre, making a pearl.

- **The best pearls** come from the Pinctada pearl oysters that live in the Pacific Ocean. The world's biggest pearl was 12 cm across and weighed 6.4 kg. It came from a giant clam.

- **Scallops** can swim away from danger by opening and shutting their shells rapidly to pump out water. But most bivalves escape danger by shutting themselves up inside their shells.

- **A giant clam** found on the Great Barrier Reef was over 1 m across and weighed more than 0.25 tonnes.

- **There are colonies** of giant clams living many thousands of metres down under the oceans, near hot volcanic vents.

◀ *There are two main kinds of seashell – univalves like these (which are a single shell), and bivalves (which come in two, hinged halves).*

Reptiles and amphibians

- **Reptiles** are scaly-skinned animals which live in many different habitats mainly in warm regions . They include crocodiles, lizards, snakes and tortoises.

- **Reptiles are cold-blooded**, but this does not mean that their blood is cold. A reptile's body cannot keep its blood warm, and it has to control its temperature by moving between hot and cool places.

- **Reptiles bask in the sun** to gain energy to hunt, and are often less active at cooler times of year.

- **A reptile's skin** looks slimy, but it is quite dry. It keeps in moisture so well that reptiles can survive in deserts. The skin often turns darker to absorb the sun's heat.

- **Although reptiles grow** for most of their lives, their skin does not, so they must slough (shed) it every now and then.

- ▶ Like all reptiles, crocodiles rely on basking in the sun to gain energy for hunting. At night, or when it is cold, they usually sleep.

- **Amphibians** are animals that live both on land and in water. They include frogs, toads, newts and salamanders.

- **Most reptiles** lay their eggs on land, but amphibians hatch out in water as tadpoles, from huge clutches of eggs called spawn.

- **Like fish**, tadpoles have gills to breathe in water, but they soon metamorphose (change), growing legs and lungs.

- **Amphibians** never stray far from water.

> ★ STAR FACT ★
> Reptiles were the first large creatures to live entirely on land, over 350 million years ago.

Pets

- **There are over 500 breeds** of domestic dog. All are descended from the wolves first tamed 12,000 years ago to help humans hunt. Dogs have kept some wolf-like traits such as guarding territory and hiding bones.

- **Many pet dogs** were originally working dogs. Collies were sheepdogs. Terriers, setters, pointers and retrievers all get their names from their roles as hunting dogs.

- **One of the lightest dog breeds** is the miniature Yorkshire terrier, under 500 g.

- **Members of the cavy family** of rodents have become popular pets, such as guinea pigs and chinchillas.

- **Chihuahuas** were named after a place in Mexico – the Aztecs thought them sacred.

▲ Powerfully built and strong-jawed, pit bulls were first bred from bulldogs and terriers as fighting dogs, by miners in the 18th century.

- **All pet golden hamsters** are descended from a single litter which was discovered in Syria in 1930.

- **Like their wild ancestors**, domestic cats are deadly hunters – agile, with sharp eyes and claws – and often catch mice and birds.

- **Cats spend** a great deal of time sleeping, in short naps, but can be awake and ready for action in an instance.

- **Tabby cats** get their name from Attab in Baghdad(Irak), where striped silk was made in the Middle Ages.

- **A female cat** is called a queen, a male is a tom, a youngster is a kitten, and a group of cats is called a clowder. A female dog is a bitch, a male is a dog a youngster is a puppy, and a group of dogs is a kennel.

Fleas and lice

- **Fleas and lice** are small wingless insects that live on birds and mammals, including humans. Dogs, cats and rats are especially prone to fleas.

- **Fleas and sucking lice** suck their host's blood.

- **Chewing lice** chew on their host's skin and hair or feathers. Chewing lice do not live on humans.

- **Fleas and lice** are often too small to see easily. But adult fleas grow to over 2 mm long.

- **A flea** can jump 30 cm in the air – the equivalent of a human leaping 200 m in the air.

- **The fleas** in flea circuses perform tricks such as jumping through hoops and pulling wagons.

- **Fleas spread** by jumping from one animal to another, to suck their blood.

> ★ STAR FACT ★
> Fleas jump with a force of 140 g – over 20 times that required to launch a space rocket.

▲ A much-magnified flea with its powerful back legs for jumping.

- **When fleas lay their eggs,** they hatch as larvae and crawl off into the host's bedding, where they spin cocoons and emerge as adults 2 weeks later.

- **Head lice** gum their nits (eggs) to hair and spread from head to head through sharing of combs and hats.

Life in woodlands

- **Woodlands** in temperate zones between the tropics and the Poles are home to many creatures.

- **Deciduous trees** lose their leaves in autumn. Evergreens keep theirs through cold winters.

- **In the leaf litter** under the trees live tiny creatures such as worms, millipedes, and ants and other insects.

▲ On a walk through a deciduous wood, you may be lucky enough to catch a glimpse of a shy young red deer as it crosses a clearing.

- **Spiders, shrews, salamanders and mice** feed on the small creatures in the leaf litter.

- **Some birds,** such as woodcocks, nest on the woodland floor and have mottled plumage to hide themselves.

- **Birds such as owls,** nuthatches, treecreepers, tits, woodpeckers and warblers live on and in trees, as well as insects such as beetles, moths and butterflies, and small mammals such as squirrels and raccoons.

- **Other woodland mammals** include badgers, chipmunks, opossums, stoats, weasels, polecats, pine martens and foxes.

- **Beavers, frogs, muskrats and otters** live near woodland streams.

- **The few large woodland mammals** include bears, deer, wolves and wild boar. Many of these have become rare because woods have been cleared away.

- **In winter,** many birds of deciduous woods migrate south, while small mammals like dormice hibernate.

The cat family

- **Tigers, lions and other** cats make up the family *Felidae*, which is part of the major group of mammals called the *Carnivora*.

- **The cat family** has about 38 species, ranging from massive Siberian tigers to the bay and black-footed cats, which are smaller than most pet cats.

- **There are seven kinds or species** of big cats – tiger, lion, leopard, snow leopard, clouded leopard, jaguar and cheetah.

- **The clouded leopard** is the smallest big cat, weighing only 15–20 kg. It lives in the dense forests of Southern and Southeast Asia. It is also the most arboreal (tree-dwelling) of the big cats.

- **The jaguar is** the only big cat in the Americas, although a large puma (cougar or mountain lion), which is classed as a 'small cat', can be bigger than a small jaguar.

- **The snow leopard** is one of the rarer big cats, weighing about 40–70 kg. It inhabits the high peaks of the Himalayas in Central Asia.

- **Tigers live** in the the forests of Southern and Southeast Asia.

▲ When a tiger roars, the sound can be heard for 4 or 5 kilometres through the forest.

- **Tigers prey on large animals** such as deer, buffalo, antelopes and wild pigs. They hunt silently at night, stalking their prey, then making a sudden bound.

- **The jaguar is one** of the most water-loving of all cats and regularly catches fish, alligators and turtles.

Most tigers have yellow eyes

In between the black stripes, the coat is amber or yellow

▼ Tigers are forest dwellers and can climb trees, but most of the time they like to lie around. On hot days, they will often lie in rivers to cool off and, unusually for a cat, they can swim quite well.

The fur on the throat, belly, and the insides of the legs is whitish

Male tigers usually have a ruff of hair around the face

Carrion-feeding birds

- **Vultures and condors** are the biggest birds of prey, but they mainly feed on dead animals – carrion.

- **There are 2 distinct groups** of carrion-feeding birds. The Old World vultures are part of the main eagle and hawk family, *Accipitridae*.

- **The New World** (American) vultures and condors make up the much smaller family *Cathartidae*.

- **Many vultures are bald**, with no head feathers to mat with blood when digging into corpses.

- **The New World vultures** have nostril holes right through the beak.

- **Vultures and condors** keep an eye on each other's soaring, and if one swoops to a meal, many more follow, from up to 50 km around.

> ★ **STAR FACT** ★
> Some vultures have such weak beaks that their fleshy meal must be rotted into a paste.

▲ *A vulture closes in to feed on a dead animal.*

- **The two condors,** Californian and Andean, are among the rarest of all birds of prey.

- **Carrion-feeding birds** spend hours soaring, scanning the ground for corpses with sharp eyes.

- **The lammergeier** is known as the bearded vulture because it has a beard of black bristles on its chin.

Strange sea creatures

- **Deep-sea anglerfish** live deep down in the ocean where it is pitch black. They lure prey into their mouths using a special fishing-rod-like fin spine with a light at its tip.

- **Anglerfish** cannot find each other easily in the dark, so when a male meets a female he stays with her until mating time.

- **Hatchet fish** have giant eyeballs that point upwards so they see prey from below as silhouettes against the surface.

- **Viperfish** shine in the dark, thousands of metres down, and look like a jet

◀ *If threatened, the dragon fish will try to stab its attacker with its poisonous spines.*

airliner at night, with rows of lights along their bodies.

- **Siphonophores** are colonies of tiny creatures that live in the deep oceans. They string themselves together in lines 20 m long and glow – so they look like fairy lights.

- **The cirrate octopod** looks like a jelly because its skin is 95% water – the water cannot be crushed by the intense pressure of the deep oceans where it lives.

- **The weedy seadragon** of Australia is a seahorse, but it looks just like a piece of flapping seaweed.

- **The sleeper shark** lives in the freezing depths of the North Atlantic and Arctic Oceans. This shark is 6.5 m long, but very slow and sluggish.

- **Flashlight fish** have light organs made by billions of bacteria which shine like headlights. The fish can suddenly block off these lights and change direction in the dark to confuse predators.

- **In the Arab-Israeli War** of 1967 a shoal of flashlight fish was mistaken for enemy frogmen and blown right out of the water.

Baby animals

- **All baby mammals** except monotremes (see strange mammals) are born from their mother's body, but most other creatures hatch from eggs.

- **Most creatures** hatch long after their parents have disappeared. Birds and mammals, though, usually look after their young.

- **Most birds** feed their hungry nestlings until they are big enough to find food themselves.

- **A pair of tits** may make 10,000 trips to the nest to feed their young.

- **Cuckoos** lay their egg in the nest of

▶ Lion cubs are looked after by several females until they are big enough to fend for themselves. Like many babies they have big paws, head and ears for their body.

another, smaller bird. The foster parents hatch it and look after it as it grows. It then pushes its smaller, foster brothers and sisters out of the nest.

- **Mammals nurse** their young (they feed them on the mother's milk). The nursing period varies. It tends to be just a few weeks in small animals like mice, but several years in large animals like elephants.

- **Many animals** play when they are young. Playing helps them develop strength and co-ordination, and practise tasks they will have to do for real when adults.

- **When they are young**, baby opossums cling all over their mother as she moves around.

- **Some baby animals**, including baby shrews and elephants, go around in a long line behind the mother.

Chameleons

- **Chameleons** are 85 species of lizard, most of which live on the island of Madagascar and in mainland Africa.

- **The smallest chameleon**, the dwarf Brookesia, could balance on your little finger. The biggest, Oustalet's chameleon, is the size of a small cat.

- **A chameleon** can look forwards and backwards at the same time, as each of its amazing eyes can swivel in all directions independently of the other.

- **Chameleons** feed on insects and spiders, hunting them in trees by day.

- **A chameleon's tongue** is almost as long as its body, but is normally squashed up inside its mouth.

- **A chameleon shoots** out its tongue in a fraction of a second to trap its victim on a sticky pad at the tip.

- **The chameleon's tongue** is fired out from a special launching bone on its lower jaw.

- **Most lizards** can change colour, but chameleons are experts, changing quickly to all sorts of colours.

▲ Most of a chameleon's bulging eyes are protected by skin.

- **Chameleons change colour** when they are angry or frightened, too cold or too hot, or sick – but they change colour less often to match their surroundings.

- **The colour of the skin** is controlled by pigment cells called melanophores, which change colour as they change size.

Life in cold regions

▲ *Other animals are the only substantial food in the Arctic wastes, so polar bears have to be carnivorous.*

- **The world's coldest places** are at the Poles in the Arctic and Antarctic, and high up mountains.

- **Only small animals** such as ice worms and insects can stand the extreme polar cold all year round.

- **Insects** such as springtails can live in temperatures as low as -38°C in Antarctica, because their body fluids contain substances that do not freeze easily.

- **Birds** such as penguins, snow petrels and skuas live in Antarctica. So do the leopard seals that eat penguins.

- **Polar seas** are home to whales, fish and shrimp-like krill.

- **Fish of cold seas** have body fluids that act like car anti-freeze to stop them freezing.

- **Mammals such as polar bears**, sea lions and walruses are so well insulated against the cold with their fur and fat that they can live on the Arctic ice much of the year.

- **Many animals** live on the icy tundra land in the far north of America and Asia. They include caribou, Arctic foxes and hares, and birds such as ptarmigans and snowy owls.

- **Arctic foxes and hares**, ermines and ptarmigans turn white in winter to camouflage them against the snow.

> ★ STAR FACT ★
> Ptarmigans can survive through the bitter
> Arctic winter by eating twigs.

Starfish and sea urchins

- **Despite their name** starfish are not fish, but belong instead to a group of small sea creatures called echinoderms.

- **Sea urchins** and sea cucumbers are also echinoderms.

- **Starfish** have star-shaped bodies and are predators that prey mostly on shellfish such as scallops and oysters. They have five, strong arms which they use to prise open their victim. The starfish then inserts its stomach into its victim and sucks out its flesh.

- **Under the arms** of a starfish are hundreds of tiny, tube-like 'feet'. Bigger tubes inside the starfish's body pump water in and out of the 'feet', flexing the arms and driving the starfish along.

- **Starfish** often drop some of their arms off to escape an enemy, but the arms eventually grow again.

◄ *Starfish that live in cooler water tend to be brown or yellow, whereas many tropical starfish can be bright red or even blue.*

- **Sea urchins** are ball-shaped creatures. Their shell is covered with bristling spines, which can be poisonous and can be up to 40 cm long in some species.

- **A sea urchin's spines** are used for protection. Urchins also have sucker-like feet for moving.

- **A sea urchin's mouth** is a hole with five teeth, on the underside of its body.

- **Sea cucumbers** have no shell, but a leathery skin and a covering of chalky plates called spicules.

- **When threatened**, a sea cucumber chucks out pieces of its gut as a decoy and swims away. It grows a new one later.

Dragonflies

- **Dragonflies** are big hunting insects with four large transparent wings, and a long slender body that may be a shimmering red, green or blue.

- **Dragonflies have** 30,000 separate lenses in each of their compound eyes, giving them the sharpest vision of any insect.

- **A dragonfly** can see something that is stationary from almost 2 m away, and something moving two to three times farther away.

- **As it swoops** in on its prey, a dragonfly pulls its legs forwards like a basket to scoop up its victim.

- **Dragonflies** often mate in mid-air, and the male may then stay hanging on to the female until she lays her eggs.

> ★ STAR FACT ★
> Dragonflies can reach speeds of almost
> 100 km/h to escape from birds.

- **Dragonfly eggs** are laid in water or in the stem of a water plant, and hatch in 2 to 3 weeks.

- **Newly-hatched dragonflies** are called nymphs and look like fatter, wingless adults.

- **Dragonfly nymphs** are ferocious hunters, often feeding on young fish and tadpoles.

- **Dragonfly nymphs** grow and moult over a period of several years before they climb on to a reed or rock to emerge as an adult.

▶ Dragonflies are big insects even today, but hundreds of millions of years ago, there were dragonflies with wings that were well over 70 cm across.

The owl families

- **The main owl group**, called the order *Strigiformes*, is divided into 2 smaller groups or families.

- **The 13 or so species of barn owls** make up one family, the *Tytonidae*.

- **The common barn owl** is the most widespread owl, on all continents except Antarctica – in fact, it is one of the most widespread of all birds.

- **All other owls** belong to the 'typical owl' family, *Strigidae*.

◀ An owl's big eyes face straight forward to focus on an object. However, owls cannot move their eyes and have to swivel their whole head to look to the side or rear.

- **Owls** are nocturnal and hunt by night, unlike the other main group of hunting birds, the raptors.

- **Small owls** eat mostly insects. Bigger owls eat mice and voles. Eagle owls can catch rabbits and other owls, and even carry away young deer.

- **In the country**, the tawny owl's diet is 90% small mammals, but many now live in towns, where their diet is mainly small birds such as sparrows.

- **The Australian owl** called the boobook is also known as the morepork – both names come from its call.

- **An owl's hearing** is four times as sharp as a cat's, and an owl can pinpoint sounds with astonishing accuracy from the slight difference in the sound levels it receives in each of its ears.

- **Most bird's eyes** look out to the sides, but an owl's huge eyes look straight forward like a human's. This is probably why the owl has been a symbol of wisdom since ancient times.

Poultry

- **Turkeys**, chickens, quail and similar birds are all kinds of poultry – farm birds bred to provide meat, eggs and feathers.

- **Chickens** were first tamed 5000 years ago, and there are now over 500 breeds, including bantams and Rhode Island reds.

- **Female chickens** and turkeys are called hens. Male chickens are called roosters or cockerels. Male turkeys are toms. Baby turkeys are poults.

- **To keep hens laying**, their eggs must be collected daily. If not, the hens will wait until they have a small

◄ Roosters are renowned for their noisy cries every morning as the sun comes up. This harsh cry is called a crow.

clutch of eggs, then try to sit on them to hatch them and raise the chicks.

- **Battery hens** spend their lives crowded into rows of cages called batteries inside buildings.

- **Free-range hens** are allowed to scratch outdoors for insects and seeds.

- **Chickens** raised only for cooking and eating are called broilers.

- **Turkeys** belong to the pheasant group. There are about 12 breeds, but all are descended from the native wild turkey of North America, first tamed by Native Americans 1000 years ago.

- **Turkeys** have a loose fold of bare, floppy skin called a wattle hanging down from the head and neck, and males have a spur on the leg.

> ★ STAR FACT ★
> Champion egg-laying hens produce more than 300 eggs each year.

Strange mammals

- **The duck-billed platypus** and the echidnas live in Australia and are the only monotremes – mammals that lay eggs.

- **Duck-billed platypuses** are strange in other ways, too. They have a snout shaped like a duck's bill and webbed feet, which is why they are so happy in water.

▼ The Tasmanian devil may be small, but can be very fierce.

- **Platypuses hatch** from eggs in a river-bank burrow.

- **Platypus babies** lick the milk that oozes out over the fur of their mother's belly.

- **Echidnas** are also known as spiny anteaters because they are covered in spines and eat ants.

- **After a female echidna** lays her single egg, she keeps it in a pouch on her body until it hatches.

- **The Tasmanian devil** is a small, fierce, Australian marsupial). It hunts at night and eats almost any meat, dead or alive.

- **Tasmanian devils** stuff their victims into their mouth with their front feet.

- **The sugar glider** is a tiny, mouse-like jungle creature which can glide for 45 m between trees.

- **The aardvark** is a strange South African mammal with a long snout and huge claws. It can shovel as fast as a mechanical digger to make a home or find ants.

What is a fish?

- **Fish** are mostly slim, streamlined animals that live in water. Many are covered in tiny shiny plates called scales. Most have bony skeletons and a backbone.

- **There are over 21,000 species** of fish, ranging from the 8 mm-long pygmy goby to the 12 m-long whale shark.

▼ Angling *(catching fish)* is a popular pastime all around the world. The fish is hooked as it bites the lure or bait.

- **Fish** are cold-blooded.

- **Fish breathe** through gills – rows of feathery brushes inside each side of the fish's head.

- **To get oxygen**, fish gulp water in through their mouths and draw it over their gills.

- **Fish** have fins for swimming, not limbs.

- **Most fish** have a pectoral fin behind each gill and two pelvic fins below, as well as a dorsal fin on top of their body, an anal fin beneath, and a caudal (tail) fin.

- **Fish let gas in** and out of their swim bladders to float at particular depths.

- **Some fish** communicate by making sounds with their swim bladder. Catfish use them like bagpipes.

Worms

- **Worms** are long, wriggling, tube-like animals. Annelids are worms such as the earthworm whose bodies are divided into segments.

- **There are 15,000 species** of annelid. Most live underground in tunnels, or in the sea.

- **The world's largest earthworm** is the giant earthworm of South Africa, which can grow up to 6.5 m.

- **Earthworms** spend their lives burrowing through soil. Soil goes in the mouth end, passes through the gut and comes out at the tail end.

- **An earthworm** is both male and female (hermaphrodite), and after two earthworms mate, both develop eggs.

- **Over half the annelid species** are marine (sea) bristleworms, such as ragworms and lugworms. They are named because they are covered in bristles, which they use to paddle over the seabed or dig into the mud.

- **The sea mouse** is a bristleworm with furry hairs.

- **Flatworms** look like ribbons or as though an annelid worm has been ironed flat. Their bodies do not have proper segments. Of the thousands of flatworm species, many live in the sea or in pond algae.

- **Flukes** are flatworms that live as parasites inside other animals. Diseases like bilharzia are caused by flukes.

- **Tapeworms** are parasitic flatworms that live inside their host's gut and eat their food.

▶ Plants would not grow half as well without earthworms to aerate the soil as they burrow in it, mix up the layers and make it more fertile with their droppings.

KEY

Habitats and lifestyles

Hunters and scavengers

Plant eaters

Sea mammals

Rodents and insect-eaters

Primates

Wild pigs and peccaries

- **To obtain fruit** that is out of reach, African bush pigs will lean against fruit trees, making them topple over.

- **The warthog** uses its huge tusks for fighting and impressing other warthogs, not for digging for food – it feeds almost exclusively on grass.

- **The fleshy 'warts'** on a male warthog's face protect its eyes from tusk blows when it is fighting.

- **The largest wild pig,** at over 2 m long, is the African giant forest hog, which weighs in at 275 kg or more.

- **Pigs** were first domesticated at least 7000 years ago in southwest Asia.

- **The babirusa,** or pig-deer, of the Indonesian islands has four tusks, two of which pierce its flesh and grow through the top of its muzzle.

- **Peccaries,** the wild pigs of South America, have complex stomachs for digesting tough plant fibres.

- **Unlike other wild pigs,** peccaries live in herds which includes the adult males.

- **When a herd of peccaries** is attacked by a predator, a single peccary may confront the attacker, allowing the rest of the herd to escape.

> ★ STAR FACT ★
> In 1975, the Chacoan peccary – known only from 10,000 year-old fossils – was found surviving in the forests of western Paraguay.

▲ Agile and powerful, the warthog forages across African woodlands and grasslands, often in family groups.

Bison

- **Hunters** on the Great Plains of North America reduced the number of bison from about 75 million to just a few hundred between about 1800 and 1900.

- **Bison bulls compete** for herd leadership by charging at each other, and have developed enormously thick skulls to withstand the blows.

- **Bison** have such bad tempers that they cannot be trained in captivity.

- **The European bison,** or wisent, browses on forest leaves of oak, willow and elm, unlike its American relations, which graze on grass.

- **Standing up to 2 m high** at the shoulder, the European bison is the continent's largest wild animal.

- **The last truly wild** European bison

▲ Male bison compete mainly by threats, which may develop into full scale battles.

was killed in 1919, but new herds – bred from zoo animals – have been established in reserves, in particular in the Bialowieza Forest in Poland.

- **In the 1800s,** the US Government approved the policy of killing bison in order to starve the Native Americans into submission.

- **The American plains bison** helped preserve the open prairies by eating the tree seedlings.

- **Saved by conservationists,** the American bison survives in small, managed herds in reservations and national parks.

- **Bison groom themselves** by rubbing their heads and bodies against tree trunks, and rolling in the dust.

Sea otters

- **Sea otters** live in the northeastern Pacific. They rarely come ashore, and sleep floating on their backs, wrapped in kelp seaweed to stop them drifting away.

- **The sea otter's thick fur** – the densest of any mammal in the world – keeps it warm in cold waters.

- **The heaviest** of all otters, the sea otter weighs up to 45 kg and reaches up to 1.4 m from nose to tail.

- **To maintain warmth and energy**, the sea otter eats up to 30% of its total weight each day, diving repeatedly for shellfish, sea urchins and octopi.

- **The sea otter** was the most recent mammal to evolve from a life on land to one in the sea.

- **In the 1700s and 1800s,** sea otters were hunted almost to extinction for their valuable fur, which was known as 'soft gold'.

- **To crack open shells,** the sea otter lies on its back and balances a rock on its stomach, using it like an anvil.

- **Sea otters** sleep, socialize and give birth on kelp beds.

- **Unique among otters**, sea otters can extend and contract the claws of their front feet, like a cat.

- **People have seen** sea otters bite open old drinks cans from the sea bed to get at octopi hiding inside.

▶ The sea otter uses both its front paws to hold food while floating on its back.

Porcupines

- **When threatened**, some African porcupines erect their detachable quills and run backwards at their enemy.

- **African crested porcupines** warn off would-be predators by vigorously shaking their tail quills, producing a sound like the rattle of a rattlesnake.

- **The North American porcupine** has very poor eyesight.

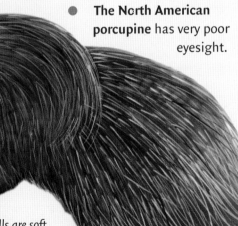

▲ A porcupine's quills are soft when it is born, but harden within a few hours.

★ STAR FACT ★
Some porcupines collect bones, which they gnaw on to sharpen their teeth. The bones provide them with phosphate.

- **Crested porcupines** are the longest lived of all rodents, the record being over 27 years.

- **American porcupines** are particularly vulnerable to attacks by fisher martens, which turn them over onto their backs to kill them, thus avoiding the quills.

- **The prehensile-tailed porcupines** of South America are active at night, and move to a new tree every 24 hours.

- **Baby porcupines** are born with soft quills to make the birth easier. Within a few hours the quills harden.

- **Some North American porcupines** have a craving for salt, and have been known to gnaw gloves, boots and saddles that are salty with sweat.

- **Old World porcupines** are not tree-climbers.

Reindeer and caribou

- **Reindeer** (Europe and Asia) and caribou (North America) are basically the same animal.

- **Reindeer** were probably first tamed in the 5th century AD by hunters, who used them as decoys when hunting wild reindeer.

- **The broad hoofs** of reindeer and caribou help them to walk on snow.

- **In 1984**, 10,000 migrating caribou drowned in Canada when dam sluices were opened.

- **Reindeer** have a well developed homing instinct, and can find their way even in blinding snowstorms.

- **Reindeer bulls fight with their feet** and rarely with their antlers, which could become locked together, leading to the starvation of both animals.

- **Reindeer are the best swimmers** of the deer family, due to the buoyancy of the hollow hairs of their coats.

- **Unlike other deer**, a reindeer's muzzle is covered in hair to help it forage in snow.

- **Reindeer dig** through the snow with their feet to find food.

> ★ STAR FACT ★
> The name 'caribou' means 'shoveller' in the language of one Canadian Indian people.

▲ Caribou bulls rarely fight with their antlers, preferring to use their feet.

Sloths

- **The sloths of South America** have a variable body temperature, and each morning need to bask in the sun above the forest canopy.

- **The sloth** has the most neck vertebrae of any mammal, and can look forwards when upside down.

- **Sloths even mate** and give birth while hanging upside down by their powerful, curved claws.

- **Sloths' fur** grows in the opposite direction to that of most mammals, pointing towards the ground so the rain runs off the body.

◄ The mother sloth carries her infant for up to 9 months on her belly, where it feeds on the leaves it can reach.

- **A sloth's large stomach** is divided into many compartments; the food inside can account for up to a third of the animal's weight.

- **A meal of leaves** may be retained in a sloth's digestive system for over a month.

- **The main predator** of the sloth is the harpy eagle.

- **Algae** grows in the grooves on a sloth's fur, helping to camouflage it in the forest greenery.

- **Sloths** have an amazing ability to heal themselves, and their wounds rarely become infected.

- **On land**, sloths can only move in an awkward, spread-eagled crawl, impeded by their curved claws.

Walruses

- **A single walrus tusk** can measure up to 1 m long and weigh 5.4 kg.

- **Walruses swim** by sweeping their huge rear flippers from side to side, each one opening in turn like a 1 m wide fan.

- **The walrus is protected from the cold** by a thick layer of blubber – a third of its total weight.

- **In the summer**, basking walruses turn a deep pink as their blood vessels dilate to radiate heat away from the body.

- **Walruses** excavate shellfish from seabed mud by squirting a high-pressure blast of water from their mouths.

- **The walrus has 300 whiskers** on each side of its moustache,

★ STAR FACT ★
Walrus pups are born 15 months after the parents have mated – 4–5 months pass before the egg starts to grow in the mother's womb.

which it uses to help it find food in murky waters.

- **A walrus uses its long tusks** to help it clamber onto ice floes – its scientific name, *Odobenus*, means 'tooth walker'.

- **In water**, a walrus turns a pale grey colour as blood leaves its skin to maintain the temperature of its body core.

- **A walrus can eat** 3,000 clams in one day.

◄ *Walruses are very sociable, and like to gather in huge groups on coastal ice or rocks.*

What are mammals?

- **Humans feel close to mammals** because they, too, are mammals, with hairy bodies, a large brain and special mammary glands for feeding their young with milk.

- **There are about 4500 species of mammals** in the world (and at least 1 million insect species!).

- **All mammals** except the duckbilled platytpus and spiny anteater give birth to live young.

- **Mammals** evolved from reptiles, but are warm blooded.

- **The two main mammal groups** are the marsupials (whose young develop in the mother's pouch) and placentals.

- **All mammals** have three little bones in their ears that transfer sound vibrations to the inner ear from the eardrum.

- **Mammals** have a variety of teeth shapes:

chisels for gnawing, long fangs for fighting and killing prey, sharp-edged slicers and flat-topped crushers.

- **The platypus and spiny anteater** are egg-laying mammals called monotremes.

- **Mammals** have a palate that enables them to breathe through their noses while chewing.

- **Mammals** give a level of maternal care beyond that of other animals.

▶ *Young mammals mature more slowly than other animal young, so they are looked after for longer.*

Tigers

- **At over 3 m long** and weighing up to 360 kg, the rare Siberian tiger is the largest living member of the cat family. Tigers originated in Siberia.

- **Tigers need a very large hunting area**, and males in northern India often patrol an area of 130 sq km or more.

- **After feeding**, tigers sometimes save the remains of a kill for a later meal, burying it under branches to hide it from scavengers or other tigers.

- **In 1945** there were only 50 Siberian tigers left in the wild; now there are 300 to 400 surviving in reserves.

- **Aggressive tigers** flash the distinctive white spots on their ears as a warning.

- **In India and Bangaladesh**, in the Sunderbans mangrove swamps, tigers keep cool in the water and ambush pigs, deer and monkeys.

- **In the early 1900s** there were probably at least 50,000 tigers; now numbers have fallen to 6000 or less, half of them living in India.

- **A tiger's stripes** camouflage it as it hunts in the tall grasses by day. But tigers also hunt at night – their night vision is at least 6 times more acute than a human's.

- **Tiger cubs** depend entirely on their mothers for food until they are about 18 months old, when they begin to make their own first kills.

◀ The tiger uses its long canine teeth to bite the throat or neck of its prey as it brings it to the ground. Its sharp-edged rear teeth cut through the meat by sliding against each other like the blades of scissors.

> ★ **STAR FACT** ★
> Tigers eat a variety of foods, ranging from fish and turtles during times of flood to locusts during locust swarms.

Huge muscles in the front legs are used for holding and killing prey

Binocular vision allows the tiger accurately to judge distance

Long rear legs help tigers to leap

◀ To keep out the cold, the Siberian tiger has an outer coat of long, pale fur over a thick undercoat

Orang-utans

- **Orang-utans** spend much more time in trees than the other great apes, and are the largest tree-dwelling mammals in the world.

- **Insatiable eaters**, orang-utans can spend an entire day feasting in one heavily laden fruit tree.

- **The name 'orang-utan'** means 'man of the forest' in the language of the local tribespeople of Southeast Asia.

- **A mature male orang-utan** makes his presence known to other orang-utans by breaking branches, bellowing and groaning. Local legends explain this as a sign of the ape's grief over losing a human bride.

- **In Sumatra**, the major predators of orang-utans are tigers at ground

▲ Orang-utans are slow breeders, and may only give birth to three or four babies in a lifetime.

level, and clouded leopards in trees.

- **Once found all over Southeast Asia**, orang-utans now live only in tropical Borneo and Sumatra.

- **Like chimpanzees**, orang-utans use sticks as tools to retrieve food from crevices and to scratch themselves.

- **Male orang-utans** have large air sacs that extend from their throats, under their arms and over their shoulders, and increase the loudness and range of their calls.

- **To help her young** move from tree to tree, a mother orang-utan pulls the branches of two trees closer together and makes a bridge with her body.

- **Orang-utans make a nest** at night, building a roof to keep off the rain.

Beavers

- **Beavers** are born with innate dam-building instincts. In zoos, they regularly 'repair' concrete dams with twigs.

- **It takes two adult beavers** about 15 minutes to gnaw their way through a tree-trunk with a 10 cm diameter.

- **Mother beavers** push tired youngsters ahead of them through the water, like swimming floats.

▼ The beaver uses its huge incisor teeth to gnaw through branches and tree trunks.

★ STAR FACT ★
European beavers took to living in burrows to avoid hunters. They are now protected by law.

- **Storing extra oxygen** in its lungs and body tissues, a beaver can remain under water for up to 15 minutes.

- **Beavers use the split claws** on their hind feet for grooming and spreading waterproof oil.

- **A beaver signals danger** by smacking the water with its tail. The noise carries over 1 km.

- **The territory-marking secretion** of the beaver contains the main ingredient in aspirin.

- **Beavers' dams** and lodges can help create environments for fish.

- **In some parts of the USA**, beavers are parachute-dropped into areas where remote rivers need damming to reduce erosion.

Aardvarks

- **When in danger**, the aardvark can dig at great speed, and can outpace a team of men armed with spades.

- **An aardvark** has several burrows on its territory, often many kilometres apart.

- **Termites and ants** form the main food of the aardvark, which digs through concrete-hard termite mounds to reach them.

- **To stop termites and dust** entering its nose, the aardvark has stiff bristles on its muzzle, and can close its nostrils.

- **A moderate blow to the head** can kill an aardvark, which depends on its acute senses and digging abilities for survival.

- **If attacked** before it has time to burrow, the aardvark may roll onto its back and lash out with all four feet at once.

- **The aardvark swallows** its food without chewing, grinding it

★ **STAR FACT** ★

'Aardvark' is Afrikaans for 'earth-pig' (but in fact aardvarks do not belong to the pig family).

up in its stomach using special muscles.

- **Baby aardvarks** depend on their mothers for about 6 months, when they learn to dig burrows.

- **Some African peoples** who also eat termites keep an aardvark claw as a charm to increase the harvest.

◀ *The aardvark usually feeds at night, eating termites in the wet season and ants in the dry season.*

Giraffes and okapis

- **The giraffe's black tongue** is almost 0.5 m long. It uses it to grip vegetation and pull it into its mouth.

- **The giraffe is the world's tallest animal** – some males reach up to 6 m in height.

- **Male giraffes stretch** up to reach leaves high in the trees, while females bend their necks to take lower leaves, thus reducing food competition.

- **Bony growths** on a male giraffe's

▶ *A giraffe's front legs are longer than its rear legs.*

skull continue to grow all its life, making its skull up to 3 times heavier than a female's.

- **The extraordinarily long necks** of giraffes have only 7 neck vertebrae, just like other mammals, but they are greatly elongated.

- **From a few weeks old**, young giraffes spend much of their time in a 'crèche', looked after by a pair of adults.

- **Female giraffes with calves** have been seen to beat severely and drive off attacking lions, using their hoofs, necks and heads as weapons.

- **To reach water**, giraffes have to spread their front legs wide apart. Special valves stop the blood rushing to and from their heads as they raise and lower them.

- **Okapis**, which are related to giraffes, closely resemble fossils of the giraffe's most recent ancestor, *Paleotragus*, from about 12 million years ago.

- **Okapis live so deep in the forests** of the Congo that they were not discovered by Europeans until the 1900s.

Wild dogs

- **The South American bush dog** pursues prey into the water, and, unlike most dogs, can swim underwater.

- **African Cape hunting dogs** live in packs in which only the dominant female has young.

- **Cape hunting dog cubs** are left in the den, protected by adult guardians, while the pack hunts, and are fed with disgorged meat when it returns.

- **Cape hunting dogs** do not creep up on prey, but approach a herd openly, selecting a single target to chase.

- **Cape hunting dogs** can run at 60 km/h for 5 km or more. They may travel 50 km a day while

▶ *Cape hunting dogs are well camouflaged; no two individuals have the same markings.*

★ STAR FACT ★
Cape hunting dog females may fight over possession of their puppies, often killing them.

hunting, and patrol a range of 1500 to 2000 sq km.

- **Indian wild dogs**, or dholes, hunt in packs of up to 30, and can drive tigers and leopards from their kills.

- **Dholes** hunt in thick undergrowth, advancing in an extended line until they have flushed out their prey.

- **The raccoon dog** of east Asia eats insects, shellfish and fruit.

- **Australian dingoes** are probably descended from Indian wolves that were domesticated in Asia and taken by Aboriginal settlers to Australia, where they reverted to the wild.

The first mammals

- **Before true mammals emerged,** some reptiles, such as the dog-like Cynodonts, had developed mammalian characteristics such as hair and specialized teeth.

- **The mammary glands** with which mammals suckle their young evolved from sweat glands – some mammal-like reptiles may have exuded a sort of milk from sweat glands for their young.

- **The earliest true mammals** appeared more than 210 million years ago and were only 15 cm long.

- **One of the best-known** of the earliest fossil mammals was an insect-eater named *Megazostrodon*. The size of a modern shrew, it hunted insects at night.

- **A major difference** between mammals and reptiles was the development of the little bones linking the eardrum and inner ear, found only in mammals.

- **In the age of the dinosaurs,** which lasted

▶ *The tiny Megazostrodon kept well hidden from predatory reptiles, and was active at night.*

★ STAR FACT ★
Within 10 million years of the extinction of the dinosaurs, most modern mammal orders, including horses and primates, had appeared.

some 160 million years, mammals stayed very small.

- **All known mammal fossils** from 210 to 66 million years ago would fit into a normal-sized bucket!

- **By the time the dinosaurs became extinct** about 65 million years ago, marsupials, placentals and monotremes had all evolved.

- **Fossils of very early mammals** came from Europe, South Africa and China.

Desert life

- **The American kangaroo rat** may never take a drink of water in its life! It derives moisture from its food and by recycling its breath.

- **Prairie dogs** have air-conditioned homes – the air in their tunnels is renewed every 10 minutes by the suction effect of the entrances being at different heights.

- **Desert ground squirrels** have hair on the pads of their feet to insulate them from burning hot sand.

- **Desert bighorn sheep** can let their daytime temperatures rise from 36.8°C to 40°C, re-radiating the excess heat at night.

- **Some desert-dwelling badgers and sheep** have a fatty layer that

▲ Living on dry plains, prairie dogs may inhabit extensive tunnel-and-nest 'towns' that cover up to 65 hectares.

insulates their internal organs from external heat.

- **The Australian fat-tailed mouse** has a carrot-shaped tail that stores fat, which it lives off during droughts.

- **Most desert mammals** rest in shade or burrows by day, emerging to seek food in the cool of night.

- **Collared peccaries**, or javelinas, are American desert pigs. In times of drought they eat cacti, spines and all.

- **The burrowing** Australian bilby licks seeds from the desert surface, and its dung pellets are up to 90% sand.

- **The long legs** of the Arabian camel raise its body to a height where air temperatures are up to 25°C cooler than ground temperatures.

Sheep and goats

- **Despite their massive curled horns,** American bighorn rams fight predators with their feet.

- **The musk ox** of the Arctic tundra is more closely related to sheep and goats than to bison or oxen.

- **Sheep and goats** were domesticated as early as 7500 BC.

- **When young sheep and goats play,** they often leap onto their mothers' backs, practising for mountain life among the rocks.

- **Goats and sheep** have scent glands on their feet that mark mountain trails, helping herds stay together.

◄ Most domestic sheep have adapted to a life of migratory grazing, moving on as the grass is cropped.

- **Bighorn rams** only fight with one another if their horns are of a similar size, ignoring larger or smaller rivals.

- **Avalanches** are the main threat to Rocky Mountain goats.

- **Of the two,** only sheep have scent glands on their faces, and only male goats have beards and a strong odour.

- **Central Asian argalis** are the largest Eurasian wild sheep, weighing up to 200 kg.

- **In a fight,** a European chamois may feign death to avoid being killed, lying flat with its neck outstretched.

▲ Both wild and domestic male goats sport distinctive beards.

Horses and asses

- **The earliest-known ancestor** of the horse, *Hyracotherium*, lived 50 million years ago, and was a forest dweller the size of a small dog.

- **Horses' earliest ancestors** evolved in America, and crossed land bridges to Asia and Europe, eventually becoming extinct in America.

- **A mule** is the offspring of a male ass and a female horse, while the rarer offspring of a male horse and female ass is called a hinny. Both mules and hinnies are unable to produce young.

- **Horses have very strong homing instincts**, and have been known to wander hundreds of kilometres to return to the place of their birth.

- **The domestic horse** is the only member of the horse family in which the mane falls to the side – in all others, including asses and zebras, it stands erect.

- **Horses' eyes** are set high in the head and far apart, giving almost all round vision. They can focus on near and far objects at the same time.

> ★ **STAR FACT** ★
> Horses were domesticated about 6000 years ago in Europe and Asia, mainly for their meat. They became transport animals from about 2000 BC.

- **The horse's large eyes** give it excellent night vision – almost as keen as that of owls.

- **Most horses sleep standing up** during the day, and at night sleep on the ground with their legs gathered under their bodies.

- **The earliest horses** had four toes per foot. These reduced as the horse moved from a forest to a plains life, and the modern horse has just a single toe.

▼ *The donkey evolved from African ass ancestors, and is capable of carrying heavy loads. All wild asses are desert dwellers, able to flourish on sparse vegetation, and survive burning hot days and icy cold nights.*

▼ *By nature horses are herd animals. In the wild a herd usually consists of one dominant stallion, accompanied by a number of mares and their young.*

Tasmanian wolf

- **The Tasmanian wolf, or thylacine,** was a meat-eating Australian marsupial that probably became extinct when the last known one died in captivity in 1936.

- **Once common** throughout Australia and New Guinea, the Tasmanian wolf retreated to Tasmania some 3000 years ago, driven out by dingoes.

- **The Tasmanian wolf** had a pouch that opened to the rear, where the young spent their first 3 months.

- **Also called the Tasmanian tiger**, because of its stripes, the Tasmanian wolf was in fact neither a wolf nor a tiger.

- **Like a kangaroo,** the Tasmanian wolf had a thick-based tail and would hop on its back legs if chased.

- **The jaws** of the Tasmanian wolf opened almost 180°, allowing it to kill an animal by crushing its skull.

- **With its immensely powerful jaws,** the Tasmanian wolf could kill a pursuing hunting dog with one bite.

- **Fossil remains** of an animal almost identical to the Tasmanian wolf were discovered in America.

- **Tasmanian wolves** may survive in the dense forest, but this remains to be proved.

> ★ **STAR FACT** ★
> Thousands of Tasmanian wolves were killed in the late 1800s, because they preyed on sheep.

▶ Some people claim to have seen Tasmanian wolves still surviving in remote parts of Tasmania.

What are rodents?

▼ The South American chinchilla has been hunted almost to extinction for its dense, soft fur, and is now sometimes raised on fur farms.

- **Rodents,** which include mice, squirrels, beavers, porcupines and guinea pigs, have two incisor teeth in each jaw that never stop growing.

- **If a rodent's teeth** are not constantly worn down by gnawing, they can curve round into the animal's skull and kill it – the name 'rodent' means 'gnawer'.

- **Some 40% of all mammal species are rodents.** They range in size from the 1.4-m long capybara to the Baluchistan pygmy jerboa, at 4.7 cm (body length).

- **The earliest-known rodents** appeared in 57-million-year-old fossil beds in both Asia and North America.

- **The house mouse** and the brown rat occur more widely than any land mammal excepts humans, and are found in all continents, including Antartica.

- **Guinea pigs** in South America and edible dormice in Europe have both been bred to be eaten by humans.

- **Female Norway lemmings** can begin to breed when only 14 days old.

- **The fastest rodents** over the ground may be kangaroo mice and jerboas, which can bound along on their hind legs at speeds of up to 48 km/h.

- **In the Miocene period** (23 to 5 million years ago), some South American rodents were the size of rhinos!

- **A female house mouse** can produce 14 litters a year.

Hippopotami

- **The lips of hippos** are up to 0.5 m wide, and contain strong muscles for grazing on short grasses.

- **Hippos feed** for 5 hours a night, and spend the next 19 hours resting in the water.

- **Hippos suckle** their young underwater and often sleep submerged, surfacing regularly to breath whilst still unconscious.

- **A pygmy hippo** is born on land in just 2 minutes, and has to be taught how to swim.

- **In dry air** the pygmy hippo loses water by evaporation at about 5 times the rate of human water loss.

- **Hippos travel** up to 30 km at night in search of food, but if frightened will run back to water to hide.

- **Hippos** are probably Africa's most dangerous animal. They kill a large number of humans each year.

- **Bull hippos** mark their territory by scattering dung with their whirling tails.

- **Aggressive hippos** warn off other hippos by opening their jaws to display their formidable tusks. They regularly fight to the death.

- **Male hippos** can weigh as much as 3200 kg.

▶ The male hippo can be extremely aggressive, opening its huge mouth wide and displaying its tusks as a warning to other males.

Rabbits and hares

- **Hares are born with fur**, with their eyes open; rabbits are born naked, with eyes shut.

- **Mother hares** visit their young for just 5 minutes a day to feed them on their rich milk.

- **Snowshoe hares** have broad, hairy hind feet for moving over snow.

- **If a hare** sees it is being stalked by a fox, it stands up to put the fox off a chase (which the hare would win).

- **The pikas** of Asia and western America 'sing' loudly.

- **Rabbits' incisors** grow constantly.

◀ Hares, like rabbits, can close and open their slit-like nostrils at will.

★ **STAR FACT** ★
Numbers of American snowshoe hares rise and fall in an 8-11 year cycle, affecting the numbers of lynxes, which depend on them as food.

- **Both sexes of hares 'box'** as part of the mating ritual.

- **Hares can reach speeds** of up to 60 km/h when running flat out.

- **Large-eared pika** is one of the highest-living mammal in the world, inhabiting mountain ranges in Asia at altitudes up to 6130 m.

▶ The snowshoe hare's large eyes help it see during dusk and after dark, when it is most active.

Elephants

- **The name 'elephant'** means 'visible from afar'.

- **Elephants communicate** over great distances by making low frequency sounds (too low for humans to hear).

- **War elephants** were used by the Carthaginian general Hannibal against the Romans in the 3rd century BC, and by the Romans invading Britain in the 1st century AD.

- **Elephants sometimes enter caves** to excavate minerals such as sodium, needed as a supplement to their diet.

- **Elephants** spend up to 18 hours a day feeding.

> ★ **STAR FACT** ★
> Stone Age rock paintings in North Africa show that elephants once lived in the Sahara region, before it became desert.

▲ *An elephant's trunk is a combination of upper lip and nose, and is used to place food into its mouth. It also doubles as a hose, squirting water down its throat and acting as a shower spray.*

▶ *The elephant's large ears help it to control its temperature, as well as aiding its acute sense of hearing. Movements of the ears are used to convey body language.*

- **Elephants are good swimmers** – some Asian elephants have been seen to swim non-stop for as much as 10 km.

- **Asian elephants** are the world's longest-lived mammals after humans, and can live to be over 70 years.

- **An African elephant** needs to eat up to 6% of its bodyweight each day – 300 kg for a 5000 kg bull!

- **An elephant uses 4 grinding teeth** at any one time, and these are replaced as they wear out - it can get through 24 molars in its lifetime.

Cheetahs

- **Unlike most cats**, cheetahs can hardly retract their claws at all. The claws grip the ground as they run, like the spikes on a sprinter's shoes.

- **A cheetah can accelerate** from 0 to 72 km/h in 2 seconds, and can reach a top speed of 120 km/h.

- **A silver vase** (c.2300 BC), found in the Caucasus, shows a cheetah in a collar, which suggests people used cheetahs then as hunting animals.

- **The 16th-century Mogul emperor Akbar** kept 1000 cheetahs, which he used to hunt blackbuck.

- **Cheetahs** have the same body length as leopards, but stand a good 35 cm taller on their long legs.

- **In the Kalahari Desert**, cheetahs can survive for 10 days without water by eating wild melons.

- **Young male cheetahs** often hunt in small groups

▶ *Cheetahs often sit on rocks or termite mounds to get a better all-round view when resting.*

(coalitions), and are healthier than solitary males.

- **A cheetah will chase a warthog** that runs, but will usually leave one that stands its ground.

- **If a cheetah does not catch its prey** in the first 300 to 400 m of the chase, it gives up and allows its heart-beat to return to normal.

- **Cheetahs avoid lions**, which will kill them.

Gorillas

▲ *The male gorilla is far larger than the female, and is the largest of all the primates – big silverbacks can weigh as much as 200 kg.*

- **Male gorillas walk on four limbs** most of the time, but will run on two legs for short distances, beating their chests, when showing off.

- **Adult gorillas** sleep in a new nest every night.

- **The mature male leader** of a gorilla group is called a

'silverback', after the saddle of white hair on its back.

- **Young male gorillas** form their own groups by kidnapping females from other groups.

- **Mountain gorillas** spend almost all their lives at 2800 to 3400 m above sea level, in damp, cloudy conditions.

- **Some gorillas supplement their plant diet** by eating handfuls of potassium- and calcium-rich soil.

- **If a gorilla cannot keep up** with the group because of a wound, the silverback slows down so it is not left behind.

- **When aggressive male gorillas** beat their chests and mock-charge one another, they give off an armpit odour powerful enough to be detected 25 m away by humans.

- **Despite their huge strength**, silverbacks are gentle with their offspring, allowing them to play on their backs.

> ★ **STAR FACT** ★
> The 'nose-prints' of gorillas are as distinctive as human fingerprints – no two are identical.

Squirrels

- **Grey squirrels** have been known to kill and eat rabbits, rats, cockerels and stoats.

- **Flying squirrels** are nocturnal, and when gliding may emit high-pitched squeaks that help them to locate a landing place.

- **North American red squirrels** tap birch and maple trees for their sweet sap in spring.

- **Many squirrel species** spread woodland trees by burying nuts and then forgetting where they put them.

- **The North American red squirrel**, or chicaree, buries green pine cones in damp soil to delay their ripening until they are needed.

- **The largest member of the squirrel family** is the alpine marmot, at 73 cm long not including the tail.

- **Southeast Asian giant squirrels** prefer to hang upside down by their hind feet while eating.

- **Chipmunks**, or ground squirrels, store huge quantities of nuts in a single cache.

- **To prevent it slipping backwards** down a tree trunk, the scaly-tailed flying squirrel presses the horny scales of its tail against the trunk.

- **An adult red squirrel** can sniff out a pine cone buried 30 cm deep.

◄ The red squirrel uses its bushy tail to help him balance when running along branches.

Mammal senses

- **Cheetahs** have a band of light-sensitive nerve cells across their retinas that give clear vision ahead and to the sides.

- **Desert mammals** such as the long-eared kit fox find sharp hearing more useful than a keen sense of smell in the dry air.

- **Polar bears can smell** seals up to 60 km away across the ice.

- **Cats have glands** between their toes that leave an identifying scent when they scratch trees.

- **Blue whales and fin whales** communicate by means of the loudest sounds produced by any living creature (up to 188 dB).

- **Baby wood-mice** emit ultrasonic distress calls in their first 10 days to summon their mother.

- **Many nocturnal mammals** have reflective areas in their eyes that help night vision.

- **Migrating whales** can sense the Earth's magnetic field, due to particles of the mineral magnetite in their bodies.

- **The exceptionally large ears** of fennec foxes can detect the sound of termites chewing beneath the ground.

- **Skunks use a powerful scent weapon** to deter their enemies.

◄ Large cats have eyes on the front of their heads rather than at the sides, helping them to focus on their prey as they hunt.

Rhinoceroses

- **The Sumatran rhino** is a relative of the woolly rhinoceros of the last Ice Age, and has reddish fur.

- **When black rhinos** are fleeing, the calf follows the mother, but when white rhinos are in flight, the mother runs behind the calf.

- **African ox-birds** ride aboard rhinos, cleaning out ticks from the folds in their hides.

- **Despite weighing 2 tonnes** or more, the rhino can run at 50 km/h, and make a 180° turn within its own body length.

- **If two rhinos feel threatened**, they stand back to back, confronting their enemies from different directions.

▶ The rhino has excellent hearing.

- **Rhinos can be heard** munching on plants from a distance of 400 m.

- **The upper lips** of the African white rhino are square, for grazing on grass; those of the African black rhino are pointed, for plucking leaves.

- **Rhinos have poor eyesight**, and cannot locate a motionless object further than 30 m away.

- **A prehistoric relative** of the rhinoceros, *Indricotherium*, stood 5.4 m tall and weighed 20 tonnes.

- **Thicker skin** on a rhino's flanks protect it from horn wounds from rivals.

Seals

- **When chasing penguins**, the leopard seal can leap 2 m high from the sea onto an ice floe.

- **Male southern elephant seals**, which weigh up to 3500 kg, have inflatable snouts used to impress females during mating displays.

- **In the 4 days after being born**, hooded seal pups double their weight from 25 kg to 50 kg.

- **The elephant seal** can dive as deep as 1500 m, and can stay under water for 1–2 hours.

- **Leopard seals** are the only seals known to make unprovoked attacks on humans, lunging through ice to get at their feet.

- **Seals can sleep** floating vertically in the water just beneath the surface,

★ STAR FACT ★
The world's largest mammal herd consists of up to 1.5 million northern fur seals, which breed on two islands in the Pacific sub-Arctic region.

rising occasionally to breathe through their nostrils.

- **When a seal dives deep**, its heartbeat slows from 55–120 beats per minute to 4–15 beats per min.

- **Crab-eater seals** have special teeth that they use like strainers to catch the shrimp-like krill on which they feed.

- **The fur seals** of the North Pacific spend up to 8 months of the year continuously at sea, feeding.

◀ The spotted seal frequents the icy waters of the North Pacific and Arctic Ocean.

Old World camels

- **Single-humped dromedaries** and twin-humped Bactrian camels can go for months without food and water, living on the fat in their humps.

- **A female dromedary** can produce 6 litres of milk a day for 9 to 18 months – the staple food for some camel-herding peoples.

- **After not drinking for many months**, a camel can drink up to 130 litres in just a few minutes.

- **Unlike other mammals**, camels have oval instead of round blood-cells. These prevent their blood thickening as their body temperature rises.

- **Evolving originally in North America**, some camel ancestors crossed land bridges to Asia to become today's Bactrian camels and dromedaries.

- **Introduced to Australia** as desert transport animals, dromedaries reverted to the wild there.

- **Domesticated in Arabia** some 6000 years ago, the dromedary, or Arabian camel, ceased to exist in

▼ A camel's average laden speed is 3–8 km/h, which it can maintain for up to 18 hours without rest.

the wild about 2000 years ago.

- **Camels do sweat**, but not until their body temperature has reached 40.5°C.

- **In the annual King's Camel Race** in Saudi Arabia, some 3000 camels are raced over a 23 km course.

- **Only about 1000** wild Bactrian camels survive, in Mongolia's Gobi Desert.

Otters

◄ The otter's coat is made up of a dense layer of underfur, with an outer layer of long guard hairs.

- **Otters enjoy playing** games, such as dropping pebbles into water and catching them on their heads!

- **The African clawless otter** can move its thumb across the other fingers to hold onto objects.

- **Clawless otters** gather tough-shelled freshwater mussels with their hands, and take them ashore to smash them on rocks.

- **When hunted by hounds**, otters have been known to

> ★ **STAR FACT** ★
> The Giant otter of Brazil is the longest of the otter family, at almost 2 m long .

drag their pursuers under water and drown them.

- **Otters have special whiskers** on their muzzles and elbows that are sensitive to water disturbances and help them to locate prey.

- **Giant otters** clear a series of 7 m wide areas around their territories before scent-marking them.

- **The male Eurasian otter** patrols a territory of up to 50 km of river bank; the female's territory is about 10 km.

- **The marine otter** of the west coast of South America is the smallest sea mammal in the world, weighing no more than 4.5 kg.

- **Some otters**, including the Cape clawless otter and the Oriental short-clawed otter, catch their prey in their paws rather than in their mouths.

Hibernation and dormancy

- **The hibernating dormouse** does not attract the attention of predators because its body temperature is so low that it gives off no body odour.

- **The core body temperature** of some hibernating bats falls below freezing – in some cases as low as -5°C – without harming them.

- **Bears are not true hibernators**, but have a moderately reduced body temperature during their winter sleep, offset by the huge amounts of food that they eat before going to sleep.

- **The raccoon dog** is the only member of the dog family to hibernate.

- **The Eastern European dormouse** and the Canadian woodchuck may spend as much as 9 months of the year in hibernation.

- **Hibernators** such as ground squirrels have internal clocks that cause them to go into hibernation at the usual time of year, even if they are kept in warm conditions with plenty of food.

★ STAR FACT ★
Hibernating mammals wake up by shivering violently, creating heat that passes to the brain, the vital organs and the rest of the body.

- **A hibernating bat's breathing rate** falls from about 200 breaths per minute to between 25 and 30 a minute for 3 minutes, followed by an 8 minute no-breathing break.

- **Alaskan ground squirrels**, born at the end of June, start to dig burrows 22 days later, and feed, fatten up and begin to hibernate by the end of August.

- **Brown fat,** found in high levels in hibernating mammals, creates heat as the temperature falls.

▼ *Many bat species are true hibernators, as is the dormouse, which may hibernate for up to 9 months, and the hedgehog, which usually sleeps through the winter. The grey squirrel is not a true hibernator, but is only active briefly on cold winter days. Eurasian badgers also become lethargic during cold spells.*

Bats

Grey squirrel

Dormouse

Eurasian badgers

Hedgehog

Monotremes

- **Monotremes** are egg-laying mammals. There are only two groups: the duckbilled platypus of Australia and the echidna, or spiny anteater, of Australia and New Guinea.

- **If harassed** on soft ground by a predator, the echidna digs down until only an area of spines is showing.

- **The platypus** is the only known mammal to detect the electric fields of its prey by means of electro-receptors in its muzzle.

- **Hunting underwater** with eyes and ears closed, the platypus eats up to 30% of its own weight each day.

- **The female echidna** has a pouch in which the young develop after hatching from their soft-shelled egg.

- **Poison** from the spurs on the male platypus's hind ankles can kill a dog within minutes.

> ★ STAR FACT ★
> The duckbilled platypus lives almost all its life either underwater or underground.

- **Before the discovery** of fossil platypus teeth in Argentina, the animal was believed only to have existed in Australia and New Guinea.

- **The platypus loses its teeth** a few weeks after birth, and thereafter grinds its food with special mouth pads.

- **The platypus's burrow** can extend 30 m from the water's edge to the nest. It blocks the entrance to deter snakes.

◄ *The duckbilled platypus swims mainly with its front legs, trailing its rear legs as a rudder.*

Badgers

- **Successive generations** of Eurasian badgers use the same den or sett, sometimes for over a century.

- **The ferret badger** is the smallest member of the badger family, and the only badger to climb trees.

- **The honey badger** is led to bee nests by the greater honey-guide bird, which attracts it with special calls, and feeds on beeswax once the badger has opened the nest.

- **The desert-dwelling American badger** can burrow fast enough to catch a ground squirrel

▶ *In damp weather, one Eurasian badger may eat several hundred earthworms per night.*

- burrowing in the ground ahead of it trying to escape.

- **A female European badger** sometimes has female helpers that baby-sit her cubs, often in their own nests, while she forages for food.

- **Despite a bear-like appearance**, badgers belong to the mammal group known as mustelids, and are related to otters and weasels.

- **The honey badger's** extremely tough skin protects it from all kinds of dangers, ranging from bee stings and porcupine quills to snake bites.

- **Badgers are enthusiastic housekeepers** – they regularly change their bedding, and also dig latrines some distance from their setts.

- **Earthworms** are one of the badger's favourite foods, and females suckling their young feed on little else.

- **Eurasian badgers** will enlarge their favourite setts. One ancient den consisted of 879 m of tunnels, with 178 entrances and 50 subterranean chambers.

Hedgehogs

- **The Eurasian hedgehog** has between 5000 and 7000 spines on its back and sides, each erected by its own muscle, creating a defence difficult for predators to penetrate.

- **When a hedgehog rolls into a ball** at the approach of danger, a special muscle draws its loose skin together (like a drawstring on a bag) over its head and rump.

- **From Roman to medieval times** in Europe, it was believed that hedgehogs often carried a supply of fruit with them, impaled on their spines.

- **Over 150,000 hedgehogs** are killed every year on the roads of France alone.

- **The moonrats** of Southeast Asia and China are closely related to hedgehogs, but have no spines.

- **The long-eared and desert hedgehogs** of Asia and North Africa dig their own individual, short burrows.

- **Hedgehogs can go without water** for long periods, and if dehydrated will drink half their bodyweight in one go.

- **A western European male hedgehog** has a foraging territory of up to 35 hectares.

- **Lack of food** rather than cooling temperatures causes a hedgehog to hibernate.

> ★ STAR FACT ★
> The hedgehog keeps up a ceaseless whistling sound while hunting for food.

▲ Scent is important to hedgehogs, as they communicate and track food by smell.

Domestic dogs

- **All modern domestic dogs**, from Chihuahuas to Great Danes, are direct descendants of grey wolves.

- **Grey wolves** were first domesticated over 12,000 years ago in Europe and Asia, for use as guards and herders.

- **Female domestic dogs** can have two litters of puppies a year; wild members of the dog family have only one.

- **The Portuguese water dog** can be trained to dive and retrieve fishing equipment in fresh or salt water.

- **Bloodhounds** can pick up a trail over two weeks old, and follow it for over 200 km.

- **The caffeine** compounds in a bar of dark chocolate can kill a dog weighing up to 5 kg.

- **St Bernard rescue dogs** work in teams of three – two to keep the victim warm, one to fetch their handler.

- **Some dogs can sense** when their owner is about to have an epileptic fit, and others can detect skin cancers before the recognized symptoms appear.

- **During World War II**, over 50,000 dogs were enlisted in the US forces, performing tasks from sentry duty to stealing enemy documents.

- **Native Americans** used dogs to drag a type of sledge.

▶ Male St Bernard dogs often weigh over 90 kg.

Polar bears

◀ Apart from pregnant females, which spend the winter in dens where they give birth, polar bears are active all through the winter months, often travelling great distances in search of food.

- **The Polar bear** is the only bear which is almost exclusively a meat-eater, other bears eat plants too.

- **While stalking a seal**, a polar bear will sometimes lie on its chest with its front legs trailing at its sides and its rump in the air, pushing itself forward with its rear legs.

- **Polar bears** can detect the scent of seal pups in dens buried 1 m deep in snow.

- **Lying in ambush** for a seal, a polar bear will sometimes cover its black nose with its paws to remain unseen against the snow and ice.

- **Polar bears** have a number of tiny protrusions and suction pads on the soles of their feet to give them a firm grip on the ice.

- **The most southerly place** that polar bears regularly visit is James Bay in Canada, which is on the same line of latitude as London.

- **Female polar bears** can put on as much as 400 kg in weight in the course of their summer feeding binge on seal cubs.

- **The polar bear** is a powerful swimmer, even though it uses only its front paws as paddles, letting its rear legs trail behind.

- **Beneath its thick white fur**, a polar bear's skin is black. Translucent hairs channel heat from the sun to the animal's skin, which absorbs the heat.

The heavy forelimbs are ideal for breaking through ice to get at seals' lairs beneath

The huge feet are used as paddles for swimming and snow shoes for crossing thin ice

Manatees and dugongs

- **Manatees and dugongs**, known as sirenians, are the only vegetarian sea mammals in the world.

- **In the days of sail**, sailors sometimes mistook manatees, which can float upright in the water, for mermaids.

- **About 90% of Florida's manatees** carry scars on their bodies caused by power-boat propellers.

- **Manatees** are very slow breeders, and currently more die

◄ Manatees have rounded tails; dugongs' are more whale-like.

each year than are born, threatening their extinction.

- **Manatees** have been used successfully to clear waterways of the fast-growing water hyacinth.

- **Stella's seacow** was a massive North Pacific sirenian, up to 9 m long and weighing 6400 kg. It was hunted to extinction in the 18th century.

- **Fossil evidence** shows that manatees and dugongs have existed for about 50 million years (much longer than seals). They are probably related to elephants.

  - **The teeth of manatees** are regularly replaced, being shed at the front as they wear out, and replaced by new ones moving forward.

  - **Amazonian manatees**, found only in the Amazon River and its tributaries, fast during the 6-month dry season.

- **The dugong** of the Indian Ocean and South Pacific feeds entirely on eel grass, which is the only flowering marine plant.

Tapirs

- **The forest-dwelling tapirs** of Asia and America are related to horses and rhinos, and probably resemble early horses.

- **Tapirs** moved across land bridges from North America to South America and Asia over 5 million years ago.

- **The Malayan tapir** has stark black and white colouring that breaks up its body outline in moonlit forests.

- **Tapirs use their long snouts as snorkels**, staying under water for several minutes to elude predators.

- **All newly born tapirs** have the same stripes and spots, which fade away within 6 months.

- **The South American mountain tapir** grazes at altitudes of over 5000 m.

- **The earliest-known tapir** lived some 55 million years ago.

- **Tapirs, horses and rhinos** are the only living members of the Perissodactyla order of

★ STAR FACT ★
The Malayan tapir walks along the bottom of rivers and lakes like a hippopotamus.

mammals, with an uneven number of toes per foot.

- **In South America**, engineers have built roads along ancient tapir trails, which accurately follow land contours.

▲ The Malayan tapir eats the young shoots of rubber trees.

Llamas and their relatives

- **First domesticated some** 500 years ago, tame llamas and alpacas were important to the Inca empire (1400–1533 AD). The vicuña remained untameable.

- **Vicuña herds** defend two permanent territories, one where they feed, and a smaller one at a higher altitude where they sleep at night.

- **The Incas** used llamas to carry secret messages tied into their fur.

- **Vicuñas** can live at altitudes of 5486 m, where the air is too thin for most mammals.

- **Unlike** in other hoofed mammals, vicuñas' incisor teeth never stop growing.

◀ *Tame domestic llamas are usually mild-tempered, but still spit to show their anger.*

- **Fine vicuña wool** was reserved for the robes of the Inca royal family and their nobles.

- **When annoyed**, llamas spit at their opponents, sometimes including a pebble as a missile in with their saliva.

- **Llama herders** use the animals' fur for rugs and ropes, their hides for shoe leather, their fat for candles, their dung for fuel, and their milk and flesh for food.

- **Baby llamas** can get up and follow their mothers just 15–30 minutes after being born.

> ★ **STAR FACT** ★
> A llama can carry a 60-kg load up to 30 km a day across high mountainous terrain.

Migration

- **Florida manatees** usually migrate south in winter, but recently they have moved instead into the warm water outlets of hydroelectric generating plants.

- **Hooded seals** usually migrate south from Greenland in the Atlantic Ocean, but in 1990 one seal ended up off California in the Pacific, having taken a wrong turn.

- **Migrating noctule bats** established themselves in Hawaii, after being blown 3000 km off course.

- **Migrating whales** travel huge distances with the aid of internal magnetic navigation.

> ★ **STAR FACT** ★
> Each year, gray whales migrate 20,000 km in all, going to and from their breeding grounds.

- **Oil pipe-lines** are serious obstacles to caribou, which follow traditional migratory routes every year.

- **Migrating European noctule bats** fly at high altitude, emitting loud, low-frequency sounds at one second intervals to keep in ground contact.

- **American grey squirrels** sometimes travel in their thousands, crossing roads, rivers and towns in their search for food.

- **Beluga whales** return to the estuaries where they were born to give birth.

- **Over 1 million wildebeest** take part in a circular seasonal migration in east Africa's Serengeti region.

▶ *The new-born gray whale calf accompanies its mother on the long journey from Mexican waters to the Arctic.*

Rats

- **New World wood rats,** or pack rats, continually gather twigs and build them into mounds near their nests.

- **Polynesian voyagers** carried rats on their boats as a form of live meat.

- **One species** of the Southeast Asian bandicoot rat has a body and tail length of almost 1 m!

- **To stop the black rat** stowing away on ships, mooring ropes are sometimes fitted with metal cones, which the rats cannot get past.

- **Baby Norwegian rats** signal to playmates that their play-fights are not serious by occasionally flipping over onto their backs.

- **Rats** constantly investigate their environment, which makes them good problem-solvers in laboratories.

- **Observers** have seen old, experienced rats deliberately

◀ *Rats are among the world's most successful mammals.*

kick traps around until they are sprung, before taking and eating the bait in safety.

- **Norwegian or brown rats** are natural burrowers, and expert at colonizing human buildings.

- **Following heavy rains** in drought regions, 19th-century Australian settlers were subjected to plagues of long-haired rats that devoured anything at ground level.

★ **STAR FACT** ★
The black rat was indirectly responsible, via its fleas, for the death of 25% of the entire human population of Europe by bubonic plague between 1347 and 1352.

Anteaters

- **To protect their long, curved digging claws,** giant anteaters have to walk awkwardly on the knuckles of their front feet.

- **Anteaters have no teeth.** They use their extremely long, sticky tongues to gather up termites after breaking into their concrete-hard mounds.

▼ *The giant anteater sleeps up to 15 hours a day, and has one of the lowest mammal temperatures at 32.7°C.*

- **The tamandua and pygmy anteaters** of South and Central America use their prehensile tails to climb trees, in search of termite and ant nests.

- **The Australian numbat** is the only marsupial adapted to feed exclusively on ants and termites. It has a long, sticky tongue but short, weak claws.

- **Giant anteaters,** over 2 m long from nose to tail tip, cover themselves with their bushy tails when sleeping.

- **Baby anteaters** ride clinging to their mother's backs until they are half her size.

- **Even jaguars are deterred** by the sharp, slashing claws of a giant anteater reared up on its hind legs.

- **The 15 cm long pygmy anteater** has jointed soles to its feet that help it to climb the trees in which it lives.

- **The mouth** of the giant anteater is so small that you could not insert a finger into it.

- **Fossils** found in Germany show that anteaters lived there over 50 million years ago.

Pandas

- **In the late 1900s**, many pandas starved to death because the fountain bamboo they ate came to the end of its 100-year growth cycle and died back.

- **Giant pandas** often give birth to twins, but in the wild one cub is always left to die.

- **Pandas** have an inefficient digestive system – up to 50% of the plant material they eat passes out of the body intact within 10 hours.

- **Although bamboo** forms the bulk of its diet, the giant panda also eats fish, small birds and rodents.

▲ The giant panda eats sitting up, pushing bamboo canes into its mouth for 16 hours a day.

> ★ STAR FACT ★
> Giant and red pandas have an extra 'thumb' that enables them to grasp their food.

- **In ancient China**, pandas were believed to have magical powers, and people wore panda masks to ward off evil spirits.

- **Reduced in number** by hunting and deforestation, there are probably fewer than 1000 giant pandas left in the wild, in forest reserves in Southeast China.

- **The giant panda** has an unsuccessful zoo breeding record, with about 20 successes in the last 50 years.

- **Much livelier** than the giant panda, the red panda is a nimble climber. It uses its long tail for balance, and when threatened rears up and hisses.

- **Giant pandas** reach a weight of up to 150 kg, but when new-born weigh only 100–150 g.

Moles and shrews

- **Shrews** have to forage and eat almost continuously, day and night, to avoid dying of starvation.

- **The Namib golden mole** 'swims' through the desert sand, using its hypersensitive hearing to locate its insect prey.

- **The pygmy white-toothed shrew**, weighing about 2 g, is the smallest living land-based mammal on the planet.

- **European desmans** are aquatic members of the mole family, with long, flat tails, waterproof fur and webbed toes.

▶ Most of a mole's food comes from the creatures that fall into its tunnels.

- **The African armoured shrew** has such strong vertebrae that it can survive being stood on by a full-grown man.

- **After their milk teeth have gone**, shrews usually only have one set of teeth. When these wear out, the shrews die.

- **Some European water shrews** have stiff hairs on their feet and tail that trap air bubbles, enabling them to scurry across the surface of water.

- **Baby shrews** may follow their mother in a line, each one holding a mouthful of the rump of the one in front.

- **The star-nosed mole** has 22 mobile, pink tentacles around the end of its snout, which help it locate prey underground.

- **The American short-tailed shrew** has enough venom in its bite to kill 200 mice.

Grizzly bears

- **The great hump** behind a grizzly's head is solid muscle, enabling it to overturn 50 kg rocks with its front paws, or kill an elk with a single blow.

- **During its winter sleep** the grizzly loses about 1 kg of bodyweight each day. Some grizzlies emerge from their sleep 50% lighter.

- **Grizzlies once ranged** across the USA, with numbers as high as 50,000–100,000; but as their terrain has been taken over by humans, their numbers have fallen to 6000–8000.

- **Most grizzlies are dark brown** in colour, but regional colouring ranges from black to very pale yellow.

- **Despite their great size**, grizzlies are nimble enough to catch squirrels and mice, and can reach a speed of over 55 km/h when charging.

▶ Grizzly mothers give birth to their cubs in their dens in winter, and go on to look after them for anything up to a further 4-5 years, teaching them to forage and hunt, and protecting them from predators.

- **Native Americans** had great respect for the grizzly, and apologized before killing it, sometimes laying out ceremonial clothes for it to wear in the spirit world.

- **Grizzlies are immensely strong**. They have been known to bite through cast iron, bend rifle barrels, and open up cars like sardine cans in search of food.

- **Originating in China**, the ancestors of the modern grizzly crossed land bridges from Asia to North America some 40,000 years ago.

- **Grizzlies** often enter their winter dens just ahead of a snowstorm, so that the snow covers up their fresh tracks and seals them in for their long winter sleep.

Guard hairs have light-coloured tips giving a 'grizzled' appearance this is how this bear gets its common name grizzly bear

★ STAR FACT ★
The huge Kodiak grizzly bear of the Alaskan coastal islands can reach a height of 3 m on its hind legs, and weigh up to 1 tonne.

Non-retractable claws

◀ Grizzlies sometimes dig huge holes to excavate food, using their powerful shoulder muscles and long, non-retractable claws.

Arctic life

- **White fur** helps creatures such as Arctic hares to hide from predators in the snow, but also helps predators such as polar bears avoid detection as they hunt.

- **The ringed seal**, the most northerly of the seals, has been reported at the North Pole itself.

- **Polar bears** and Arctic foxes have tiny ears to reduce the loss of body heat in the icy Arctic.

- **Narwhals and belugas** migrate from the Arctic to warm estuaries and fjords to give birth, returning to the pack ice in late summer.

- **The bulky Arctic musk ox** has a double coat of dense wool overlaid with thick hair, and can stay in the Arctic all year, surviving temperatures of -70°C.

- **During blizzards**, musk oxen form a circle with the calves protected in the centre from the wind and snow.

- **The walrus** is a permanent inhabitant of the Arctic region, spending much of its life on the pack ice.

- **The ringed seal** gives birth in a snow cave, entered from the water through a hole in the ice.

- **Inuit hunters** fear a female walrus defending her calf more than they fear a polar bear.

- **In winter and spring**, Arctic foxes depend on scavenging from polar bear seal-kills – but can end up on the menu themselves!

◄ *A walrus's thick layer of blubber keeps it warm in sub-zero Arctic temperatures.*

Lemurs

- **All lemurs** live on the island of Madagascar, where they evolved in isolation, separated from the African mainland by the 300 km wide Mozambique Channel.

- **In lemur groups** the females are the more aggressive protectors of territory than the males.

- **Early European travellers** to Madagascar described a giant lemur, now extinct, that was as large as a calf.

- **Contesting male lemurs** transfer scent from their wrist glands onto their tails, then use their tails to hurl scent 'bombs' over their heads at their rivals.

▶ *The ring-tailed lemur uses its distinctive tail to signal to others of its species. It may live in groups of up to 30 individuals.*

- **Lemurs were able to evolve** into their many species on Madagascar mainly because they had no competition from monkeys or other primates.

- **Long after Madagascar broke away** from Africa 65–50 million years ago, the lemurs' ancestors crossed the slowly widening channel on rafts of floating vegetation.

- **The aye-aye**, a close relative of the lemurs, has huge ears and can hear grubs chewing wood beneath bark. It extracts them with an elongated middle finger.

- **The indri** is the largest lemur, at up to 1 m from its nose tip to its almost tail-less rump.

- **Fat-tailed dwarf lemurs** sleep through the dry season in July and August, living on the fat stored in the thick bases of their tails.

- **Lemurs groom** using a special claw on one finger, and their front teeth, which resemble a comb.

Capybaras and coypus

- **The South American capybara** is the world's largest rodent, a water-loving giant up to 134 cm long and 64 kg in weight.

- **Capybaras graze** in large groups on river banks. At the first sign of danger they dash into the water and the adults surround the babies.

- **South American coypu females** suckle their young while swimming, from rows of teats high on their sides.

- **Coypu** were hunted almost to extinction in the 1800s for their thick, soft fur, overlain with coarse hairs.

- **Captive farming of coypu** for what was called 'nutria' fur began in the 1920s. Many countries now have feral populations established by escaped captives.

- **The male capybara** has a hairless scent gland on its snout called the morillo (Spanish for 'small hill').

▲ The capybara spends much of its life in the water, and has webbed feet.

- **Capybaras mate in the water**, but give birth on land. All the females in a group feed the young if they have milk.

- **Catholic priests** once allowed capybaras to be eaten during Lent, because they considered them to be close relatives of fish (which were permitted to be eaten).

- **A capybara can stay under water** for up to 5 minutes, sleeping there with only its nose sticking out.

- **Some extinct capybara** weighed as much as a grizzly.

The weasel family

- **In years of vole plagues**, the European common weasel may have up to three litters, because food is available.

- **Pest control** of American prairie dogs has led to the extinction of the black-footed ferret in much of its range.

- **Tribesmen in Burma** are reported to have used trained weasels to kill wild geese and the young of wild goats.

- **The 25 kg wolverine**, the largest weasel close relative,

★ STAR FACT ★
The American least weasel, at 15 cm long and weighing 30 g, is the world's smallest carnivore.

has large feet for hunting reindeer in deep snow.

- **Male weasels** are often twice the size of females, and eat different prey, reducing food competition.

- **Bred for the fur trade**, many American mink escaped into the European countryside, replacing European mink and depleting water vole populations.

- **Ferrets**, traditionally used in Europe to catch rabbits, are a domesticated form of the European polecat.

- **Black-footed ferret young** are cared for by their mother in a separate burrow until they are self-sufficient.

- **In New Zealand**, introduced weasels have almost wiped out some native birds by eating their eggs.

◀ A mink's broad diet includes fish, bringing it into direct competition with otters.

Toothed whales

- **Beluga whales** are the only white whales. They were once called 'sea canaries' by seamen, because their bird-like calls can be heard above the water's surface.

- **Sperm whales** will form a defensive circle, heads to the centre, around young or wounded group members, and beat off predators with their tails.

- **Beaked whales** feed mainly on cuttlefish and squid – one bottle-nosed whale was found to have the remains of 10,000 cuttlefish in its stomach.

- **All dolphins are toothed whales.** The orca – the largest member of the dolphin family – sometimes half-beaches itself to catch seals at the water's edge.

- **Beaked whales will dive to 500 m** or more to escape orcas, staying in the depths for an hour or more until the danger has passed.

- **Spending 85% of the day** under the sea's surface, bottle-nosed whales have been recorded diving to well over 1 500 m in their search for their squid prey.

- **Beluga whales** are frequently stranded in coastal shallows as the tide retreats, and wait patiently for the next tide to refloat them.

> ★ STAR FACT ★
> The male strap-toothed whale has two teeth in its lower jaw that grow to wrap around its upper jaw, severely restricting its ability to open its beak-like mouth.

- **The massive sperm whale**, which weighs up to 70 tonnes, has the largest brain of any mammal on Earth. Fat deposits in its brain case help to focus the sounds the whale produces by echolocation.

- **Toothed whales** cooperate with one another far more than baleen whales do, often working together to herd prey into a tight mass for easy feeding.

▼ Orcas are found throughout the world's oceans. They travel in close-knit social groups of up to 40 individuals, and hunt cooperatively, herding prey fish such as salmon into a close-packed mass before attacking them.

Extremely tall dorsal fin (straight and vertical in males, curved in females)

Pale markings help break up the body's outline

What are marsupials?

- **Marsupials** are born in a tiny, undeveloped form, and many spend months in a protective pouch, attached to a teat.

- **Marsupials** probably originated in America some 100 million years ago, at a time when America and Australia were still joined.

- **The red kangaroo** is the largest living marsupial today.

- **Marsupial mouse**, marsupial rat and marsupial mole are the popular names of some Australian marsupials, but they are not in fact related to mice, rats or moles.

- **Marsupials** have slightly lower body temperatures than most

▲ *Opossums use their long toes and prehensile tails for grasping branches.*

other mammals, and have smaller brains than placentals of a similar size.

- **Two thirds of all marsupials** live in Australia and New Guinea; one third are mainly South American opossums.

- **One marsupial,** the Australian numbat, eats only termites and ants.

- **The wombat's pouch** faces backwards, so that the young are protected from pieces of flying earth when the mother is digging.

- **In Australia**, kangaroos fill the plains-grazing niche occupied elsewhere by antelopes and gazelles (placental mammals).

- **Many small marsupials,** including some opossums, do not have pouches.

Leopards and jaguars

- **A leopard** can carry a prey animal three times its own weight up a tree, out of reach of scavengers.

- **Black panthers** are leopards with black pigmentation. Any leopard litter may include a black cub.

- **The South American jaguar** is America's only big cat.

- **A frozen leopard** carcase was found on Mount Kilimanjaro, Africa, at an altitude of 5692 m.

- **The jaguar** catches not only fish, but also otters, turtles, alligators and frogs.

- **Snow leopards**, which inhabit the mountains of Central Asia, have never been known to roar.

- **The snow leopard** has paws cushioned with hair to act as snow shoes. In the Himalayas it seldom goes below 2000 m, and sometimes goes as high as 5500 m.

- **Leopards** have survived successfully partly because they will eat almost anything, from crabs to baboons.

- **By far the best climber** of the big cats, the leopard sometimes drops straight out of a tree onto its victim.

- **The jaguar** was worshipped as a god by early South American cultures.

▶ *The leopard is by far the best climber of the big cats, and often sleeps in the branches, as well as storing food there and mounting a look-out.*

Armadillos and pangolins

- **The South American three-banded armadillo** can roll itself up into an impenetrable ball.

- **For swimming across rivers**, some armadillos increase their buoyancy by inflating their intestines with air.

- **The giant armadillo** has up to 100 small teeth.

- **The African giant pangolin** has a long tongue that extends internally as far as its pelvis.

- **The 9-banded armadillo** has four identical, same-sex young per litter, all developed from 1 egg.

- **The armadillo's armour** is made up of small bone plates covered in heavy skin; the pangolin's consists of overlapping plates of horn.

▶ *Armadillos walk mainly on their hind legs, with their forelegs just brushing the ground.*

> ★ STAR FACT ★
> Stone Age people used the 1.5 m high shell of the *Glyptodon*, an armadillo, as a shelter.

- **The long-tailed tree pangolin** and the white-bellied tree pangolin hardly ever leave the trees.

- **Pangolins** often use only their back legs when running.

- **The long-tailed tree pangolin** has 37–46 tail vertebrae – a mammal record for the most tail bones.

Domestic cattle

- **European domestic cattle** are descended from the aurochs, a large wild ox seen in ancient cave drawings.

- **The wild auroch** was domesticated about 6500 BC.

▲ *The wild ancestors of modern European cattle were domesticated, mainly for milk, some 8500 years ago by nomadic tribes-people.*

- **Humped zebu** are the main domestic cattle of Asia.

- **In India**, zebu are considered holy by Hindus, and are allowed to roam free, eat fruit off market stalls, and sleep in the roads.

- **Domesticated water buffalo** in Egypt, India and Southeast Asia are powerful draught animals, and are also regularly milked.

- **India** is the country with the most domestic cattle: more than 270 million.

- **A large feral population** of domesticated water buffalo lives in northern Australia.

- **Masai cattle herders** in Kenya regularly take blood from the throats of their cattle and drink it.

- **In Tibet**, domesticated yaks thrive at altitudes well over 6000 m, providing meat, milk and transport.

- **Domestic cattle** sleep for up to 8 minutes at a time, for a maximum total of 60 minutes in 24 hours.

Kangaroos

- **Female kangaroos** suckling young of different ages at the same time are able to produce milk of different concentrations for the individual youngsters.

- **Hopping** is a good way to travel fast, but to go slowly a kangaroo has to use its tail as a fifth supporting leg.

- **Some tree kangaroos** can leap to the ground from as high as 30 m without coming to harm.

- **New-born kangaroos** are deaf as well as naked and blind.

- **Flat out**, some kangaroos can reach a speed of almost 65 km/h, making huge hops of over 8 m in length.

- **When bounding**, most kangaroos can only move their hind

▼ A moving kangaroo uses its large, muscular tail as a counter-balance.

long hind legs make the kangaroo the fastest marsupial

legs both at the same time, but when swimming can move them alternately.

- **Hare wallabies** are small members of the kangaroo family weighing only 1–4.5 kg.

- **Rock wallabies** live on rocky outcrops. Their rough-soled feet are fringed with stiff hairs, enabling them to climb steep rock faces.

- **When male kangaroos fight,** they support themselves on their tails and deliver slashing kicks with their hind legs.

★ STAR FACT ★
Prehistoric kangaroos in Australia included a giant that stood 2.4 m tall and weighed 270 kg, and at least one meat-eating species.

Voles and lemmings

- **At up to 2 kg**, the American muskrat is 130 times heavier than most voles.

- **Every 3 or 4 years** some vole and lemming species undergo population explosions, followed by high numbers of deaths from stress and food shortages.

- **The mole-lemming** of the Central Asian steppes digs tunnels using its protruding incisor teeth.

- **Eurasian water voles** live in river bank burrows with entrances below the level of the water's surface.

- **At the peak** of a lemming population explosion, lemmings devastate the local vegetation – and the next summer predators can find them more easily.

- **At 1 m below the snow's surface**, a lemming's winter nest can be 10°C, while outside it is below freezing.

- **Some species of voles and lemmings** have their first litters when they are only 5 weeks old themselves.

- **The collared lemming** is the only rodent to change the colour of its coat to white in winter.

- **Lemmings** will swim across any water in their path as they migrate in search of new food sources; if the water is too wide to cross, they drown – hence the myth of lemmings committing mass suicide.

- **A fox can hear** and smell voles moving under the snow.

▼ The European water vole stores food for the winter.

Communication

▲ *Members of the dog family use ear positions as part of their language.*

● **Whales' low frequency** calls travel thousands of km through the water.

● **Some whales** communicate with complex 'songs'. All the individuals in one ocean region sing the same song.

● **Some of the puppies** from the litter of a poodle bred with a jackal had the poodle's 'language'; others had the jackal's. But the two groups could not communicate with one another.

● **Male chimps** establish their status by seeing who can make the most noise.

● **One chimp** learned to use 130 gestures of American Sign Language.

● **Cats and dogs** erect the hair on parts of their bodies to impress rivals and mates, or frighten off predators.

● **The gorilla groups** over 90% of all vocal signals and calls are made by the males.

● **A well-fed lion** can walk head-up through a herd of antelope without panicking them, but if its head is low, the antelope run, knowing it is hunting.

● **The sifaka lemur** has one alarm call to warn of birds of prey, and another to warn of snakes.

● **Many young mammals** have a 'play' body language just for mock fights.

◀ *Chimps communicate with a wide range of facial expressions.*

Old World monkeys

● **Japanese macaques** sit in hot springs in winter to keep warm.

● **Some female red colobus monkeys** in Gambia gang up to attack, and even kill, strange males.

● **The Old World monkeys** of Africa and Asia rest by sitting down, and have tough pads on their bottoms to prevent sores developing.

● **Some colobus monkeys** gnaw on the charcoal of burned trees to help neutralize the toxins in some leaves.

◀ *Old World monkeys forage for plant food during the day, and rest by night.*

● **Red colobus monkeys** often travel in mixed groups with diana monkeys, as the diana monkeys are better at spotting the chimps that prey on colobus monkeys.

● **Talapoin monkeys** in Central Africa live in forests that are frequently flooded. Excellent swimmers, they often sleep on branches overhanging the water.

● **In Japan,** in areas where humans regularly feed macaques, the birth-rate of the animals rockets, leading to groups of up to 1000.

● **The Hanuman grey langur** of India is protected by religious law, in honour of Hanuman, the monkey god.

● **Some Japanese macaques** have learned to dip food in the sea to clean and salt it, and have become good swimmers in the process.

★ **STAR FACT** ★
The Barbary macaque is the only primate, apart from humans, living in Europe.

Lions

- **The largest-known wild lion** was an African male man-eater, shot in 1936, and weighing 313 kg (the average male lion weighs 150–190 kg).

- **Male lions** have the job of protecting the pride, leaving the hunting to the females most of the time. But the males insist on eating first from any kills!

▲ Lion cubs suckle from their mother for the first six months of their lives, but begin to eat meat at three months old.

▶ Only male lions have a mane, which shows off their size, and also protects them during fights. The females are the main hunters in the pride.

★ STAR FACT ★

A male lion can eat up to 30 kg of meat at one sitting, and then will not need to eat again for several days.

- **Lions** are the only big cats that lead social lives, cooperating in hunting and sharing their prey.

- **Lions usually kill large prey** such as zebra by suffocating them, biting their throats and holding them around the neck with their paws.

- **When a foreign male** takes over a pride of lions by driving off its leading male, he kills cubs under about 6 months old and mates with their mothers.

- **Lions** spend most of their time sleeping, usually dozing for about 20 hours of the day.

- **Once widespread** throughout Southwest Asia and India, the only lions now surviving outside Africa are a few Asiatic lions in the Indian Gir Forest wildlife reserve.

- **The roar** of a male lion, used to intimidate rivals and locate pride members is audible 8 km away.

- **A male lion** will not usually allow other pride members to share a kill until he has had enough, though he may make an exception for small cubs.

Parental care of mammals

- **Many mammals carry** their young around with them. Some bats even go hunting with a youngster aboard.

- **Mother whales** have to nudge and encourage newly born young up to the surface to take their first breath, often aided by 'aunts' from the same pod.

- **In wild dog packs**, several females may take turns to suckle and guard all the young in the group.

- **Sperm whale** offspring may suckle for up to 15 years.

- **Elephant young** are born after 22 months. Several of the herd cows help the new baby to stand.

- **Mother cheetahs** teach their young how to hunt by bringing small live prey back for them to practice on.

- **A big cat female** carries her young by holding the entire head in her mouth, in a gap behind her teeth.

- **Young kangaroos** leave the pouch at 5–11 months, but continue to stick their head in to suckle for 6 months.

- **Many cats**, large and small, start to train their young by allowing them to attack their twitching tails.

> ★ STAR FACT ★
> Baby gorillas may only climb on the silver-back while they still have a white rump tuft.

◀ The baby baboon depends on its mother for food and transport, but is also protected from danger by certain males in the group.

Dolphins

- **Groups of common dolphins**, travelling and feeding together, may number up to 2000 individuals.

- **Orcas**, or killer whales, are actually the largest species of dolphin, though they feed on other dolphin species.

- **There are five species** of freshwater dolphin living in Asian and South American rivers. Most catch fish by sound rather than sight.

- **Dolphins** have been known to aid humans by keeping them afloat and driving off attacking sharks.

- **Spinner dolphins** are named for the acrobatic leaps they perform, spinning up to 7 times in mid air.

- **The Atlantic hump-backed dolphin** helps fishermen in West Africa by driving shoals of mullet into their nets.

- **In Mexico's Baja California**, bottle-nosed dolphins chase fish up onto the shore, then roll up onto the beach, completely out of the water, to grab them.

- **Military observers** once recorded a group of dolphins swimming at 64 km/h in the bow wave of a warship.

- **The striped dolphin**, seen in ancient Greek paintings, leaps up to 7 m to perform somersaults and spins.

- **The Yangtse dolphin**, or baiji, is one of the world's rarest mammals – probably less than 300 survive.

◀ Many dolphin species 'spy-hop', holding their heads out of the water as they check on their surroundings for predators and potential food.

Moose and elk

- **The world's largest deer** (called moose in North America and elk in Europe) stand up to 2 m tall at the shoulder.

- **Moose escape wolves** by retreating to marshes and lakes, but in winter the wolves can follow them across the ice.

- **The prehistoric Irish elk**, which became extinct 10,000 years ago, had massive antlers up to 4.3 m across.

- **Moose** have reached Isle Royale in Lake Superior, USA, by swimming across 32 km of water.

- **To protect her calf** from wolves, the mother moose shepherds it into shallow water and stands

▶ Two male elk spar with their antlers, which they lose and regain every year.

> ★ STAR FACT ★
> The moose has been known to dive to 5.5 m, staying under water for 30 seconds, to reach water plants and roots.

between it and the wolves, which usually give up.

- **A moose will use its great weight** to push over young trees to get at twigs and shoots.

- **A moose eats** the equivalent of 20,000 leaves a day.

- **The antlers** of a moose are 'palmate', with broad areas like hands.

- **A young moose** stays with its mother for almost a year, but she chases it away just before she is about to give birth to a new calf.

Australasian marsupials

- **The brush-tailed possum** is Australia's most common marsupial. It often moves into the lofts of houses.

- **Kangaroos** are not restricted to Australia – several tree-kangaroo species live in Papua New Guinea.

- **Australian marsupial moles** strongly resemble true moles, but have different ancestors.

▶ The stocky wombat is related to the koala, but cannot climb trees and digs large burrows.

> ★ STAR FACT ★
> Kangaroos are serious competitors with sheep for grass, because with front teeth in both jaws instead of just one, they crop it much closer.

- **Wombats live in burrows** and weigh up to 40 kg (but one fossil wombat weighed in at a hefty 100 kg).

- **The Tasmanian devil** is the largest surviving marsupial carnivore, eating mainly carrion.

- **The Australian pygmy possum** sleeps so soundly that you can pick it up without it waking.

- **The muscular tail** of the long-tailed dunnart is up to 210 mm long (twice its body length).

- **Some bandicoots** (nocturnal, rat-like marsupials) have a gestation period of just 12.5 days – a mammal record.

- **The striped possum** digs for grubs in tree-bark with an elongated finger.

Ice Age mammals

- **Woolly mammoths** adapted to Ice Age conditions by developing a thick coat of dark hair, and using their enormous tusks to sweep snow off the grasses they ate.

- **The woolly rhinoceros** was up to 5 m long, and roamed the tundras of northern Europe and Asia. Like the mammoth, it featured in the cave drawings of hunters.

- **Several Ice Age mammals** became giant-sized to help them combat the cold, including aurochs – the giant ancestors of modern cattle.

- **Many mammoths** are so well preserved in the Siberian permafrost that their flesh is still edible, and their last meals remain in their stomachs.

- **On the tundra** at the edge of the ice sheets, some mammals migrated south in winter; others, like the huge European cave bear, hibernated in their lairs.

- *Smilodon*, a large sabre-toothed cat, inhabited Ice Age North America, dying out along with many of the large animals it preyed on.

- **Many mammal species died out** between 12,000 and 10,000 years ago, as the last Ice Age ended. But some survived, including musk-oxen, horses, hyenas and saiga antelopes.

- **The Ice Age bison** were similar

▲ Sabre-toothed Smilodon ranged from Canada to Argentina. It used its huge upper canine teeth to slice through the tough hides of large prey animals and bite out big chunks of flesh.

> ★ STAR FACT ★
> Cave bears used the same caves for many generations. One cave in Austria contained the bones of up to 50,000 individual bears.

to modern bison, but had sweeping 1-m long horns on either side of their heads.

- **The giant short-faced bear**, which inhabited North America until the end of the last Ice Age, was twice the size of the Kodiak bear, had long legs and weighed up to 1 tonne.

▲ The woolly mammoth had small ears to prevent heat-loss, and beneath its hairy skin was a thick layer of heat-preserving fat.

Mongooses, civets, genets

- **African banded mongooses** gang up together to repel and attack predators such as jackals.

- **The Malaysian binturong** is related to civets, and is the only Old World mammal with a prehensile tail, which it uses as a brake when descending trees.

- **The palm civet** of Asia is known as the toddy cat, because it has a taste for a fermented alcoholic drink.

- **Civets** were once kept captive in Ethiopia and 'milked' of their strong-smelling musk, which was used in the perfume industry.

- **A mongoose will tire out a cobra** by making quick movements, then kill it.

- **The dwarf mongoose** marks its territory by doing a handstand to deposit a scent mark as high as possible on a rock or bush.

- **Common genets** are found in France and Spain. They may have been introduced in medieval times as pets and rat-catchers, by the Moors of North Africa.

▲ The banded mongoose lives and forages in large groups, leaving a baby-sitting adult back in the den to guard the young.

- **Otter civets**, like true otters, have webbed feet and closable nostrils. They catch fish and can climb trees.

- **Largest of the civet-mongoose family**, the fossa of Madagascar has a cat-like head and retractable claws.

- **In fights** against members of the same species, some mongooses curl over and present their posterior to their opponent, biting at him between their hindlegs.

Camouflage

- **Stripes** benefit both predators and prey by breaking up the body shape, for example in tigers and zebras.

- **The simplest camouflage** makes an animal a similar colour to its surroundings, such as the white of a polar bear in snow.

- **Some whales and dolphins** are dark on top and light underneath, camouflaging them against the dark of deep water or the light of the sky.

- **Some camouflage** mimics the broken shapes of light shining through trees, as in the dappled markings of giraffes.

- **The young** of many mammal species, such as lions and pigs, have early camouflage markings that disappear as the animals grow older.

★ STAR FACT ★
Not all camouflage is visual – some mammals roll in dung to disguise their own scents.

- **The coats of Arctic foxes** and hares change from dark in summer to white in winter.

- **Bold markings**, such as the contrasting shapes of the oryx, camouflage by breaking up body outline.

- **The bobcat's spots** camouflage it in rocks, while the similar-shaped plain lynx merges with forest.

- **The elephant's huge grey form** disappears as it stands still in the shadows.

◄ The orca's light underparts make it less visible from underneath against the water's surface in daytime.

New World marsupials

- **American marsupials** are nearly all from the opossum family, which has lived in America for 55 million years.
- **Opossums** have spread successfully northwards as far as Canada, but are vulnerable to frostbitten ears and tails.
- **When attacked**, the opossum goes into a death-like trance, called 'playing 'possum'.
- **Opossums entwine** their prehensile tails around those of their young when carrying them.
- **The Virginia opossum** usually has 13 teats in its pouch, but often gives birth to a higher number of young. Those that are not able to attach to a teat soon die.
- **The yapok**, or water opossum, is the only mainly aquatic marsupial. It has webbed rear feet.
- **The monito del monte** is a rat-sized marsupial unrelated

▲ Opossums eat fruit, flowers and nectar, as well as insects.

to opossums, and found in Chile's cool forests.

- **Once a baby opossum** has attached itself to a teat, it cannot let go until it is fully developed.
- **The newly born mouse opossum** is no larger than a grain of rice – the smallest new-born mammal.

> ★ STAR FACT ★
> The Maya civilization of Central America believed the opossum to be a magical animal.

Mountain lions or pumas

- **The mountain lion**, or puma, is the widest-ranging American mammal, occurring from Canada in the north to southern Chile in the south.
- **Mountain lions** are the largest American desert carnivores.

▶ The puma is the largest of the so-called small cats, and its prey ranges from mice to full-grown deer.

- **The Patagonian puma** has a hunting territory of up to 100 sq km. Its main prey is the llama-like guanaco.
- **As a form of territorial marking**, pumas build little piles of soil or vegetation called scrapes.
- **Although the size of a leopard**, the mountain lion is classified as a small cat because it can purr.
- **In the Sierra Nevada**, the main prey of mountain lions is the mule deer, which can be twice the lion's weight.
- **High altitude varieties** of mountain lion may be much larger (113 kg) than those living lower down (45 kg).
- **Below the timber line**, the mountain lion hunts by night. At higher altitudes it may have to hunt by day.
- **There are few reports** of mountain lion attacks on humans, but attacks have increased as humans have taken over more of the mountain lion's territories.
- **Mountain lions** are solitary, avoiding one another except to mate. When the young leave their mother, they relocate at least 45 km away.

Black bears

- **American black bears** vary in colour from black, through brown, cinnamon, honey and ice-grey, to white, according to regional races.

- **Beavers are a favourite food** of some black bears, because of their high fat content.

- **In autumn**, feeding up for the winter sleep, black bears put on up to 1.5 kg per day.

- **Black bears mate** in the summer, but the fertilized egg does not begin to develop until the autumn, and the cubs are born in January or February.

- **'Nuisance' bears** that have learned to beg and scavenge garbage in U.S.

▶ *Black bears occasionally raid people's beehives and orchards, as well as city dumps.*

national parks have to be tranquillized and moved to new areas some distance away.

- **The most northerly** Canadian black bears have a varied diet ranging from caribou and seals to birds' eggs and tiny shrimp.

- **The sun bear** of Southeast Asia is the world's smallest bear, at 27–65 kg. It specializes in gathering honey and insects with its long tongue.

- **South America's only bear** is the spectacled bear, which builds feeding and sleeping platforms in the branches of fruit trees.

- **The black sloth bear** of India has a mobile snout and closable nostrils for dealing with ants.

★ **STAR FACT** ★
Asiatic black bears are constipated when they awake from their winter hibernation, and in Russia drink birch tree sap as a laxative.

Mole rats

- **Unlike most rodents**, mole rats live for several years.

- **Mole rats** have extremely loose skin, which enables them to turn round in the tightest of tunnels.

- **Naked mole rats** have no fur. They live in colonies, like some insects, with a queen that bears all the young, and workers that dig the tunnels.

- **Mole rats**, unlike moles, dig with their protruding

▶ *Naked mole rats enjoy stable temperatures of around 29°C in their humid burrows, when outside surface temperatures can be as high as 60°C.*

front teeth. Lip folds prevent them swallowing earth.

- **Mole rats' eyes** are probably blind, but they may use the eye surface to detect air currents in the burrow.

- **Mole rats** have been observed biting off the growing sprouts of roots and tubers before storing them, thus preventing them losing nutritive value before use.

- **Blind mole rats** of the eastern Mediterranean have skin-covered eyes. They dig individual tunnel systems up to 350 m long.

- **Naked mole rats** cooperate to dig tunnels, several moving the soil to the surface and one kicking it out of the hole.

- **The 'queen'** of a naked mole rat colony suppresses the breeding ability of other females by means of chemical signals.

- **The Cape dune mole rat** moves up to half a tonne of soil in just 1 month.

Prehistoric elephants

- **Platybelodon**, which lived up to 14 million years ago, had huge, shovel-like lower teeth for scooping up and cutting water plants, and a short, broad trunk.

- **Remains of 91-cm tall elephants** were found on Malta.

- **The last woolly mammoths** were a dwarf species that died out less than 7000 years ago.

- **Two million years ago**, *Deinotherium* may have used its curled tusks for scraping bark from trees.

- **The elephant *Gomphotheres*** had four straight tusks, and lived in Europe, Africa and Pakistan.

- **Forest-dwelling *Anancus*** had straight tusks up to 4 m long, which it used for digging up roots.

- **At one time**, more commercial ivory came from frozen mammoths in Siberia than from modern elephants.

> ★ STAR FACT ★
> One of the earliest-known elephant ancestors, *Moeritherium*, lived about 38 million years ago.

- **Some Stone Age Siberian people** built huts from the tusks and long bones of the mammoths they hunted.

- **Mastodons** had smaller bodies and tusks than mammoths, and had a different diet.

▲ Platybelodon was a swamp elephant that devoured huge amounts of water plants, scooping them up with its lower jaw.

The mating game

- **In some species** of Australian marsupial mouse, the male dies after a two-week mating period.

- **A beaver** stays with its mate for many years, producing a new litter each year.

- **A male hedgehog** courts a female by circling her, sometimes wearing a deep groove in the soil, until she accepts him.

- **Male Californian sea-lions** bark to guard their mating territory. Underwater, the barks produce bursts of bubbles.

- **The hooded seal** impresses females by inflating a nostril lining into a red balloon.

- **The red markings** on a male mandrill's blue and red

▼ A male narwhal's tusk can be up to 3 m long, and is actually one of its only two teeth.

face become brighter during the mating season.

- **To attract potential mates**, orang-utan males emit a series of loud roars that tail off into groans.

- **White rhino males** have strict territorial boundaries. They try to keep receptive females within the territory, but if a female strays outside, he will not follow her.

- **Hippos prefer to mate in the water**, with the female often completely submerged, and having to raise her head to breath every so often.

> ★ STAR FACT ★
> Narwhal males compete for mates by 'fencing' with their long, spiral tusks.

Bats

- **The earliest insect-eating bat fossil** is 50 million years old, and the earliest fruit bat fossil only 35 million years old, so they probably evolved from different ancestors.

- **The bumblebee bat** of Thailand is the world's smallest mammal. Its body is just 3 cm long, and it weighs only 2 g.

- **In one North American cave**, 10 million Mexican free-tailed bats give birth each year to 10 million young over a period of about a week.

- **Bat species** form 22% of all the world's mammals, and are by far the most common rainforest mammal.

- **In some bat species**, males are known sometimes to produce milk, but it is not known if they ever suckle the young.

- **A resting bat** emits 10 sound pulses per second, rising to 30 per second as it flies, 60 per second when approaching an object, and 200 per second when approaching an insect.

- **Australia's ghost bat** is the continent's only meat-eating bat. It hunts and devours frogs, birds, lizards, small mammals, and even other bats.

- **The bulldog bat** feeds on fish, grabbing them from the surface of the water with its specially elongated toes.

- **Many tropical nectar- and pollen-eating bats** are important pollinators of plants, including some trees. They transfer the pollen from one plant to another as they feed inside the flowers.

▲ The only mammals capable of powered flight, bats come in a diverse range of shapes and sizes – but all have excellent hearing. Shown here are: (1) the red bat, (2) the Mexican fishing bat, (3) the African yellow-winged bat, (4) the noctule bat, (5) the long-eared bat, (6) the hoary bat, (7) the horse or hammer-headed bat, (8) the lesser horseshoe bat and (9) the spotted bat.

★ STAR FACT ★
The vampire bat uses razor-sharp teeth to make tiny cuts in the limbs of sleeping mammals, and then laps up the blood.

Baleen whales

- **Baleen whales** include blue whales, the planet's largest mammals – the heaviest known weighed over 190 tonnes.

- **Blue whale calves** grow about 1000 times faster in the womb than human babies.

▼ *Baleen whales' pleated lower jaws take in masses of water per gulp.*

- **Humpback whales** have been seen to leap out of the water as many as 100 times in quick succession.

- **Right whales** were so-named because they were the 'right' ones to hunt – heavy with oil, meat and baleen.

- **Despite being protected** since the 1940s, there are less than 320 northern right whales surviving.

- **The baleen plates** of modern baleen whales evolved about 30 million years ago.

- **Right whales** force a constant current of water through their baleen plates to trap their food – krill organisms.

- **Bowhead whales** are estimated to eat up to 1500 kg of filtered-out food organisms daily for 130 days at a time.

- **Women's corsets** were once made out of baleen plates.

Buffaloes

- **The African buffalo** will stalk and attack a human even if unprovoked, and will mob lions and kill their cubs if it gets the chance.

- **The wild Asiatic buffalo** can weigh up to 1200 kg, and has the longest horns of any living animal, sometimes exceeding a 4-m spread.

- **African buffaloes** have a wide range of vocal communications, including signals for moving off, direction-changing, danger and aggressive intent.

- **In Australia in the dry season**, female feral water buffaloes leave their calves with a 'nursemaid' on the edge of the plains where they graze.

- **The African savannah buffalo** can weigh up to 875 kg, and herds can number several thousand.

- **A wounded African buffalo** will ambush its hunter, exploding out of cover in an unstoppable charge.

- **Needing to drink every day**, African buffaloes never stray more than 15 km from water.

- **Buffaloes rarely fight**. Contests consist of tossing the head, pawing the ground and circling, before one bull walks away.

- **Blind or crippled buffaloes** are sometimes observed living healthily in the herd, whereas loners would soon die.

- **In the rinderpest cattle epidemic** of the 1890s, up to 10,000 African buffaloes died for every one animal that survived.

▼ *Swamp mud helps protect a water buffalo's skin from heat and insects.*

Lynxes and bobcats

- **Bobcats and lynxes** are closely related, but the lynx inhabits northern conifer forests and swamps, and the bobcat prefers rocky regions with dense undergrowth.

- **Lynxes have shorter tails** than bobcats, and their longer legs help them to move through deep snow.

- **Chased by dogs**, the bobcat often takes to water, where it is a superior swimmer to its pursuers.

- **In experiments**, bobcats with clipped ear-tufts heard less well, suggesting the tufts aid their hearing.

- **Lynxes have thick fur** on the soles of their feet to keep them warm and help prevent slipping on icy surfaces.

- **The bobcat** is only found in America, but the lynx has populations across Europe and Asia.

> ★ STAR FACT ★
> Snow hares provide 70% of the North American lynx's diet. Lynx numbers fluctuate with the 10-year population cycle of the snow hare.

▲ Its long ear tufts help the lynx to hear its main prey, the snow hare, and long legs enable it to chase its prey through deep snow.

- **Bobcat kittens** are taught to hunt by the age of 7 months. At 12 months the mother drives them away.

- **Unlike the lynx**, the bobcat flourishes in deserts.

- **The bobcat may live up to 20 years**, eating rabbits, prairie dogs, rattlesnakes and crayfish.

Koalas

- **Koala numbers** started to rise after European settlers reduced the numbers of dingoes.

- **Male koalas mark their territories** by rubbing their large chest gland, which females lack, onto tree trunks.

- **The koala feeds** mainly on eucalyptus leaves.

> ★ STAR FACT ★
> A koala weighs less than 0.5 g at birth, and remains in its mother's pouch for 7 months.

- **Koalas** are the sole living representatives of their family, but are distantly related to wombats.

- **The koala grips branches** with its sharp-clawed hands by opposing the first 2 fingers to the other 3.

- **Koalas spend 80% of their day** asleep in the trees.

- **When its body temperature** nears 37°C, the koala licks its paws and rubs cooling saliva onto its face.

- **The name 'koala'** comes from an Aboriginal word meaning 'no drink' – it gets most of the moisture it needs from the leaves it eats.

- **A giant koala**, twice the size of today's animals, existed over 40,000 years ago.

◄ Although resembling a bear, koalas are not related to the bear family.

Chimpanzees

- **Chimps have a strict social ladder**, with dominant males at the top. These top males recognize property rights, and never steal food from their inferiors.

- **Observers** have noted chimpanzees carefully lifting a fellow chimp's eyelid to remove a speck of grit.

- **Chimps are the best tool-users** after humans. They use grass stems to fish for termites in their mounds, stones and anvils to crack nuts, and chewed leaves as sponges for gathering water.

- **Chimpanzees** actively hunt for meat, especially when plant food is scarce, and collaborate to catch colobus monkeys, young baboons, birds and rodents.

- **If a chimpanzee** finds a tree laden with fruit, it drums on a tree trunk and makes loud panting cries to summon other chimps from many kilometres away for a share of the feast.

- **Bands of male chimpanzees** have been observed attacking and killing all the males in a neighbouring band. Up to a third of adult male chimp deaths result from territorial disputes.

> ★ STAR FACT ★
> Chimpanzees reach puberty at about 10 years, give birth every 4 or 5 years, and may live into their 50s.

▲ Grooming is a very important activity amongst chimps. It helps to create strong bonds between individuals, and to establish the group's pecking order.

- **Bonobos**, or pygmy chimpanzees, are found in the dense forests along the Congo River. They are darker than other chimps, with longer legs and smaller heads, and walk upright more often.

- **A bonobo named Kanzi**, a very successful participant in language experiments, also learned how to light a barbecue and cook his own sausages.

- **Chimps eat** a range of plants as medicines, to get rid of conditions such as stomach aches and parasitic worms.

◀ With a large brain and intense curiosity, the chimp can absorb a considerable amount of information, and is also able to learn by imitation.

Life on the plains

- **In the 1800s**, a vast springbok herd, 25 km wide and 160 km long, crossed the plains of southern Africa.

- **The Argentine maned wolf** has extremely long legs for hunting in the tall pampas grasses.

- **The African springhare** resembles a miniature kangaroo. It grazes at night on floodplains.

- **The world's biggest** grouping of large land mammals takes place every year on Africa's Serengeti plains, with the migration of 1.5 million wildebeest and 1 million other hoofed animals.

- **Savannah buffalo** graze on tall, coarse grasses, reducing them to

the height preferred by other grazers.

- **New-born wildebeest** have a strong instinct to approach anything that moves – even, fatally, hyenas or lions.

- **As herds of wildebeest** trample and manure the ground, they stimulate the rapid regrowth of grasses.

- **If young wild dogs tire** while hunting on Africa's Okavango flood plain, the adults hide them and return for them later.

- **The American pronghorn antelope** can see the white warning patches on the rump of another pronghorn from several kilometres away.

- **The Bactrian camel** of Central Asia eats salty plants avoided by other grazers.

◄ *The pronghorn communicates over long distances.*

New World monkeys

- **The howler monkey** has a special throat bone that enables it to produce its distinctive deep roar.

- **The pygmy marmoset** of the upper Amazon Basin is the world's smallest monkey, weighing 125 g.

- **Unlike Old World monkeys**, most New World monkeys have prehensile tails, and can suspend their whole bodies from them when travelling or feeding.

- **New World monkeys** have broad noses with sideways-pointing nostrils; Old World monkeys' noses are narrow, with downward-pointing nostrils.

- **The pygmy marmoset** uses its teeth to gouge holes in tree bark so that it can extract the gum – a

major part of its diet.

- **The South American night monkey** is the only truly nocturnal monkey.

- **The capuchin** is the brainiest New World monkey. In captivity, it soon learns to use tools to obtain food.

- **Marmosets and tamarins** always give birth to twins, carried mainly by the father.

- **Titi monkeys** live in small family groups, and all sleep together with their tails entwined.

▼ *The howler monkey makes ear-shattering calls to warn off rivals.*

> **★ STAR FACT ★**
> Spider monkeys hang by their tails from low branches over rivers to drink.

Heat regulation

- **Fruit bats** are susceptible to heat stroke, so to keep themselves cool, some lick themselves all over and fan cool air at their bodies with their wings.

- **The oryx** has special blood vessels in its nose to keep its blood temperature low in the desert heat.

- **Large-eared desert species** such as fennec foxes use their ears as radiators to get rid of body heat.

- **The desert bighorn sheep** draws air over a thickly veined area of its throat to cool its blood.

- **Wallowing in mud** keeps pigs cool and protects their skin from the sun.

▶ Little kit foxes of the American prairies use their huge ears to help them cool down.

- **A hippos' skin** exudes a red, lacquer-like substance to protect it from sunburn.

- **During hot spells**, kangaroos lick their wrists a lot, so that the evaporation of the saliva causes cooling.

- **Indian zebu cattle** have more sweat glands than western cattle, and maintain a lower body temperature, making them common in China, Africa and South America.

- **The eland's temperature** can rise several degrees without causing sweating, allowing it to conserve 5 litres of water daily.

- **After feeding their young**, mother bats often leave them in the heat of the cave and perch near the cooler entrance.

Fruit bats

- **In Southwest Asia**, some date farmers protect their fruit from fruit bat raiders by covering the dates with bags of woven palm leaves.

- **Island fruit bats** are vulnerable to tropical storms that can blow them far out to sea. This is how some species reached islands in the first place.

- **Fruit bats** enjoy eating fruit in mangrove forests, where sea-water minerals supplement their diet.

- **Large fruit bats** strip the leaves from the trees in which they roost to give them a clearer view.

- **Male hammer-headed bats** gather together in riverside trees called leks, so that the females can choose a mate from among them. As they hang, the males flap their wings and call out.

- **The Queensland tube-nosed bat** has tube-like nostrils projecting 5–6 mm from its face. These may act as snorkels as it feeds on pulpy fruit.

- **Fruit bats eat their own weight** in fruit each day, and are important seed-dispersers, spitting out seeds as they eat.

- **Australian black fruit bats** chew leaves to get protein, but spit them out after swallowing the juice to make flying easier.

- **Spectacled flying foxes** sometimes drink sea-water as they skim by, and have been snapped up by saltwater crocodiles.

★ STAR FACT ★
The largest fruit bat is the Indian flying fox, which has a wingspan of up to 150 cm.

▶ Unlike echolocating bats, fruit bats, navigate visually, and live on a plant diet.

Wolves

- **In wolf packs**, only the dominant female normally mates and has cubs. The female wolves sometimes fight to establish who is to be the pack mother.

- **Forest wolves stay all year** in their own territory, while tundra wolves are nomadic, following the migrations of prey such as caribou.

- **Wolves howl** to avoid territorial fights – if they know where another pack is, they usually steer clear of it.

- **Grey wolves** often go for a week without food. They only average one kill in every 10 hunting expeditions.

- **Although they normally hunt large prey** such as deer, wolves will also eat carrion, berries and even fish.

- **Wolf packs** may number 20 or so where moose are plentiful, but only 6 or 7 where deer are the main prey.

- **Tundra wolves** hunt larger prey than wolves further south, and tend to be larger themselves.

- **A pack's dominant pair** scent mark the home range (up to 1000 sq km) by urinating about every 3 mins.

▲ *The grey wolf is the ancestor of the domestic dog, and still occasionally mates with dogs such as huskies.*

- **Wolves** migrated into Europe, Asia and Africa from North America some 7 million years ago.

- **Wolves cull the old and weak** members in a herd of prey animals, improving the herd's overall health.

Raccoons

- **In many suburban areas** of the USA, raccoons have moved into sheds and roof spaces, emerging at night to raid garbage cans.

- **Hunting raccoons** with 'coon dogs at night is popular in the southern states of the USA, but raccoons have been known to lure dogs into water and then drown them.

- **Raccoons** use their slender-fingered front paws to capture frogs and crayfish.

▲ *The raccoon's distinctive 'mask' fits its reputation as a night-time bandit, thief and garbage raider.*

★ **STAR FACT** ★
At one time raccoon skins were used as currency in parts of Tennessee, USA.

- **Raccoons have a weakness** for sweet corn, raiding crops just ahead of the farmer.

- **The crab-eating raccoon** of South America leads a semi-aquatic life, and is also a good tree climber.

- **Raccoons** belong to a family that includes long-tailed kinkajous, coatis and cacomistles in the Americas, and the red pandas in Asia.

- **In the northern part of their range**, raccoons may retire to their nests in winter for a month or two.

- **Captive raccoons** appear to wash food before eating it, but in the wild a raccoon's underwater manipulations are to locate food rather than to wash it.

- **In urban areas**, raccoons sometimes carry off garbage cans, even untying rope knots to remove lids.

Gibbons

▲ *From earliest infancy the gibbon spends nearly all its life above ground in the trees.*

- **The gibbons of Southeast Asia** are the smallest and most agile of the apes. They pair for life, and each couple has its own song of whoops and wails.

- **Swinging by their long arms**, gibbons hurtle through the forest, flying up to 15 m between hand-holds.

- **With the longest arms**, relative to body size, of all the primates, gibbons often hang by just one arm.

- **No-one** has been able to keep up with gibbons to time how fast they swing arm over arm (brachiation).

- **Siamangs** are the largest gibbons, at up to 15 kg.

- **About 2 million years ago** there was only one gibbon species, but Ice Age changes in sea levels created forest islands, where separate species developed.

- **A gibbon sleeps** sitting up on a branch with its head between its bent knees, not in a nest like great apes.

- **Gibbons** are more closely related to orang-utans than to the chimps and gorillas of Africa.

- **Gibbons have extremely flexible** shoulder joints, and can rotate through 360° while hanging from one arm.

> ★ **STAR FACT** ★
> In the black gibbon species, the male is all black, the female light cream with a black face.

Hyenas

- **After making a successful kill**, the spotted ('laughing') hyena emits a blood-curdling, laugh-like cry.

- **The aardwolf** is a small, insect-eating member of the hyena family. One specimen was found to have over 40,000 termites in its stomach.

- **Often portrayed as a skulking scavenger**, the spotted hyena is in fact an aggressive hunter, and is also capable of driving lions from their kills at times.

- **The hyena's powerful jaws** can crush large bones, which its digestive system dissolves in a few hours.

- **Hyenas may suckle** their young for more than 1 year, compared to 2 months in the dog family.

- **All hyenas hide surplus food** for later – sometimes even underwater in the case of the spotted hyena.

- **Hyenas** are more closely related to mongooses than to members of the dog family.

- **In South Africa**, brown hyenas, or 'beach wolves', beachcomb for dead crabs, fish and sea mammals.

- **A female brown hyena** was once seen to take a springbok carcase from a leopard, and drive the leopard up a tree.

- **Brown and striped hyenas** erect their long manes to make them look larger when displaying aggression.

▶ *The spotted hyena can chase a wildebeest for 5 km at up to 60 km/h.*

Gazelles and antelopes

- **The smallest antelope**, the West African royal antelope, is only the size of a brown hare, and weighs between 1.5 and 3 kg.

- **When the Indian blackbuck antelope** runs flat out, it reaches 80 km/h, making 8-m long strides. The Indian aristocracy once used trained cheetahs to hunt them.

- **When a dominant greater kudu bull lies down**, he suddenly loses all authority, and female and young bull kudus often harass and annoy him with impunity.

- **The giant eland** of West and Central Africa is the largest of all antelopes, reaching 3.5 m in length, 1.85 m at the shoulder, and weighing up to 940 kg.

- **The American pronghorn antelope** has been timed running at 56 km/h for 6 km, and up to 88.5 km/h over short distances less than 1 km.

- **When migrating** to new grazing grounds, herds of wildebeest sometimes number up to 1.3 million individuals, and the herd may measure as much as 40 km in length.

- **The Arabian oryx** is a desert specialist, with a pale,

▶ A fleeing springbok may leap vertically in an activity known as 'pronking', confusing predators and giving the springbok a better view.

heat-reflecting coat and splayed hoofs for walking in soft sand. Its small size enables it to shelter in the shade of shrubby trees.

- **The spiral-horned antelopes**, which include elands, kudus and bongos, are found only in Africa, and are an offshoot of the ancestors of domestic cattle.

- **The springbok** is famous for its spectacular, stiff-legged leaps while running – a display activity known as 'pronking'.

> ★ **STAR FACT** ★
> The pronghorn is not a true antelope, and is more closely related to the deer family.

▶ The male pronghorn has several scent glands for marking territory, including glands beneath the ears, on the rump, above the tail and between the toes.

Large eyes give a 360° field of vision

▲ The Indian blackbuck is one of the world's fastest animals, with entire herds travelling at up to 80 km/h for 1 km at a time.

Coyotes and jackals

- **Silver-backed jackals** lived in Africa's Olduvai Gorge some 1.7 million years ago, and still live in the region.

- **The coyote** is probably the only predator whose range is increasing across North America.

- **Coyotes can live to be over 14 years old** in the wild, and over 21 years old in captivity.

- **Jackals are fearless defenders** of their family groups – a single jackal will attack a hyena five times its weight.

- **Farmers who poison coyotes** to reduce attacks on their livestock may be increasing the numbers of attacks, by killing the coyote's natural prey.

- **Native Americans** celebrated the cunning 'trickster' coyote, and told myths about its cleverness.

- **The golden jackal** of Eurasia and Africa is fond of fruit,

> ★ STAR FACT ★
> Young coyotes may spend a year helping to raise their younger brothers and sisters.

▶ A keen hunter, the coyote's prey ranges from mice to sheep.

eating figs, berries, grapes and desert dates, as well as animal prey.

- **When fighting** a predator or stealing a kill, pairs of jackals employ a 'yo-yo' technique, dashing in from each side alternately.

- **Without a 'helper'**, an average of one silver-backed jackal pup survives each litter, but with a helper 3 survive, and with 3 helpers an average of 6 survive.

Gliders

- **Gliding mammals** include the flying squirrels of America and Asia, the scaly-tailed squirrels of Africa, and the marsupial gliding possums of Australia.

- **The Australian feather-tailed glider** is the smallest gliding mammal, weighing just 12 g.

- **Gliding mammals** achieve their glides by means of a hairy membrane

◀ The southern flying squirrel fluffs out its tail and uses it as a rudder in mid-air.

> ★ STAR FACT ★
> The longest glide by a gliding mammal ever recorded was 450 m by a giant flying squirrel.

called a patagium that joins the fore and hind limbs, and acts like a parachute.

- **The Southeast Asian colugo's** glide membrane stretches from the neck to fingers, toes and tail-tip.

- **When flying squirrels** come in to land on a tree trunk, they brake by turning their tail and body under, like the landing flaps on an aircraft's wing.

- **Africa's scaly-tailed flying squirrels** live in colonies of up to 100, and glide from tree to tree after dark.

- **Australia's gliders** feed on sap and gum, biting through tree bark and lapping up the sweet liquids.

- **Some flying squirrels,** when they land, quickly move to the opposite side of the tree trunk to avoid predators.

- **The colugo** is virtually helpless on the ground.

Tenrecs and otter shrews

- **Tenrecs evolved** live on the island of Madagascar. Their physical appearance ranges from hedgehog look-alikes to shrews and web-footed otters.

- **Otter shrews**, close relatives to tenrecs, evolved separately on the African mainland. One species features in folklore as half mammal and half fish.

- **The body temperature** of tenrecs and otter shrews falls close to the surrounding air temperature while they are resting, enabling them to save energy.

- **The common tenrec** rears more young than any other mammal on the planet, with litters of up to 24.

- **Some tenrecs** find their way around at night by using a form of echolocation, based on a series of fast clicking noises made with the tongue.

- **The web-footed** tenrec was thought to be extinct, but is was recently re-discovered in the wild in Eastern Madagascar.

- **The insect-eating rice tenrec** resembles a mole, with its large front feet for digging and small eyes and ears.

- **The common tenrec**, weighing up to 1.5 kg, is the world's largest insectivore, and a ferocious fighter. It uses sharp neck spines to spike its attackers.

- **When alarmed**, baby common tenrecs rub together the quills on their backs to make a vibrating noise.

◀ Long-tailed tenrecs live in the forests of Madagascar.

Deer and chevrotains

- **The tiny Chinese water deer** is unique in the deer family in giving birth to as many as seven fawns at a time.

- **Chevrotains**, or mouse-deer, are in a separate family from true deer. They eat fish and meat as well as plants.

- **Reindeer** are the only deer species in which the females have antlers, using them to find moss under the snow.

★ STAR FACT ★

In the Middle Ages, the kings of Europe planted royal forests specially for deer-hunting.

- **Male musk deer** use their long, down-curved canine teeth when fighting rival males in the mating season.

- **The antlers** that male deer use for fighting are shed each year, regrowing the following spring.

- **Indian chital deer** seek out langur monkeys, feeding on the leafy stems thrown down by the monkeys above.

- **When competing for females**, red deer stags prefer to roar at each other rather than fight and risk an injury.

- **Newly grown antlers** are covered with a protective skin known as 'velvet', which stags rub off against trees.

- **On the Scottish island of Rhum**, red deer supplement their plant diet by snacking on Manx shearwater chicks.

◀ Most deer have large, mobile ears that are constantly alert.

The smaller cats

- **The fishing cat** of Southeast Asia and India inhabits marshes and swamps, and has slightly webbed paws. It preys on fish, crayfish, birds and small mammals.

- **The Iriomote cat** is probably the world's rarest cat. Less than 100 exist, on a remote, mountainous island off southern Japan.

- **The caracal** is a lynx-like African cat weighing up to 20 kg. It can kill antelopes twice its own weight.

- **The black-footed cat** of South Africa is the smallest wild cat. It spends the day in disused burrows, and eats spiders and beetles as well as small rodents.

- **The serval** is a cat of tall grasses, with very

▶ *The long-legged caracal is a good jumper and climber, and even takes sleeping birds, including eagles.*

long legs and neck. It locates prey with its prominent ears, catching it with a high, fox-like pounce.

- **The secretive Andean mountain cat** lives at altitudes of up to 5000 m, protected from the cold by its fine fur and long, bushy tail.

- **The Central American margay** specializes in hunting birds high in the treetops, and is the best of all cat climbers, with flexible legs and ankles.

- **The sand cat** of Africa and Asia does not need to drink, and has hairy foot-pads for walking in hot sand.

- **Unlike most small cats**, the ocelot runs down its prey instead of ambushing it, and is an excellent swimmer.

- **The smaller cats purr**, but cannot roar.

Baboons

- **Baboons' feet** are more suited to walking than grabbing branches.

- **Some East African baboons** cooperate in hunting and killing small antelopes, but are unwilling to share the catch.

- **Male Hamadryas baboons** herd their females all the time to keep them from other males.

◀ *The male mandrill has a bright blue and red face for attracting females.*

> ★ STAR FACT ★
> Olive baboon males fighting over females will enlist the help of a third male.

- **The olive baboons** of the East African highlands live in troops of up to 140 individuals.

- **When old male Hamadryas baboons** are defeated by younger males, they lose weight, and their distinctive grey mantle changes to the colour of the females' hair.

- **Chacma baboons**, found in the far south of Africa, often enter water to feed on water plants or shellfish.

- **For their first few weeks**, baby baboons hang upside down from their mother's chest, but by 4 or 5 months they are riding on her back, like jockeys.

- **The ancient Egyptians** sometimes trained Hamadryas baboons to harvest figs.

- **Baboons** in South Africa's Kruger National Park will risk electric fence shocks to steal food from tourists.

Domestic cats

- **Domestic cats** probably evolved from African wild cats, which were domesticated as early as 4000 BC in Egypt.

- **The ancient Egyptians revered cats**, and believed they held the daylight in their eyes.

- **Clay tiles** in a Roman temple in Britain bear the imprint of cats' paws. It is likely that the Romans introduced domestic cats to the British Isles.

- **The long-haired Turkish Van cat** is sometimes called the swimming cat, and is known in Turkey for attending lakeside picnics, playing in the shallows.

- **Some 98% of the patched cats** known as tortoiseshells, or calico cats, are females.

- **The Maine Coon**, the oldest breed of domestic cat in the USA, may have Viking origins.

▶ *Domestic cats have retained their wild hunting instincts, and are major predators of garden birds.*

- **In 1950 a 4-month-old kitten** followed some climbers to the summit of the Matterhorn in the Swiss Alps.

- **Siamese cats** were once found only in Thailand's temples and palaces. One king's favourite cat was entombed with him, but it later escaped.

- **In November 1939**, in Devon, a tabby cat called Puss celebrated its 36th birthday, and died the next day.

- **In the 10th-century**, a kitten was worth 2 pence before it caught its first mouse, and 4 pence afterwards.

Skunks

- **The skunk squirts a sticky spray** at its enemy from glands under its tail. It can reach a target up to 6 m away, and is accurate up to 2 m.

- **The skunk's spray**, which consists of 7 different chemical components, can cause temporary blindness.

- **Before spraying**, a skunk warns its enemy by stamping its feet. The spotted skunk does a handstand and walks with its hind legs in the air.

- **Skunks** belong to the same family as

weasels and polecats, all of which have smelly sprays, but the skunk's spray is the smelliest of all.

- **Vets** recommend that dogs which have been sprayed by a skunk should be given a bath in tomato juice.

- **Most predators avoid skunks**, but it is a favourite prey of the great horned owl, which has a poor sense of smell and catches it at night!

- **In the USA**, skunks are major carriers of rabies.

- **Skunks have little fear of humans** and are often sold as pets – after a de-scenting operation.

- **Skunks are great diggers**. They use their long, straight claws to rip apart rotten logs for grubs, and to dig in sand and mud for turtle eggs.

- **Skunks sleep in communal dens** when temperatures reach freezing, with up to 20 skunks in a den.

◀ *The skunk eats mainly live prey, such as insects and small mammals, and also enjoys fruit and birds' eggs.*

Meerkats

- **Young meerkats** care for their younger brothers and sisters while their mother forages for food to maintain her milk supply.

- **Grey meerkats** often share their burrow systems with ground squirrels.

- **If surprised in open ground** by a hawk, the adults in a meerkat pack will cover the young with their bodies.

- **The grey meerkat** attacks intruders without warning or threats, and kills with an energetic shaking, followed by a neck bite.

▶ *The meerkat lives in cooperative groups of up to 30 individuals in a complex warren system.*

> ★ **STAR FACT** ★
> Meerkat warrens can cover an area of up to 25 m by 32 m, with 90 separate entrances.

- **Meerkats** enthusiastically attack and eat scorpions, first rendering them harmless by biting off their tail stings.

- **Meerkats warm themselves up** in the morning sun, standing tall on their hind feet and tails, while constantly on the lookout for enemies.

- **Meerkats dig** for many food items, such as beetles, moth pupae, termites and spiders.

- **Living in the arid regions** of South Africa, the meerkat sometimes obtains moisture by chewing Tsama melons and digging up plant roots.

- **Faced with attack**, the normally slim meerkat becomes almost spherical, its hair bristling, tail up and back arched as it growls, spits and rocks to and fro.

Mice

- **In the early 1940s**, a huge population of house mice in California had a density of about 200,000 per hectare.

- **The Andes fishing mouse** – only discovered in 1994 – fishes in streams at an altitude of at least 3600 m.

- **The Australian pebble mound mouse** builds large piles of rounded stones, and then takes up residence in them.

- **The Oldfield mouse** has an escape tunnel leading from its nest near to the surface, so it can escape intruders by breaking through the apparent 'dead end'.

- **The water mice** of Central America have webbed, hairy feet that help them dive for water snails and fish.

- **American grasshopper mice** defend their territory by standing on their hind legs, shrieking at rival mice.

- **Grasshopper mice** are sometimes kept as pets to clear a house of insect pests such as cockroaches.

- **An ancient Greek legend** tells how a Cretan army owed its success to divine mice, which gnawed through the shield straps of the enemy.

- **The Old World harvest mouse** climbs through tall grasses using its grasping tail and flexible feet.

- **American kangaroo mice** have long, hairy hind feet and a long tail, and often travel in a series of leaps.

◀ (1) Burrowing house mouse, (2) field mouse, (3) climbing harvest mouse.

Foxes

- **The larder of one Arctic fox** was found to contain 50 lemmings and 40 little auks, all lined up with tails pointing the same way and their heads bitten off.

- **African bat-eared foxes** have huge ears for radiating heat away from the body.

- **Arctic foxes** live only 480 km from the North Pole.

- **The grey fox** of North and Central America is the oldest surviving member of the dog family, first appearing up to 9 million years ago.

- **The African fennec fox's** 15-cm long ears are the largest of any carnivore.

- **The American grey fox** leaps with ease between tree branches.

- **Some foxes roll about** and chase their tails to 'charm' rabbits, which seem fascinated and come closer, allowing the fox to make a grab.

- **The red fox** has adapted with great success to urban life, even moving into houses via cat flaps.

- **When locating insects** beneath the ground, the bat-eared fox cups its large ears, gradually pinpointing the exact position of the prey before digging.

- **In early autumn,** up to 90% of the red fox's diet may consist of apples, blackberries and other fruits.

◄ *Although basically a night hunter, the red fox is often seen during the day, and shows up sharply against winter snow.*

Zebras

- **A zebra's stripes** are as individual as human fingerprints – no two zebras are exactly the same.

- **The quagga** was a South African zebra that only had stripes on the front part of its body.

- **The home range** of Grevy's zebra, which roams desert and savannah terrains in northeastern Kenya, sometimes exceeds 10,000 sq km.

- **The zebra** can be a formidable foe, driving off lions, and even killing humans to defend its foals.

- **The plains zebra** lived north of the Sahara, in Algeria and Tunisia, up until 10,000 years ago, when it was replaced by the African wild ass.

- **Grevy's zebra** is a large species with narrowly spaced stripes and very large, mule-like ears.

- **A plains zebra herd's stallion** will challenge any potential rival coming within 50–100 m of his herd.

- **The quagga** once existed in very large herds, but became extinct through over-hunting in the 1870s.

- **Mountain zebras** follow ancient trails to mountain springs and pools in the dry season, and dig for subsurface water in stream beds.

- **Chapman's zebra** has shadow stripes – light, greyish stripes that alternate with the dark main stripes.

▲ *Horses are sociable and like physical contact and mutual grooming*

INDEX

ACKNOWLEDGEMENTS

The publisher would like to thank the following artists whose work appears in this book:
Chris Buzer (Galante Studio), Jim Channell, Brian Delf, Fiametta Dogi (Scientific Illustrations), Chris Forsey, L R Galante (Galante Studio), Shami Ghale, Roger Goringe, Alan Hancocks, Alan Harris, Mike Hughes, Ian Jackson, Emma Louise Jones, Roger Kent (Illustration), Steve Kirk, Mick Loates (Linden Artists), Kevin Maddison, Alan Male (Linden Artists), Janos Marffy, Gill Platt, Terry Riley, Steve Roberts, Eric Robson, Guy Smith (Mainline Design), Sara Smith, Rudi Vizi, Christian Webb (Temple Rogers), Steve Weston, Mike White (Temple Rogers)

The publisher would like to thank the following sources for the use of their photographs:
Page 41 (T/R) Kobal Collection/Amblin/Universal; 130 (B/R) Corbis; 143 (B/R) Corbis; 151 (B/R) Corbis; 166 (T/C) Science Photo Library

All other photographs are from: MKP Archives; Corbis Professional Collections; Corel Corporation; Photodisk